The Data Journalism Handbook

*Edited by Jonathan Gray, Liliana Bounegru, and
Lucy Chambers*

O'REILLY®

Beijing · Cambridge · Farnham · Köln · Sebastopol · Tokyo

The Data Journalism Handbook

Edited by Jonathan Gray, Liliana Bounegru, and Lucy Chambers

A project of the European Journalism Centre and the Open Knowledge Foundation.

Printed in the United States of America.

Published by O'Reilly Media, Inc., 1005 Gravenstein Highway North, Sebastopol, CA 95472.

O'Reilly books may be purchased for educational, business, or sales promotional use. Online editions are also available for most titles (*http://my.safaribooksonline.com*). For more information, contact our corporate/institutional sales department: 800-998-9938 or *corporate@oreilly.com*.

Editor: Shawn Wallace	**Cover Designer:** Karen Montgomery
Production Editor: Kristen Borg	**Interior Designer:** David Futato
Proofreader: O'Reilly Production Services	**Illustrator:** Kate Hudson

July 2012:   First Edition.

Revision History for the First Edition:
    2012-07-11   First release
See *http://oreilly.com/catalog/errata.csp?isbn=9781449330064* for release details.

ISBN: 978-1-449-33006-4

[LSI]

1342013318

Table of Contents

Preface

For the Great Unnamed

The Data Journalism Handbook was born at a 48 hour workshop led by the European Journalism Centre and the Open Knowledge Foundation at MozFest 2011 in London. It subsequently spilled over into an international, collaborative effort involving dozens of data journalism's leading advocates and best practitioners.

Figure P-1. How it all began

In the six months that passed between the book's inception to its first full release, hundreds of people have contributed in various ways. While we have done our best to keep track of them all, we have had our fair share of anonymous, pseudonymous, and untraceable edits.

To all of those people who have contributed and are not listed below, we say two things. Firstly, thank you. Secondly, can you please tell us who you are so that we can give credit where credit is due?

Contributors

The following people have drafted or otherwise directly contributed to text in the current version of the book (and illustrations are by graphic designer Kate Hudson):

- Gregor Aisch, Open Knowledge Foundation
- Brigitte Alfter, Journalismfund.eu
- David Anderton, Freelance Journalist
- James Ball, the Guardian
- Caelainn Barr, Citywire
- Mariana Berruezo, Hacks/Hackers Buenos Aires
- Michael Blastland, Freelance Journalist
- Mariano Blejman, Hacks/Hackers Buenos Aires
- John Bones, Verdens Gang
- Marianne Bouchart, Bloomberg News
- Liliana Bounegru, European Journalism Centre
- Brian Boyer, Chicago Tribune
- Paul Bradshaw, Birmingham City University
- Wendy Carlisle, Australian Broadcasting Corporation
- Lucy Chambers, Open Knowledge Foundation
- Sarah Cohen, Duke University
- Alastair Dant, the Guardian
- Helen Darbishire, Access Info Europe
- Chase Davis, Center for Investigative Reporting
- Steve Doig, Walter Cronkite School of Journalism, Arizona State University
- Lisa Evans, the Guardian
- Tom Fries, Bertelsmann Stiftung
- Duncan Geere, Wired UK
- Jack Gillum, Associated Press
- Jonathan Gray, Open Knowledge Foundation
- Alex Howard, O'Reilly Media
- Bella Hurrell, BBC
- Nicolas Kayser-Bril, Journalism++

- John Keefe, WNYC
- Scott Klein, ProPublica
- Alexandre Léchenet, Le Monde
- Mark Lee Hunter, INSEAD
- Andrew Leimdorfer, BBC
- Friedrich Lindenberg, Open Knowledge Foundation
- Mike Linksvayer, Creative Commons
- Mirko Lorenz, Deutsche Welle
- Esa Mäkinen, Helsingin Sanomat
- Pedro Markun, Transparência Hacker
- Isao Matsunami, Tokyo Shimbun
- Lorenz Matzat, OpenDataCity
- Geoff McGhee, Stanford University
- Philip Meyer, Professor Emeritus, University of North Carolina at Chapel Hill
- Claire Miller, WalesOnline
- Cynthia O'Murchu, Financial Times
- Oluseun Onigbinde, BudgIT
- Djordje Padejski, Knight Journalism Fellow, Stanford University
- Jane Park, Creative Commons
- Angélica Peralta Ramos, La Nacion (Argentina)
- Cheryl Phillips, The Seattle Times
- Aron Pilhofer, New York Times
- Lulu Pinney, Freelance Infographic Designer
- Paul Radu, Organised Crime and Corruption Reporting Project
- Simon Rogers, the Guardian
- Martin Rosenbaum, BBC
- Amanda Rossi, Friends of Januária
- Martin Sarsale, Hacks/Hackers Buenos Aires
- Fabrizio Scrollini, London School of Economics and Political Science
- Sarah Slobin, Wall Street Journal
- Sergio Sorin, Hacks/Hackers Buenos Aires
- Jonathan Stray, The Overview Project
- Brian Suda, (optional.is)
- Chris Taggart, OpenCorporates
- Jer Thorp, The New York Times R&D Group

- Andy Tow, Hacks/Hackers Buenos Aires
- Luk N. Van Wassenhove, INSEAD
- Sascha Venohr, Zeit Online
- Jerry Vermanen, NU.nl
- César Viana, University of Goiás
- Farida Vis, University of Leicester
- Pete Warden, Independent Data Analyst and Developer
- Chrys Wu, Hacks/Hackers

What This Book Is (And What It Isn't)

This book is intended to be a useful resource for anyone who thinks that they might be interested in becoming a data journalist—or just dabbling in data journalism.

Lots of people have contributed to writing it, and through our editing we have tried to let their different voices and views shine through. We hope that it reads like a rich and informative conversation about what data journalism is, why it is important, and how to do it.

Lamentably, the act of reading this book will not supply you with a comprehensive repertoire of all the knowledge and skills you need to become a data journalist. This would require a vast library manned by hundreds of experts able to answer questions on hundreds of topics. Luckily this library exists; it is called the Internet. Instead, we hope this book will give you a sense of how to get started and where to look if you want to go further. Examples and tutorials serve to be illustrative rather than exhaustive.

We count ourselves very lucky to have had so much time, energy, and patience from all of our contributors and have tried our best to use this wisely. We hope that—in addition to being a useful reference source—the book does something to document the passion and enthusiasm, the vision and energy of a nascent movement. The book attempts to give you a sense of what happens behind the scenes, the stories behind the stories.

The Data Journalism Handbook is a work in progress. If you think there is anything which needs to be amended or is conspicuously absent, then please flag it for inclusion in the next version. It is also freely available under a Creative Commons Attribution-ShareAlike (*http://creativecommons.org/licenses/by-sa/3.0/*) license at www.datajournalismhandbook.org, and we strongly encourage you to share it with anyone that you think might be interested in reading it.

— *Jonathan Gray, Open Knowledge Foundation (@jwyg), Liliana Bounegru, European Journalism Centre (@bb_liliana), and Lucy Chambers, Open Knowledge Foundation (@lucyfedia), March 2012*

Conventions Used in This Book

The following typographical conventions are used in this book:

Italic
> Indicates new terms, URLs, email addresses, filenames, and file extensions.

> This icon signifies a tip, suggestion, or general note.

> This icon indicates a warning or caution.

Safari® Books Online

 Safari Books Online is an on-demand digital library that delivers expert content in both book and video form from the world's leading authors in technology and business.

Technology professionals, software developers, web designers, and business and creative professionals use Safari Books Online as their primary resource for research, problem solving, learning, and certification training.

Safari Books Online offers a range of product mixes and pricing programs for organizations, government agencies, and individuals. Subscribers have access to thousands of books, training videos, and prepublication manuscripts in one fully searchable database from publishers like O'Reilly Media, Prentice Hall Professional, Addison-Wesley Professional, Microsoft Press, Sams, Que, Peachpit Press, Focal Press, Cisco Press, John Wiley & Sons, Syngress, Morgan Kaufmann, IBM Redbooks, Packt, Adobe Press, FT Press, Apress, Manning, New Riders, McGraw-Hill, Jones & Bartlett, Course Technology, and dozens more. For more information about Safari Books Online, please visit us online.

How to Contact Us

Please address comments and questions concerning this book to the publisher:

O'Reilly Media, Inc.
1005 Gravenstein Highway North
Sebastopol, CA 95472
800-998-9938 (in the United States or Canada)
707-829-0515 (international or local)
707-829-0104 (fax)

We have a web page for this book, where we list errata, examples, and any additional information. You can access this page at:

http://oreil.ly/data-journalism-handbook

To comment or ask technical questions about this book, send email to:

bookquestions@oreilly.com

For more information about our books, courses, conferences, and news, see our website at *http://www.oreilly.com*.

Find us on Facebook: *http://facebook.com/oreilly*

Follow us on Twitter: *http://twitter.com/oreillymedia*

Watch us on YouTube: *http://www.youtube.com/oreillymedia*

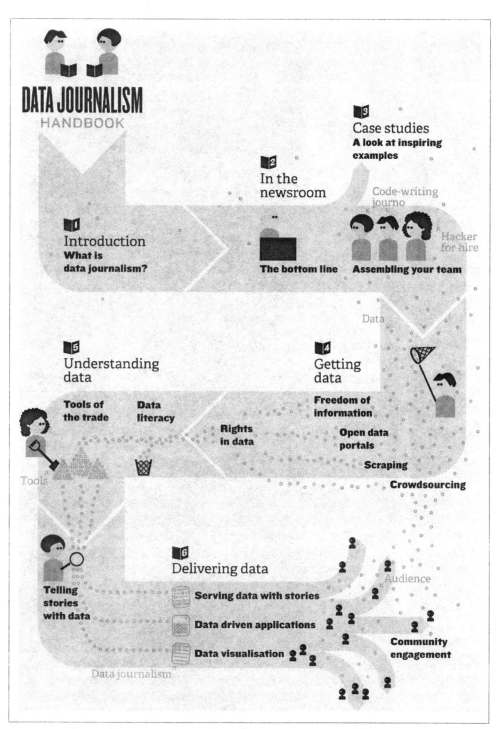

Figure P-2. The Handbook at a glance: Infographic impresario Lulu Pinney created this superb poster, which gives an overview of the contents of The Data Journalism Handbook

CHAPTER 1

Introduction

What is data journalism? What potential does it have? What are its limits? Where does it come from? In this section we look at what data journalism is and what it might mean for news organizations. Paul Bradshaw (Birmingham City University) and Mirko Lorenz (Deutsche Welle) say a bit about what is distinctive about data journalism. Leading data journalists tell us why they think it is important and what their favorite examples are. Finally Liliana Bounegru (European Journalism Centre) puts data journalism into its broader historical context.

What Is Data Journalism?

What is data journalism? I could answer, simply, that it is journalism done with data. But that doesn't help much.

Both "data" and "journalism" are troublesome terms. Some people think of "data" as any collection of numbers, most likely gathered on a spreadsheet. 20 years ago, that was pretty much the only sort of data that journalists dealt with. But we live in a digital world now, a world in which almost anything can be (and almost everything is) described with numbers.

Your career history, 300,000 confidential documents, everyone in your circle of friends; these can all be (and are) described with just two numbers: zeroes, and ones. Photos, video, and audio are all described with the same two numbers: zeroes and ones. Murders, disease, political votes, corruption, and lies: zeroes and ones.

What makes data journalism different to the rest of journalism? Perhaps it is the new possibilities that open up when you combine the traditional "nose for news" and ability to tell a compelling story with the sheer scale and range of digital information now available.

And those possibilities can come at any stage of the journalist's process: using programming to automate the process of gathering and combining information from local government, police, and other civic sources, as Adrian Holovaty did with Chicago-Crime (*http://chicago.everyblock.com/crime/*) and then EveryBlock (*http://www.every block.com/*).

Or using software to find connections between hundreds of thousands of documents, as The Telegraph did with MPs' expenses (*http://tgr.ph/mps-expenses*).

Data journalism can help a journalist tell a complex story through engaging infographics. For example, Hans Rosling's spectacular talks on visualizing world poverty with Gapminder (*http://www.gapminder.org/*) have attracted millions of views across the world. And David McCandless' popular work in distilling big numbers—such as putting public spending into context, or the pollution generated and prevented by the Icelandic volcano—shows the importance of clear design at Information is Beautiful (*http://www.informationisbeautiful.net/*).

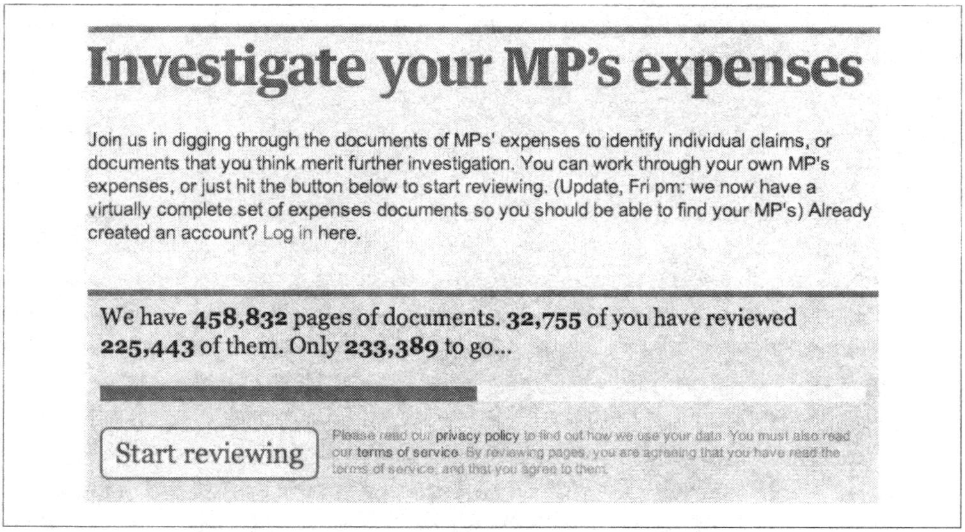

Investigate your MP's expenses

Join us in digging through the documents of MPs' expenses to identify individual claims, or documents that you think merit further investigation. You can work through your own MP's expenses, or just hit the button below to start reviewing. (Update, Fri pm: we now have a virtually complete set of expenses documents so you should be able to find your MP's) Already created an account? Log in here.

We have **458,832** pages of documents. **32,755** of you have reviewed **225,443** of them. Only **233,389** to go...

Start reviewing — Please read our **privacy policy** to find out how we use your data. You must also read our **terms of service**. By reviewing pages, you are agreeing that you have read the terms of service, and that you agree to them.

Figure 1-1. Investigate your MP's expenses (the Guardian)

Or it can help explain how a story relates to an individual, as the BBC and the Financial Times now routinely do with their budget interactives (where you can find out how the budget affects you, rather than "Joe Public"). And it can open up the news-gathering process itself, as the Guardian does so successfully in sharing data, context, and questions with their Datablog (*http://www.guardian.co.uk/news/datablog*).

Data can be the source of data journalism, or it can be the tool with which the story is told—or it can be both. Like any source, it should be treated with skepticism; and like any tool, we should be conscious of how it can shape and restrict the stories that are created with it.

— *Paul Bradshaw, Birmingham City University*

Why Journalists Should Use Data

Journalism is under siege. In the past we, as an industry, relied on being the only ones operating a technology to multiply and distribute what had happened overnight. The printing press served as a gateway. If anybody wanted to reach the people of a city or region the next morning, they would turn to newspapers. This era is over.

Today, news stories are flowing in as they happen, from multiple sources, eyewitnesses, and blogs, and what has happened is filtered through a vast network of social connections, being ranked, commented on—and more often than not, ignored.

This is why data journalism is so important. Gathering, filtering, and visualizing what is happening beyond what the eye can see has a growing value. The orange juice you drink in the morning, the coffee you brew: in today's global economy, there are invisible connections between these products, other people, and you. The language of this network is data: little points of information that are often not relevant in a single instance, but massively important when viewed from the right angle.

Right now, a few pioneering journalists already demonstrate how data can be used to create deeper insights into what is happening around us and how it might affect us.

Data analysis can reveal "a story's shape" (Sarah Cohen), or provides us with a "new camera" (David McCandless). By using data, the job of journalists shifts its main focus from being the first ones to report to being the ones telling us what a certain development might actually mean. The range of topics can be wide. The next financial crisis that is in the making. The economics behind the products we use. The misuse of funds or political blunders, presented in a compelling data visualization that leaves little room to argue with it.

This is why journalists should see data as an opportunity. They can, for example, reveal how some abstract threat (such as unemployment) affects people based on their age, gender, or education. Using data transforms something abstract into something everyone can understand and relate to.

They can create personalized calculators to help people to make decisions, be this buying a car, a house, deciding on an education or professional path in life, or doing a hard check on costs to stay out of debt.

They can analyze the dynamics of a complex situation like a riot or political debate, show fallacies, and help everyone to see possible solutions to complex problems.

Becoming knowledgeable in searching, cleaning, and visualizing data is transformative for the profession of information gathering, too. Journalists who master this will experience that building articles on facts and insights is a relief. Less guessing, less looking for quotes; instead, a journalist can build a strong position supported by data, and this can affect the role of journalism greatly.

Additionally, getting into data journalism offers a future perspective. Today, when newsrooms downsize, most journalists hope to switch to public relations. Data journalists or data scientists, though, are already a sought-after group of employees, not only in the media. Companies and institutions around the world are looking for "sensemakers" and professionals who know how to dig through data and transform it into something tangible.

There is a promise in data, and this is what excites newsrooms, making them look for a new type of reporter. For freelancers, proficiency with data provides a route to new offerings and stable pay, too. Look at it this way: instead of hiring journalists to quickly fill pages and websites with low value content, the use of data could create demand for interactive packages, where spending a week on solving one question is the only way to do it. This is a welcome change in many parts of the media.

There is one barrier keeping journalists from using this potential: training themselves to work with data through all the steps—from a first question to a big data-driven scoop.

Working with data is like stepping into vast, unknown territory. At first look, raw data is puzzling to the eyes and to the mind. Such data is unwieldy. It is quite hard to shape it correctly for visualization. It needs experienced journalists, who have the stamina to look at often confusing or boring raw data and "see" the hidden stories in there.

— *Mirko Lorenz, Deutsche Welle*

The Survey

The European Journalism Centre conducted a survey (*http://bit.ly/ddjnet-survey*) to find out more about training needs of journalists. We found there is a big willingness to get out of the comfort zone of traditional journalism and invest time in mastering new skills. The results from the survey showed us that journalists see the opportunity, but need a bit of support to cut through the initial problems that keep them from working with data. There is a confidence that should data journalism become more universally adopted, the workflows, tools, and results will improve quite quickly. Pioneers such as the Guardian, The New York Times, the Texas Tribune, and Die Zeit continue to raise the bar with their data-driven stories.

Will data journalism remain the preserve of a small handful of pioneers, or will every news organization soon have its own dedicated data journalism team? We hope this handbook will help more journalists and newsrooms to take advantage of this emerging field.

Figure 1-2. European Journalism Centre survey on training needs

Why Is Data Journalism Important?

We asked some of data journalism's leading practitioners and proponents why they think data journalism is an important development. Here is what they said.

Filtering the Flow of Data

When information was scarce, most of our efforts were devoted to hunting and gathering. Now that information is abundant, processing is more important. We process at two levels: 1) analysis to bring sense and structure out of the never-ending flow of data and 2) presentation to get what's important and relevant into the consumer's head. Like science, data journalism discloses its methods and presents its findings in a way that can be verified by replication.

— *Philip Meyer, Professor Emeritus, University of North Carolina at Chapel Hill*

New Approaches to Storytelling

Data journalism is an umbrella term that, to my mind, encompasses an ever-growing set of tools, techniques, and approaches to storytelling. It can include everything from traditional computer-assisted reporting (using data as a "source") to the most cutting-edge data visualization and news applications. The unifying goal is a journalistic one: providing information and analysis to help inform us all about important issues of the day.

— *Aron Pilhofer, New York Times*

Like Photo Journalism with a Laptop

"Data journalism" only differs from "words journalism" in that we use a different kit. We all sniff out, report, and relate stories for a living. It's like "photo journalism"; just swap the camera for a laptop.

— *Brian Boyer, Chicago Tribune*

Data Journalism Is the Future

Data-driven journalism is the future. Journalists need to be data-savvy. It used to be that you would get stories by chatting to people in bars, and it still might be that you'll do it that way sometimes. But now it's also going to be about poring over data and equipping yourself with the tools to analyze it and pick out what's interesting. And keeping it in perspective, helping people out by really seeing where it all fits together, and what's going on in the country.

— *Tim Berners-Lee, founder of the World Wide Web*

Number-Crunching Meets Word-Smithing

Data journalism is bridging the gap between stat technicians and wordsmiths. Locating outliers and identifying trends that are not just statistically significant, but relevant to de-compiling the inherently complex world of today.

— *David Anderton, freelance journalist*

Updating Your Skills Set

Data journalism is a new set of skills for searching, understanding, and visualizing digital sources in a time when basic skills from traditional journalism just aren't enough. It's not a replacement of traditional journalism, but an addition to it.

In a time when sources are going digital, journalists can and have to be closer to those sources. The Internet opened up possibilities beyond our current understanding. Data journalism is just the beginning of evolving our past practices to adapt to the online.

Data journalism serves two important purposes for news organizations: finding unique stories (not from news wires), and executing the watchdog function. Especially in times of financial peril, these are important goals for newspapers to achieve.

From the standpoint of a regional newspaper, data journalism is crucial. We have the saying "a loose tile in front of your door is considered more important than a riot in a far-away country." It hits you in the face and impacts your life more directly. At the same time, digitization is everywhere. Because local newspapers have this direct impact in their neighborhood and sources become digitalized, a journalist must know how to find, analyze and visualize a story from data.

— *Jerry Vermanen, NU.nl*

A Remedy for Information Asymmetry

Information asymmetry—not the lack of information, but the inability to take in and process it with the speed and volume that it comes to us—is one of the most significant problems that citizens face in making choices about how to live their lives. Information taken in from print, visual, and audio media influence citizens' choices and actions. Good data journalism helps to combat information asymmetry.

— *Tom Fries, Bertelsmann Foundation*

An Answer to Data-Driven PR

The availability of measurement tools and their decreasing prices—in a self-sustaining combination with a focus on performance and efficiency in all aspects of society—have led decision-makers to quantify the progresses of their policies, monitor trends, and identify opportunities.

Companies keep coming up with new metrics showing how well they perform. Politicians love to brag about reductions in unemployment numbers and increases in GDP. The lack of journalistic insight in the Enron, Worldcom, Madoff, or Solyndra affairs is proof of many a journalist's inability to clearly see through numbers. Figures are more likely to be taken at face value than other facts, as they carry an aura of seriousness even when they are entirely fabricated.

Fluency with data will help journalists sharpen their critical sense when faced with numbers and will hopefully help them gain back some terrain in their exchanges with PR departments.

— *Nicolas Kayser-Bril, Journalism++*

Providing Independent Interpretations of Official Information

After the devastating earthquake and subsequent Fukushima nuclear plant disaster in 2011, the importance of data journalism has been driven home to media people in Japan, a country which is generally lagging behind in digital journalism.

We were at a loss when the government and experts had no credible data about the damage. When officials hid SPEEDI data (predicted diffusion of radioactive materials) from the public, we were not prepared to decode it even if it were leaked. Volunteers began to collect radioactive data by using their own devices, but we were not armed with the knowledge of statistics, interpolation, visualization, and so on. Journalists need to have access to raw data, and to learn not to rely on official interpretations of it.

— *Isao Matsunami, Tokyo Shimbun*

Dealing with the Data Deluge

The challenges and opportunities presented by the digital revolution continue to disrupt journalism. In an age of information abundance, journalists and citizens alike all need better tools, whether we're curating the samizdat of the 21st century in the Middle East, processing a late night data dump, or looking for the best way to visualize water quality for a nation of consumers. As we grapple with the consumption challenges presented by this deluge of data, new publishing platforms are also empowering everyone to gather and share data digitally, turning it into information. While reporters and editors have been the traditional vectors for information gathering and dissemination, the flattened information environment of 2012 now has news breaking online first, not on the news desk.

Around the globe, in fact, the bond between data and journalism is growing stronger. In an age of big data, the growing importance of data journalism lies in the ability of its practitioners to provide context, clarity, and—perhaps most important—find truth in the expanding amount of digital content in the world. That doesn't mean that the integrated media organizations of today don't play a crucial role. Far from it. In the information age, journalists are needed more than ever to curate, verify, analyze, and synthesize the wash of data. In that context, data journalism has profound importance for society.

Today, making sense of big data, particularly unstructured data, will be a central goal for data scientists around the world, whether they work in newsrooms, Wall Street, or Silicon Valley. Notably, that goal will be substantially enabled by a growing set of common tools, whether they're employed by government technologists opening Chicago, healthcare technologists, or newsroom developers.

— *Alex Howard, O'Reilly Media*

Our Lives Are Data

Good data journalism is hard, because good journalism is hard. It means figuring out how to get the data, how to understand it, and how to find the story. Sometimes there are dead ends, and sometimes there's no great story. After all, if it were just a matter of pressing the right button, it wouldn't be journalism. But that's what makes it worthwhile, and—in a world where our lives are increasingly data—essential for a free and fair society.

— *Chris Taggart, OpenCorporates*

A Way to Save Time

Journalists don't have time to waste transcribing things by hand and messing around trying to get data out of PDFs, so learning a little bit of code (or knowing where to look for people who can help) is incredibly valuable.

One reporter from Folha de São Paulo was working with the local budget and called me to thank us for putting up the accounts of the municipality of São Paolo online (two days work for a single hacker!). He said he had been transcribing them by hand for the past three months, trying to build up a story. I also remember solving a "PDF issue" for *Contas Abertas*, a parliamentary monitoring news organization: 15 minutes and 15 lines of code solved a month's worth of work.

— *Pedro Markun, Transparência Hacker*

An Essential Part of the Journalists' Toolkit

I think it's important to stress the "journalism" or reporting aspect of "data journalism." The exercise should not be about just analyzing or visualizing data for the sake of it, but to use it as a tool to get closer to the truth of what is going on in the world. I see the ability to be able to analyze and interpret data as an essential part of today's journalists' toolkit, rather than a separate discipline. Ultimately, it is all about good reporting, and telling stories in the most appropriate way.

Data journalism is another way to scrutinize the world and hold the powers that be to account. With an increasing amount of data available, it is now more important than ever that journalists are aware of data journalism techniques. This should be a tool in the toolkit of any journalist, whether learning how to work with data directly, or collaborating with someone who can.

Its real power is in helping you to obtain information that would otherwise be very difficult to find or to prove. A good example of this is Steve Doig's story that analyzed damage patterns from Hurricane Andrew. He joined two different datasets: one mapping the level of destruction caused by the hurricane, and one showing wind speeds. This allowed him to pinpoint areas where weakened building codes and poor construction practices contributed to the impact of the disaster. He won a Pulitzer Prize for the story in 1993 (*http://www.pulitzer.org/awards/1993*) and it's still a great example of what is possible.

Ideally, you use the data to pinpoint outliers, areas of interest, or things that are surprising. In this sense, data can act as a lead or a tip off. While numbers can be interesting, just writing about the data is not enough. You still need to do the reporting to explain what it means.

— *Cynthia O'Murchu, Financial Times*

Adapting to Changes in Our Information Environment

New digital technologies bring new ways of producing and disseminating knowledge in society. Data journalism can be understood as the media's attempt to adapt and respond to the changes in our information environment, including more interactive, multidimensional storytelling enabling readers to explore the sources underlying the news and encouraging them to participate in the process of creating and evaluating stories.

— *César Viana, University of Goiás*

A Way to See Things You Might Not Otherwise See

Some stories can only be understood and explained through analyzing—and sometimes visualizing—the data. Connections between powerful people or entities would go unrevealed, deaths caused by drug policies would remain hidden, environmental policies that hurt our landscape would continue unabated. But each of the above was changed because of data that journalists have obtained, analyzed, and provided to readers. The data can be as simple as a basic spreadsheet or a log of cell phone calls, or complex as school test scores or hospital infection data, but inside it all are stories worth telling.

— *Cheryl Phillips, The Seattle Times*

A Way To Tell Richer Stories

We can paint pictures of our entire lives with our digital trails. From what we consume and browse, to where and when we travel, to our musical preferences, our first loves, our children's milestones, even our last wishes – it all can be tracked, digitized, stored in the cloud, and disseminated. This universe of data can be surfaced to tell stories, answer questions and impart an understanding of life in ways that currently surpass even the most rigorous and careful reconstruction of anecdotes.

— *Sarah Slobin, Wall Street Journal*

You Don't Need New Data to Make a Scoop

Sometimes the data is already public and available, but no one has looked at it closely. In the case of the Associated Press's report on 4,500 pages of declassified documents describing the actions of private security contractors during the Iraq war, the material was obtained by an independent journalist over several years, using Freedom of Information requests addressed to the U.S. State Department. They scanned the paper results and uploaded them to DocumentCloud, which made it possible for us to do our comprehensive analysis.

— *Jonathan Stray, The Overview Project*

Some Favorite Examples

We asked some of our contributors for their favorite examples of data journalism and what they liked about them. Here they are.

Do No Harm in the Las Vegas Sun

My favorite example is the Las Vegas Sun's 2010 Do No Harm series on hospital care (*http://www.lasvegassun.com/hospital-care/*). The Sun analyzed more than 2.9 million hospital billing records, which revealed more than 3,600 preventable injuries, infections and surgical mistakes. They obtained data through a public records request and identified more than 300 cases in which patients died because of mistakes that could have been prevented. It contains different elements, including an interactive graphic (*http://bit.ly/lvsun-surgery*) that allows the reader to see (by hospital) where surgical injuries happened more often than would be expected; a map (*http://bit.ly/lvsun-infections*) with a timeline that shows infections spreading hospital by hospital; and an interactive graphic (*http://bit.ly/lvsun-events*) that allows users to sort data by preventable injuries or by hospital to see where people are getting hurt. I like it because it is very easy to understand and navigate. Users can explore the data in a very intuitive way.

It also had a real impact: the Nevada legislature responded with six pieces of legislation (*http://bit.ly/lvsun-milestone*). The journalists involved worked very hard to acquire and clean up the data. One of the journalists, Alex Richards, sent data back to hospitals and to the state at least a dozen times (*http://bit.ly/poynter-webgold*) to get mistakes corrected.

— *Angélica Peralta Ramos, La Nación (Argentina)*

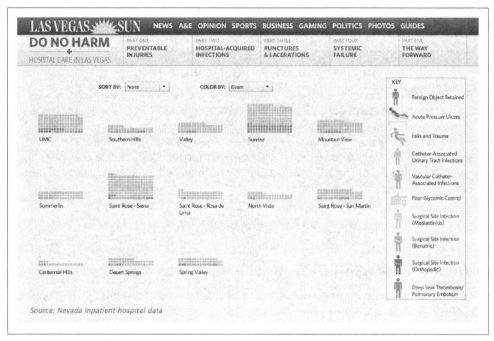

Figure 1-3. *Do No Harm (The Las Vegas Sun)*

Government Employee Salary Database

I love the work that small independent organizations are performing every day, such as ProPublica or the Texas Tribune, who have a great data reporter in Ryan Murphy. If I had to choose, I'd pick the Government Employee Salary Database project from the Texas Tribune (*http://bit.ly/texastrib-employee*). This project collects 660,000 government employee salaries into a database for users to search and help generate stories from. You can search by agency, name, or salary. It's simple, meaningful, and is making inaccessible information public. It is easy to use and automatically generates stories. It is a great example of why the Texas Tribune gets most of its traffic from the data pages.

— *Simon Rogers, the Guardian*

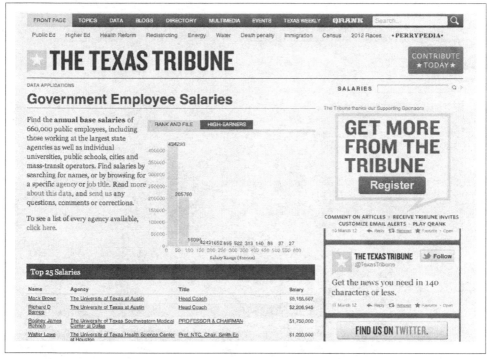

Figure 1-4. *Government Employee Salaries (The Texas Tribune)*

Full-Text Visualization of the Iraqi War Logs, Associated Press

Jonathan Stray and Julian Burgess' work on Iraq War Logs (*http://bit.ly/jstray-war logs*) is an inspiring foray into text analysis and visualization using experimental techniques to gain insight into themes worth exploring further within a large textual dataset.

By means of text-analytics techniques and algorithms, Jonathan and Julian created a method that showed clusters of keywords contained in thousands of US-government reports on the Iraq war leaked by WikiLeaks, in a visual format.

Though there are limitations to this method and the work is experimental, it is a fresh and innovative approach. Rather than trying to read all the files or reviewing the War Logs with a preconceived notion of what may be found by inputting particular keywords and reviewing the output, this technique calculates and visualizes topics/keywords of particular relevance.

With increasing amounts of textual (emails, reports, etc.) and numeric data coming into the public domain, finding ways to pinpoint key areas of interest will become more and more important. It is an exciting subfield of data journalism.

— *Cynthia O'Murchu, Financial Times*

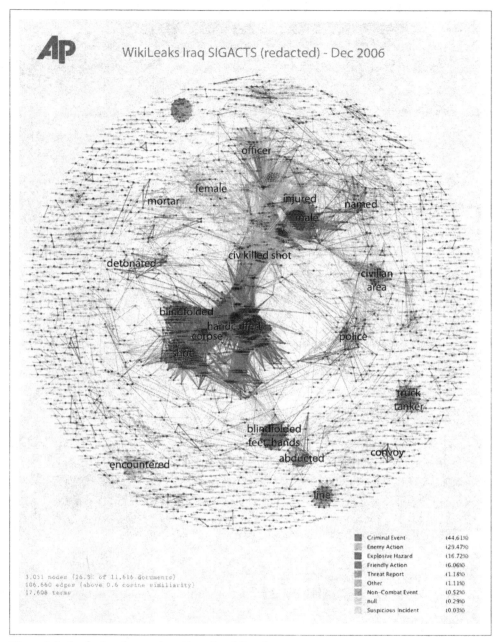

Figure 1-5. Analyzing the war logs (Associated Press)

Murder Mysteries

One of my favorite pieces of data journalism is the *Murder Mysteries* project by Tom Hargrove of the Scripps Howard News Service (*http://bit.ly/murder-mysteries*). From government data and public records requests, he built a demographically detailed database of more than 185,000 unsolved murders, and then designed an algorithm to search it for patterns suggesting the possible presence of serial killers. This project has it all: hard work, a database better than the government's own, clever analysis using social science techniques, and interactive presentation of the data online so readers can explore it themselves.

— *Steve Doig, Walter Cronkite School of Journalism, Arizona State University*

Figure 1-6. Murder Mysteries (Scripps Howard News Service)

Message Machine

I love ProPublica's Message Machine story (*http://bit.ly/message-machine*) and nerd blog post (*http://bit.ly/nerd-blog-post*). It all got started when some Twitterers expressed curiosity about having received different emails from the Obama campaign. The folks at ProPublica noticed, and asked their audience to forward any emails they got from the campaign. The presentation is elegant, a visual diff of several different emails that were sent out that evening. It's awesome because they gathered their own data (admittedly a small sample, but big enough to tell the story). But it's even more awesome because they're telling the story of an emerging phenomenon: big data used in political campaigns to target messages to specific individuals. It is just a taste of things to come.

— *Brian Boyer, Chicago Tribune*

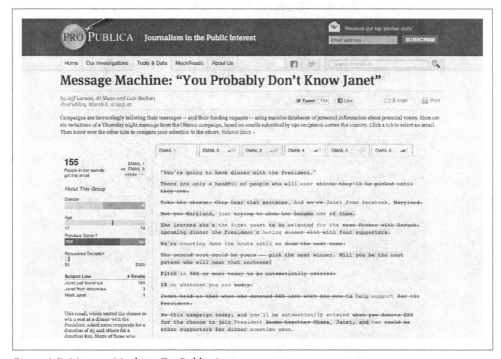

Figure 1-7. Message Machine (ProPublica)

Chartball

One of my favorite data journalism projects is Andrew Garcia Phillips' work on Chartball (*http://www.chartball.com/*). Andrew is a huge sports fan with a voracious appetite for data, a terrific eye for design, and the capacity to write code. With Chartball he visualizes not only the sweep of history, but details the success and failures of individual players and teams. He makes context, he makes an inviting graphic, and his work is deep and fun and interesting—and I don't even care much for sports!

— *Sarah Slobin, Wall Street Journal*

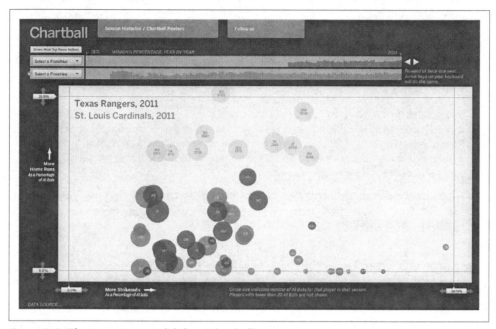

Figure 1-8. Charting victory and defeat (Chartball)

Data Journalism in Perspective

In August 2010 some colleagues at the European Journalism Centre and I organized what we believe was one of the first international data journalism conferences (*http://bit.ly/ddj-conf*), which took place in Amsterdam. At this time there wasn't a great deal of discussion around this topic and there were only a couple of organizations that were widely known for their work in this area.

The manner in which media organizations like the Guardian and The New York Times handled the large amounts of data released by WikiLeaks is one of the major steps that brought the term into prominence. Around that time, the term started to enter into more widespread usage (along with "computer-assisted reporting") to describe how journalists were using data to improve their coverage and to augment in-depth investigations into a given topic.

Speaking to experienced data journalists and journalism scholars on Twitter (*http://bit .ly/smfrogers-status*) it seems that one of the earliest formulations of what we now recognize as data journalism was in 2006 by Adrian Holovaty, founder of EveryBlock, an information service that enables users to find out what has been happening in their area, on their block. In his short essay "A fundamental way newspaper sites need to change" (*http://www.holovaty.com/writing/fundamental-change/*), he argues that journalists should publish structured, machine-readable data, alongside the traditional "big blob of text":

> For example, say a newspaper has written a story about a local fire. Being able to read that story on a cell phone is fine and dandy. Hooray, technology! But what I really want to be able to do is explore the raw facts of that story, one by one, with layers of attribution, and an infrastructure for comparing the details of the fire with the details of previous fires: date, time, place, victims, fire station number, distance from fire department, names and years experience of firemen on the scene, time it took for firemen to arrive, and subsequent fires, whenever they happen.

But what makes this distinctive from other forms of journalism that use databases or computers? How, and to what extent is data journalism different from other forms of journalism from the past?

Computer-Assisted Reporting and Precision Journalism

Using data to improve reportage and delivering structured (if not machine-readable) information to the public has a long history. Perhaps most immediately relevant to what we now call data journalism is *computer-assisted reporting*, or CAR, which was the first organized, systematic approach to using computers to collect and analyze data to improve the news.

CAR was first used in 1952 by CBS to predict the result of the presidential election. Since the 1960s, (mainly investigative, mainly US-based) journalists have sought to independently monitor power by analyzing databases of public records with scientific methods. Also known as "public service journalism," advocates of these computer-assisted techniques have sought to reveal trends, debunk popular knowledge and reveal injustices perpetrated by public authorities and private corporations. For example, Philip Meyer tried to debunk received readings of the 1967 riots in Detroit to show that it was not just less educated Southerners who were participating. Bill Dedman's "The Color of Money" stories in the 1980s revealed systemic racial bias in lending policies of major financial institutions. In his "What Went Wrong" article, Steve Doig sought to analyze the damage patterns from Hurricane Andrew in the early 1990s, to understand the effect of flawed urban development policies and practices. Data-driven reporting has brought valuable public service, and has won journalists famous prizes.

In the early 1970s the term *precision journalism* was coined to describe this type of news-gathering: "the application of social and behavioral science research methods to the practice of journalism" (from *The New Precision Journalism* by Philip Meyer; *http://bit.ly/precision-journalism*). Precision journalism was envisioned to be practiced in mainstream media institutions by professionals trained in journalism and social sciences. It was born in response to "new journalism," a form of journalism in which fiction techniques were applied to reporting. Meyer suggests that scientific techniques of data collection and analysis, rather than literary techniques, are what is needed for journalism to accomplish its search for objectivity and truth.

Precision journalism can be understood as a reaction to some of journalism's commonly cited inadequacies and weaknesses: dependence on press releases (later described as "churnalism"), bias towards authoritative sources, and so on. These are seen by Meyer as stemming from a lack of application of information science techniques and scientific methods such as polls and public records. As practiced in the 1960s, precision journalism was used to represent marginal groups and their stories. According to Meyer (*http://bit.ly/p-meyer*):

> Precision journalism was a way to expand the tool kit of the reporter to make topics that were previously inaccessible, or only crudely accessible, subject to journalistic scrutiny. It was especially useful in giving a hearing to minority and dissident groups that were struggling for representation.

An influential article (*http://bit.ly/oxford-influential*) published in the 1980s about the relationship between journalism and social science echoes current discourse around data journalism. The authors, two US journalism professors, suggest that in the 1970s and 1980s, the public's understanding of what news is broadens from a narrower conception of "news events" to "situational reporting" (or reporting on social trends). For example, by using databases of census data or survey data, journalists are able to "move beyond the reporting of specific, isolated events to providing a context which gives them meaning."

As we might expect, the practice of using data to improve reportage goes back as far as data has been around. As Simon Rogers points out (*http://bit.ly/facts-are-sacred*), the first example of data journalism at the Guardian dates from 1821. It is a leaked table of schools in Manchester listing the number of students who attended and the costs per school. According to Rogers, this helped to show the real number of students receiving free education, which was much higher than official numbers showed.

Another early example in Europe is Florence Nightingale and her key report, "Mortality of the British Army" (*http://bit.ly/mortality-army*), published in 1858. In her report to Parliament, she used graphics to advocate improvements in health services for the British army. The most famous is her "coxcomb," a spiral of sections each representing deaths per month, which highlighted that the vast majority of deaths were from preventable diseases rather than bullets.

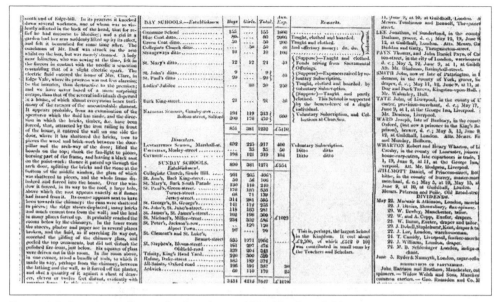

Figure 1-9. Data journalism in the Guardian in 1821 (the Guardian)

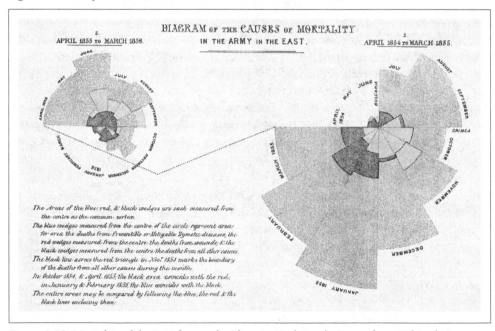

Figure 1-10. Mortality of the British army by Florence Nightingale (image from Wikipedia)

Data Journalism and Computer-Assisted Reporting

At the moment there is a "continuity and change" debate going on around the label "data journalism" and its relationship with previous journalistic practices that employ computational techniques to analyze datasets.

Some argue that there is a difference between CAR and data journalism. They say that CAR is a technique for gathering and analyzing data as a way of enhancing (usually investigative) reportage, whereas data journalism pays attention to the way that data sits within the whole journalistic workflow. In this sense data journalism pays as much —and sometimes more—attention to the data itself, rather than using data simply as a means to find or enhance stories. Hence we find the Guardian Datablog or the Texas Tribune publishing datasets alongside stories—or even just datasets by themselves— for people to analyze and explore.

Another difference is that in the past, investigative reporters would suffer from a poverty of information relating to a question they were trying to answer or an issue that they were trying to address. While this is of course still the case, there is also an overwhelming abundance of information that journalists don't necessarily know what to do with. They don't know how to get value out of data. A recent example is the Combined Online Information System, the UK's biggest database of spending information. The database was long sought after by transparency advocates, but baffled and stumped many journalists upon its release. As Philip Meyer recently wrote to me: "When information was scarce, most of our efforts were devoted to hunting and gathering. Now that information is abundant, processing is more important."

On the other hand, some argue that there is no meaningful difference between data journalism and computer-assisted reporting. It is by now common sense that even the most recent media practices have histories, as well as something new in them. Rather than debating whether or not data journalism is completely novel, a more fruitful position would be to consider it as part of a longer tradition, but responding to new circumstances and conditions. Even if there might not be a difference in goals and techniques, the emergence of the label "data journalism" at the beginning of the century indicates a new phase wherein the sheer volume of data that is freely available online —combined with sophisticated user-centric tools, self-publishing, and crowdsourcing tools—enables more people to work with more data more easily than ever before.

Data Journalism Is About Mass Data Literacy

Digital technologies and the web are fundamentally changing the way information is published. Data journalism is one part in the ecosystem of tools and practices that have sprung up around data sites and services. Quoting and sharing source materials is in the nature of the hyperlink structure of the Web, and the way we are accustomed to navigating information today. Going further back, the principle that sits at the foundation of the hyperlinked structure of the Web is the citation principle used in academic works. Quoting and sharing the source materials and the data behind the story is one of the basic ways in which data journalism can improve journalism, what WikiLeaks founder Julian Assange calls "scientific journalism."

By enabling anyone to drill down into data sources and find information that is relevant to them, as well as to to verify assertions and challenge commonly received assumptions, data journalism effectively represents the mass democratization of resources, tools, techniques, and methodologies that were previously used by specialists; whether investigative reporters, social scientists, statisticians, analysts, or other experts. While currently quoting and linking to data sources is particular to data journalism, we are moving towards a world in which data is seamlessly integrated into the fabric of media. Data journalists have an important role in helping to lower the barriers to understanding and delving into data, and increasing the data literacy of their readers on a mass scale.

At the moment the nascent community of people who call themselves data journalists is largely distinct from the more mature CAR community. Hopefully in the future, we will see stronger ties between these two communities, in much the same way that we see new NGOs and citizen media organizations like ProPublica and the Bureau of Investigative Journalism work hand in hand with traditional news media on investigations. While the data journalism community might have more innovative ways to deliver data and present stories, the deeply analytical and critical approach of the CAR community is something that data journalism could certainly learn from.

— *Liliana Bounegru, European Journalism Centre*

CHAPTER 2

In The Newsroom

How does data journalism sit within newsrooms around the world? How did leading data journalists convince their colleagues that it is a good idea to publish datasets or launch data-driven news apps? Should journalists learn how to code, or work in tandem with talented developers? In this section we look at the role of data and data journalism at the Australian Broadcasting Corporation, the BBC, the Chicago Tribune, the Guardian, the Texas Tribune, and the Zeit Online. We learn how to spot and hire good developers, how to engage people around a topic through hackathons and other events, how to collaborate across borders, and business models for data journalism.

The ABC's Data Journalism Play

The Australian Broadcasting Corporation is Australia's national public broadcaster. Annual funding is around $1 billion dollars (AUS), which delivers seven radio networks, 60 local radio stations, three digital television services, a new international television service, and an online platform to deliver this ever-expanding offering of digital and user-generated content. At last count, there were over 4,500 full time equivalent staff, and nearly 70% of them make content.

We are a national broadcaster fiercely proud of our independence; although funded by the government, we are separated at arm's length through law. Our traditions are independent public service journalism. The ABC is regarded as the most trusted news organization in the country.

These are exciting times; under a managing director (the former newspaper executive Mark Scott), content makers at the ABC have been encouraged to be "agile," as the corporate mantra puts it.

Of course, that's easier said than done.

But one initiative in recent times designed to encourage this has been a competitive staff pitch for money to develop multiplatform projects.

This is how the ABC's first ever data journalism project was conceived.

Sometime early in 2010, I wandered into the pitch session to face three senior "ideas" people with my proposal.

I'd been chewing it over for some time, greedily lapping up the data journalism that the now legendary Guardian Datablog was offering, and that was just for starters.

It was my argument that no doubt within 5 years, the ABC would have its own data journalism unit. It was inevitable, I opined. But the question was how we would get there, and who was going to start.

For those readers unfamiliar with the ABC, think of a vast bureaucracy built up over 70 years. Its primary offering was always radio and television. With the advent of a website, in the last decade this content offering unfurled into text, stills, and a degree of interactivity previously unimagined. The web space was forcing the ABC to rethink how it cut the cake (money) and what kind of cake it was baking (content).

It is of course a work in progress.

But something else was happening with data journalism. Government 2.0 (which as we discovered, is largely observed in the breach in Australia) was starting to offer new ways of telling stories that were hitherto buried in the zeros and ones.

I said all of this to the folks attending my pitch. I also said that we needed to identify new skill sets and train journalists in new tools. We needed a project to hit play.

And they gave me the money.

On the 24th of November 2011, the ABC's multiplatform project and ABC News Online went live with "Coal Seam Gas by the Numbers" (*http://bit.ly/abc-coal*).

Figure 2-1. Coal Seam Gas by the Numbers (ABC News Online)

It was made up of five pages of interactive maps, data visualizations, and text.

It wasn't exclusively data journalism, but a hybrid of journalisms that was born of the mix of people on the team and the story, which is raging as one of the hottest issues in Australia.

The jewel was an interactive map showing coal seam gas wells and leases in Australia. Users could search by location and switch between modes to show leases or wells. By zooming in, users could see who the explorer was, the status of the well, and its drill date. Another map showed the location of coal seam gas activity compared to the location of groundwater systems in Australia.

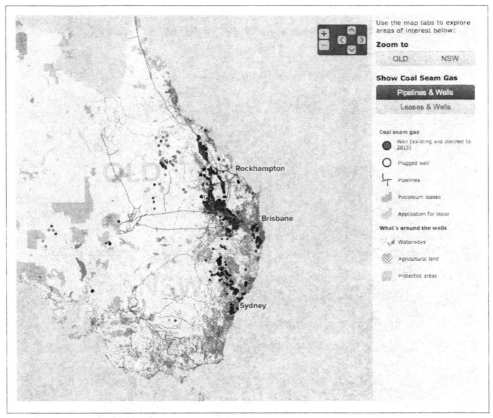

Figure 2-2. Interactive map of gas wells and leases in Australia (ABC News Online)

We had data visualizations that specifically addressed the issue of waste salt and water production that would be generated depending on the scenario that emerged.

Another section of the project investigated the release of chemicals into a local river system.

Our Team

- A web developer and designer
- A lead journalist
- A part-time researcher with expertise in data extraction, Excel spreadsheets, and data cleaning
- A part-time junior journalist
- A consultant executive producer

- A academic consultant with expertise in data mining, graphic visualization, and advanced research skills
- The services of a project manager and the administrative assistance of the ABC's multiplatform unit
- Importantly, we also had a reference group of journalists and others whom we consulted on an as-needed basis

Where Did We Get the Data From?

The data for the interactive maps were scraped from shapefiles (a common kind of file for geospatial data) downloaded from government websites.

Other data on salt and water were taken from a variety of reports.

The data on chemical releases was taken from environmental permits issued by the government.

What Did We Learn?

"Coal Seam Gas by the Numbers" was ambitious in content and scale. Uppermost in my mind was what did we learn, and how might we do it differently next time?

The data journalism project brought a lot of people into the room who do not normally meet at the ABC: in lay terms, the hacks and the hackers. Many of us did not speak the same language or even appreciate what the other group did. Data journalism is disruptive!

The practical things:

- Co-location of the team is vital. Our developer and designer were offsite and came in for meetings. This is definitely not optimal! Place everyone in the same room as the journalists.
- Our consultant EP was also on another level of the building. We needed to be much closer, just for the drop-by factor.
- Choose a story that is solely data-driven.

The Big Picture: Some Ideas

Big media organzations need to engage in capacity building to meet the challenges of data journalism. My hunch is that there are a lot of geeks and hackers hiding in media technical departments desperate to get out. So we need "hack and hacker meets" workshops where the secret geeks, younger journalists, web developers, and designers come out to play with more experienced journalists for skill-sharing and mentoring. Task: download this dataset and go for it!

Ipso facto, data journalism is interdisciplinary. Data journalism teams are made of people who would not have worked together in the past. The digital space has blurred the boundaries.

We live in a fractured, distrustful body politic. The business model that formerly delivered professional independent journalism—imperfect as it is—is on the verge of collapse. We ought to ask ourselves, as many now are, what might the world look like without a viable fourth estate? The American journalist and intellectual Walter Lippman remarked in the 1920's that "it is admitted that a sound public opinion cannot exist without access to news." That statement is no less true now. In the 21st century, everyone's hanging out in the blogosphere. It's hard to tell the spinners, liars, dissemblers, and vested interest groups from the professional journalists. Pretty much any site or source can be made to look credible, slick, and honest. The trustworthy mastheads are dying in the ditch. And in this new space of junk journalism, hyperlinks can endlessly take the reader to other more useless but brilliant-looking sources that keep hyperlinking back into the digital hall of mirrors. The technical term for this is: bullshit baffles brains.

In the digital space, everyone's a storyteller now, right? Wrong. If professional journalism—and by that I mean those who embrace ethical, balanced, courageous truth-seeking storytelling—is to survive, then the craft must reassert itself in the digital space. Data journalism is just another tool by which we will navigate the digital space. It's where we will map, flip, sort, filter, extract, and see the story amidst all those zeros and ones. In the future we'll be working side by side with the hackers, the developers, the designers, and the coders. It's a transition that requires serious capacity building. We need news managers who "get" the digital/journalism connection to start investing in the build.

— *Wendy Carlisle, Australian Broadcasting Corporation*

Data Journalism at the BBC

The term "data journalism" can cover a range of disciplines and is used in varying ways in news organizations, so it may be helpful to define what we mean by "data journalism" at the BBC. Broadly, the term covers projects that use data to do one or more of the following:

- Enable a reader to discover information that is personally relevant
- Reveal a story that is remarkable and previously unknown
- Help the reader to better understand a complex issue

These categories may overlap, and in an online environment, can often benefit from some level of visualization.

Make It Personal

On the BBC News website, we have been using data to provide services and tools for our users for well over a decade.

The most consistent example, which we first published in 1999, is our school league tables (*http://bbc.in/school-league-tables*), which use the data published annually by the government. Readers can find local schools by entering a postcode, and compare them on a range of indicators. Education journalists also work with the development team to trawl the data for stories ahead of publication.

When we started to do this, there was no official site that provided a way for the public to explore the data. But now that the Department for Education has its own comparable service, our offering has shifted to focus more on the stories that emerge from the data.

The challenge in this area must be to provide access to data in which there is a clear public interest. A recent example of a project where we exposed a large dataset not normally available to the wider public was the special report "Every death on every road" (*http://bbc.in/road-deaths*). We provided a postcode search, allowing users to find the location of all road fatalities in the UK in the past decade.

We visualized some of the main facts and figures (*http://bbc.in/police-data*) that emerge from the police data and, to give the project a more dynamic feel and a human face, we teamed up with the London Ambulance Association and BBC London radio and TV to track crashes across the capital as they happened. This was reported live online (*http://bbc.in/road-deaths-feed*), as well as via Twitter using the hashtag #crash24, and collisions were mapped (*http://bbc.in/road-deaths-map*) as they were reported.

Simple Tools

As well as providing ways to explore large datasets, we have also had success creating simple tools for users that provide personally relevant snippets of information. These tools appeal to the time-poor, who may not choose to explore lengthy analysis. The ability to easily share a personal fact is something we have begun to incorporate as standard.

A lighthearted example of this approach is our feature "The world at 7 billion: What's your number?" (*http://bbc.in/KQsSzB*), published to coincide with the official date at which the world's population exceeded 7 billion. By entering their birth date, the user could find out what "number" they were, in terms of the global population, when they were born and then share that number via Twitter or Facebook. The application used data provided by the UN population development fund. It was very popular, and became the most shared link on Facebook in the UK in 2011.

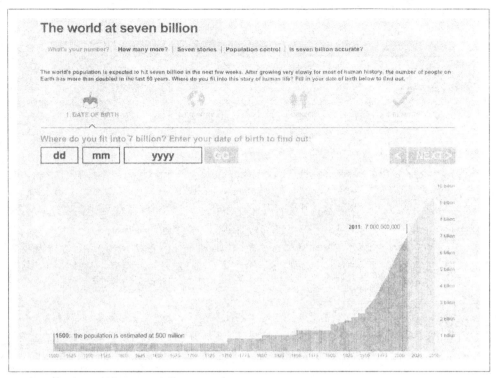

Figure 2-3. The world at seven billion (BBC)

Another recent example is the BBC budget calculator (*http://bbc.in/JepssY*), which enabled users to find out how better or worse off they will be when the Chancellor's budget takes effect—and then share that figure. We teamed up with the accountancy firm KPMG LLP, who provided us with calculations based on the annual budget, and then we worked hard to create an appealing interface that would encourage users to complete the task.

Mining The Data

But where is the journalism in all this? Finding stories in data is a more traditional definition of data journalism. Is there an exclusive buried in the database? Are the figures accurate? Do they prove or disprove a problem? These are all questions a data journalist or computer-assisted reporter must ask themselves. But a great deal of time can be taken up sifting through a massive dataset in the hope of finding something remarkable.

In this area, we have found it most productive to partner with investigative teams or programs that have the expertise and time to investigate a story. The BBC current affairs program Panorama spent months working with the Centre for Investigative Journalism, gathering data on public sector pay. The result was a TV documentary and a special report online, "Public Sector pay: The numbers" (*http://bbc.in/IKPrL2*), where all the data was published and visualized with sector by sector analysis.

As well as partnering with investigative journalists, having access to numerous journalists with specialist knowledge is essential. When a business colleague on the team analyzed the spending review cuts data put out by the government, he came to the conclusion that it was making them sound bigger than they actually were. The result was an exclusive story, "Making sense of the data" (*http://bbc.in/LcuGFV*) complemented by a clear visualization (*http://bbc.in/IIADrj*), which won a Royal Statistical Society award.

Understanding An Issue

But data journalism doesn't have to be an exclusive no one else has spotted. The job of the data visualization team is to combine great design with a clear editorial narrative to provide a compelling experience for the user. Engaging visualizations of the right data can be used to give a better understanding of an issue or story, and we frequently use this approach in our storytelling at the BBC. One technique used in our UK claimant count tracker is to heat-map data over time to give a clear view of change (*http://bbc.in/ KF7IKU*).

The data feature "Eurozone debt web" (*http://bbc.in/IIAHHI*) explores the tangled web of intra-country lending. It helps to explain a complicated issue in a visual way, using color and proportional arrows combined with clear text. An important consideration is to encourage the user to explore the feature or follow a narrative, without making him feel overwhelmed by the numbers.

Team Overview

The team that produces data journalism for the BBC News website is comprised of about 20 journalists, designers, and developers.

As well as data projects and visualizations, the team produces all the infographics and interactive multimedia features on the news website. Together, these form a collection of storytelling techniques we have come to call *visual journalism*. We don't have people who are specifically identified as data journalists, but all editorial staff on the team have to be proficient at using basic spreadsheet applications such as Excel and Google Docs to analyze data.

Central to any data projects are the technical skills and advice of our developers and the visualization skills of our designers. While we are all either a journalist, designer, or developer "first," we continue to work hard to increase our understanding and proficiency in each other's areas of expertise.

The core products for exploring data are Excel, Google Docs, and Fusion Tables. The team has also, but to a lesser extent, used MySQL, Access databases, and Solr to explore larger datasets; and used RDF and SPARQL to begin looking at ways in which we can model events using Linked Data technologies. Developers will also use their programming language of choice, whether that's ActionScript, Python, or Perl, to match, parse, or generally pick apart a dataset we might be working on. Perl is used for some of the publishing.

We use Google, Bing Maps, and Google Earth, along with Esri's ArcMAP, for exploring and visualizing geographical data.

For graphics we use the Adobe Suite including After Effects, Illustrator, Photoshop, and Flash, although we would rarely publish Flash files on the site these days as JavaScript—particularly JQuery and other JavaScript libraries like Highcharts, Raphael and D3—increasingly meets our data visualization requirements.

— *Bella Hurrell and Andrew Leimdorfer, BBC*

How the News Apps Team at the Chicago Tribune Works

The news applications team at the Chicago Tribune is a band of happy hackers embedded in the newsroom. We work closely with editors and reporters to help: 1) research and report stories, 2) illustrate stories online and 3) build evergreen web resources for the fine people of Chicagoland.

It's important that we sit in the newsroom. We usually find work via face-to-face conversations with reporters. They know that we're happy to help write a screen scraper for a crummy government website, tear up a stack of PDFs, or otherwise turn non-data into something you can analyze. It's sort of our team's loss leader; this way we find out about potential data projects at the outset.

Unlike many teams in this field, our team was founded by technologists for whom journalism was a career change. Some of us acquired a masters degree in journalism after several years of coding for business purposes, and others were borrowed from the open government community.

We work in an agile fashion. To make sure we're always in sync, every morning begins with a 5-minute stand-up meeting. We frequently program in pairs; two developers at one keyboard are often more productive than two developers at two keyboards. Most projects don't take more than a week to produce, but on longer projects we work in week-long iterations, and show our work to stakeholders (reporters and editors usually) every week. "Fail fast" is the mantra. If you're doing it wrong, you need to know as soon as possible, especially when you're coding on a deadline!

There's a tremendous upside to hacking iteratively, on a deadline: we're always updating our toolkit. Every week we crank out an app or two, then, unlike normal software shops, we can put it to the back of our mind and move on to the next project. It's a joy we share with the reporters, and every week we learn something new.

Figure 2-4. The Chicago Tribune news applications team (photo by Heather Billings)

All app ideas come from the reporters and editors in the newsroom. This, I believe, sets us apart from app teams in other newsrooms, who frequently spawn their own ideas. We've built strong personal and professional relationships in the newsroom, and folks know that when they have data, they come to us.

Much of our work in the newsroom is reporter support. We help reporters dig through data, turn PDFs back into spreadsheets, screen-scrape websites, etc. It's a service that we like to provide because it gets us in early on the data work that's happening in the newsroom. Some of that work becomes a news application: a map, table, or sometimes a larger-scale website.

Before, we linked to the app from the written story, which didn't result in much traffic. These days apps run near the top of our website, and the app links through to the story, which works nicely for both the app and the story. There is a section of the website for our work (*http://www.chicagotribune.com/news/data/*), but it's not well-trafficked. But that's not surprising. "Hey, today I want some data!," isn't a very big use case.

We love page views, and we love the accolades of our peers, but that's weak sauce. The motivation should always be impact; on people's lives, on the law, on holding politicians to account, and so on. The written piece will speak to the trend and humanize it with a few anecdotes. But what's the reader to do when they've finished the story? Is their family safe? Are their children being educated properly? Our work sings when it helps a reader find his or her *own* story in the data. Examples of impactful, personalized work that we've done include our Nursing Home Safety Reports (*http://nursinghomes .apps.chicagotribune.com/*) and School Report Card (*http://schools.chicagotribune .com/*) apps.

— *Brian Boyer, Chicago Tribune*

Behind the Scenes at the Guardian Datablog

When we launched the Datablog, we had no idea who would be interested in raw data, statistics, and visualizations. As someone rather senior in my office said, "why would anyone want that?"

The Guardian Datablog (*http://www.guardian.co.uk/datablog*), which I edit, was to be a small blog offering the full datasets behind our news stories. Now it consists of a front page (*http://guardian.co.uk/data*); searches of world government and global development data; data visualizations by Guardian graphic artists and from around the Web, and tools for exploring public spending data. Every day, we use Google spreadsheets to share the full data behind our work; we visualize and analyze that data, and then use it to provide stories for the newspaper and the site.

As a news editor and journalist working with graphics, it was a logical extension of work I was already doing, accumulating new datasets and wrangling with them to try to make sense of the news stories of the day.

The question I was asked has been answered for us. It has been an incredible few years for public data. Obama opened up the US government's data vaults as his first legislative act, and his example was soon followed by government data sites around the world: Australia, New Zealand, and the British government's Data.gov.uk.

We've had the MPs expenses scandal, Britain's most unexpected piece of data journalism—the resulting fallout has meant that Westminster is now committed to releasing huge amounts of data every year.

We had a general election where each of the main political parties was committed to data transparency, opening our own data vaults to the world. We've had newspapers devoting valuable column inches to the release of the Treasury's COINS database.

At the same time, as the Web pumps out more and more data, readers from around the world are more interested in the raw facts behind the news than ever before. When we launched the Datablog, we thought the audiences would be developers building applications. In fact, it's people wanting to know more about carbon emissions, Eastern European immigration, the breakdown of deaths in Afghanistan, or even the number of times the Beatles used the word "love" in their songs (613).

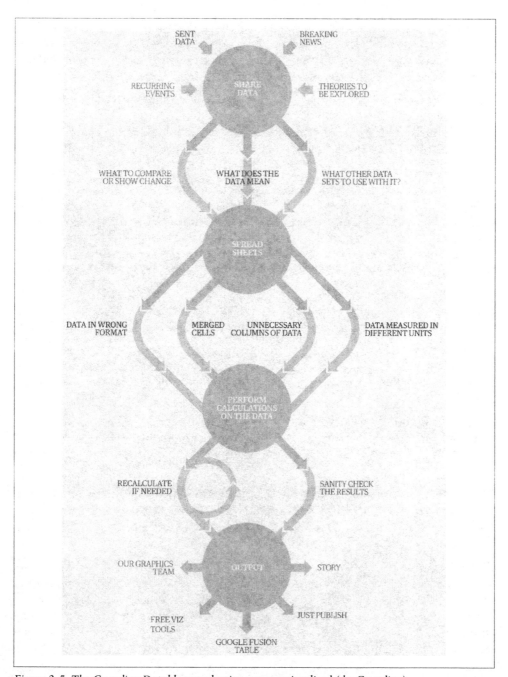

Figure 2-5. The Guardian Datablog production process visualized (the Guardian)

Gradually, the Datablog's work has reflected and added to the stories we faced. We crowdsourced 458,000 documents relating to MPs' expenses and we analyzed the detailed data of which MPs had claimed what. We helped our users explore detailed Treasury spending databases and published the data behind the news.

But the game-changer for data journalism happened in spring 2010, beginning with one spreadsheet: 92,201 rows of data, each one containing a detailed breakdown of a military event in Afghanistan. This was the WikiLeaks war logs. Part one, that is. There were to be two more episodes to follow: Iraq and the cables. The official term for the first two parts was SIGACTS: the US military Significant Actions Database.

News organizations are all about geography—and proximity to the news desk. If you're close, it's easy to suggest stories and become part of the process; conversely, out of sight is literally out of mind. Before WikiLeaks, we were placed on a different floor, with graphics. Since WikiLeaks, we have sat on the same floor, next to the newsdesk. It means that it's easier for us to suggest ideas to the desk, and for reporters across the newsroom to think of us to help with stories.

It's not that long ago journalists were the gatekeepers to official data. We would write stories about the numbers and release them to a grateful public, who were not interested in the raw statistics. The idea of us allowing raw information into our newspapers was anathema.

Now that dynamic has changed beyond recognition. Our role is becoming interpreters; helping people understand the data, and even just publishing it because it's interesting in itself.

But numbers without analysis are just numbers, which is where we fit in. When Britain's prime minister claims the riots in August 2011 were not about poverty, we were able to map the addresses of the rioters with poverty indicators to show the truth behind the claim.

Behind all of our data journalism stories is a process. It's changing all the time as we use new tools and techniques. Some people say the answer is to become a sort of super hacker, write code, and immerse yourself in SQL. You can decide to take that approach. But a lot of the work we do is just in Excel.

Firstly, we locate the data or receive it from a variety of sources, from breaking news stories, government data, journalists' research and so on. We then start looking at what we can do with the data; do we need to mash it up with another dataset? How can we show changes over time? Those spreadsheets often have to be seriously tidied up—all those extraneous columns and weirdly merged cells really don't help. And that's assuming it's not a PDF, the worst format for data known to humankind.

Often official data comes with the official codes added in; each school, hospital, constituency, and local authority has a unique identifier code.

Countries have them too (the UK's code is GB, for instance). They're useful because you may want to start mashing datasets together, and it's amazing how many different spellings and word arrangements can get in the way of that. There's Burma and Myanmar, for instance, or Fayette County in the US (there are 11 of these in states from Georgia to West Virginia). Codes allow us to compare like with like.

At the end of that process is the output: will it be a story or a graphic or a visualization, and what tools will we use? Our top tools are the free ones that we can produce something quickly with. The more sophisticated graphics are produced by our dev team.

This means that we commonly use Google charts for small line graphs and pies, or Google Fusion Tables to create maps quickly and easily.

It may seem new, but it's really not.

In the very first issue of the Manchester Guardian (on Saturday May 5th, 1821), the news was on the back page, like all papers of the day. The first item on the front page was an ad for a missing Labrador.

Amid the stories and poetry excerpts, a third of that back page is taken up with, well, facts. A comprehensive table of the costs of schools in the area never before "laid before the public," writes "NH."

NH wanted his data published because otherwise the facts would be left to untrained clergymen to report. His motivation was that, "Such information as it contains is valuable; because, without knowing the extent to which education ... prevails, the best opinions which can be formed of the condition and future progress of society must be necessarily incorrect." In other words, if the people don't know what's going on, how can society get any better?

I can't think of a better rationale now for what we're trying to do. Now what once was a back page story can now make front page news.

— *Simon Rogers, the Guardian*

Data Journalism at the Zeit Online

The PISA based Wealth Comparison (*http://bit.ly/Pisa_Wealth*) project is an interactive visualization that enables comparison of standards of living in different countries. It uses data from the OECD's comprehensive world education ranking report, PISA 2009 (*http://bit.ly/Pisa_2009*), published in December 2010. The report is based on a questionnaire which asks fifteen year-old pupils about their living situation at home.

The idea was to analyze and visualize this data to provide a unique way of comparing standards of living in different countries.

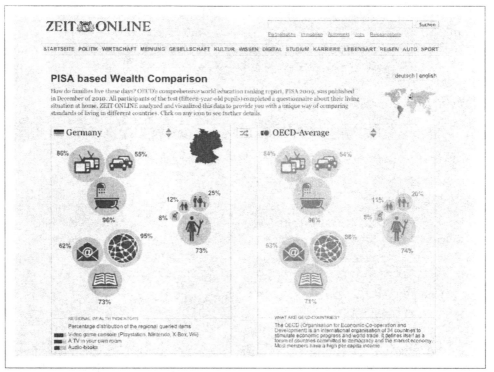

Figure 2-6. PISA based Wealth Comparison (Zeit Online)

First, our in-house editorial team decided which facts seemed to be useful to make living standards comparable and should be visualized, including:

- Wealth (number of TVs, cars and available bathrooms at home)
- Family situation (whether there are grandparents living with the family, percentage share of families with only one child, unemployment of parents, and mother's job status)
- Access to knowledge sources (Internet at home, frequency of using email and quantity of owned books)
- Three additional indicators on the level of development of each country

With the help of the internal design team, these facts were translated into self-explanatory icons. A front end design was built to make comparison between the different countries possible, by looking at them like they were playing cards.

Next we contacted people from the German Open Data Network (*http://opendata-net work.org/*) to find developers who could help with the project. This community of highly motivated people suggested Gregor Aisch, a very talented information designer, to code the application that would make our dreams come true (without using Flash, which was very important to us!). Gregor created a very high quality and interactive visualization with a beautiful bubble-style, based on the Raphaël-Javascript Library (*http://raphaeljs.com/*).

The result of our collaboration was a very successful interactive that got a lot of traffic. It is easy to compare any two countries, which makes it useful as a reference tool. This means that we can reuse it in our daily editorial work. For example, if we are covering something related to the living situation in Indonesia, we can quickly and easily embed a graphic comparing the living situation in Indonesia and Germany (*http://bit.ly/Pisa _Indonesia_Germany*). The know-how transferred to our in-house team was a great investment for future projects.

At the Zeit Online, we've found that our data journalism projects (*http://www.zeit.de/ datenjournalismus*) have brought us a lot of traffic and have helped us to engage audiences in new ways. For example, there was a lot of coverage about the situation at the nuclear plant in Fukushima after the tsunami in Japan. After radioactive material escaped from the power plant, everyone within 30 kilometers of the plant was evacuated. People could read and see a lot about the evacuations. Zeit Online found a innovative way to explain the impact of this to our German audience. We asked: how many people live near a nuclear power plant in Germany? How many people live within a radius of 30 kilometers? A map shows how many people would have to be evacuated in a similar situation in Germany (*http://bit.ly/near_nuclear*). The result: lots and lots of traffic; in fact, the project went viral in the social media sphere. Data journalism projects can be relatively easily adapted to other languages. We created an English language version about proximity to nuclear power plants in the US, which was a great traffic motor. News organizations want to be recognized as trusted and authoritative sources amongst their readers. We find that data journalism projects combined with enabling our readers to look and reuse the raw data brings us a high degree of credibility.

For two years the R&D Department and the Editor-in-Chief at the Zeit Online, Wolfgang Blau, have been advocating data journalism as an important way to tell stories. Transparency, credibility, and user engagement are important parts of our philosophy. That is why data journalism is a natural part of our current and future work. Data visualizations can bring value to the reception of a story, and are an attractive way for the whole editorial team to present their content.

For example, on November 9th, 2011, Deutsche Bank pledged to stop financing cluster bomb manufacturers. But according to a study by non-profit organization Facing Finance, the bank continued to approve loans to producers of cluster munitions after that promise was made. Our visualization (*http://zeit.de/wirtschaft/cluster-munition*) based on the data shows our readers the various flows of money. The different parts of the Deutsche Bank company are arranged at the top, with the companies accused of involvement in building cluster munitions at the bottom. In between, the individual loans are represented along a timeline. Rolling over the circles shows the details of each transaction. Of course the story could have been told as a written article. But the visualization enables our readers to understand and explore the financial dependencies in a more intuitive way.

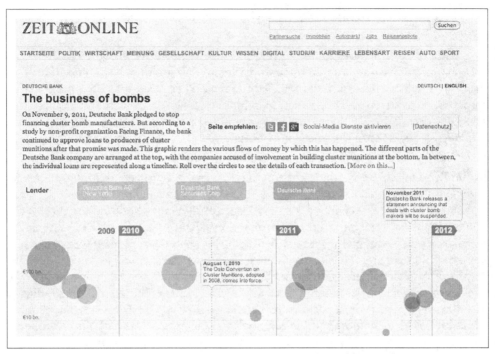

Figure 2-7. The business of bombs (Zeit Online)

To take another example: the German Federal Statistic Office (*https://www.destatis.de/ EN/Homepage.html*) has published a great dataset on vital statistics for Germany, including modeling various demographic scenarios up until 2060 (*http://bit.ly/German _Federal_Statistics*). The typical way to represent this is a population pyramid, such as the one from the Federal Statistics Agency (*https://www.destatis.de/bevoelkerungspyra mide/*).

With our colleagues from the science department, we tried to give our readers a better way to explore the projected demographic data about our future society. With our visualization (*http://www.zeit.de/wissen/altersstruktur*), we present a statistically representative group of 40 people of different ages from the years 1950 till 2060. They are organized into eight different groups. It looks like a group photo of German society at different points in time. The same data visualized in a traditional population pyramid gives only a very abstract feeling of the situation, but a group with kids, younger people, adults, and elderly people means our readers can relate to the data more easily. You can just hit the play button to start a journey through eleven decades. You can also enter your own year of birth and gender to become part of the group photo: to see your demographic journey through the decades and your own life expectancy.

— *Sascha Venohr, Zeit Online*

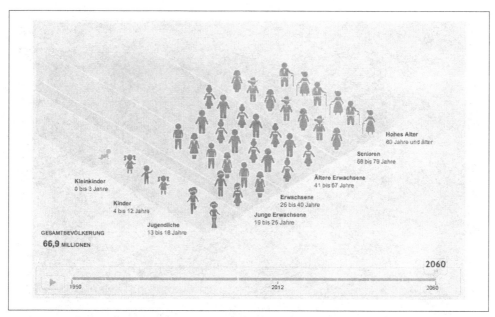

Figure 2-8. Visualizing demographic data (Zeit Online)

How to Hire a Hacker

One of the things that I am regularly asked by journalists is "how do I get a coder to help me with my project?" Don't be deceived into thinking that this is a one-way process; civic-minded hackers and data-wranglers are often just as keen to get in touch with journalists.

Journalists are power-users of data driven tools and services. From the perspective of developers, journalists think outside the box to use data tools in contexts developers haven't always considered before (feedback is invaluable!). They also help to build context and buzz around projects and help to make them relevant. It is a symbiotic relationship.

Fortunately, this means that whether you are looking to hire a hacker or looking for possible collaborations on a shoestring budget, there will more than likely be someone out there who is interested in helping you.

So how do you find them? Says Aron Pilhofer from The New York Times:

> You may find that your organzation already has people with all the skills you need, but they are not necessarily already in your newsroom. Wander around, visit the technology and IT departments, and you are likely to strike gold. It is also important to appreciate coder culture: come across someone who has a computer that looks like the one in Figure 2-9...then you are probably onto a winner.

Figure 2-9. Badge of honor: hackers are often easy to spot (photo by Lucy Chambers)

Here are a few more ideas:

Post on job websites

Identify and post to websites aimed at developers who work in different programming languages. For example, the Python Job Board (*http://www.python.org/community/jobs/*).

Contact relevant mailing lists

For example, the NICAR-L (*http://bit.ly/nicar-subscribe*) and Data Driven Journalism (*http://bit.ly/ddj-list*) mailing lists.

Contact relevant organizations

For example, if you want to clean up or scrape data from the web, you could contact an organization such as Scraperwiki (*https://scraperwiki.com/*), who have a great address book of trusted and willing coders.

Join relevant groups/networks

Look out for initiatives such as Hacks/Hackers (*http://hackshackers.com/*) which bring journalists and techies together. Hacks/Hackers groups are now springing up all around the world. You could also try posting something to their jobs newsletter (*http://bit.ly/hacks-hackers-jobs*).

Local interest communities
You could try doing a quick search for an area of expertise in your area (e.g. "java-script" + "london"). Sites such as Meetup.com can also be a great place to start.

Hackathons and competitions
Whether or not there is prize money available, app and visualization competitions and development days are often fruitful ground for collaboration and making connections.

Ask a geek!
Geeks hang around with other geeks. Word of mouth is always a good way to find good people to work with.

— *Lucy Chambers, Open Knowledge Foundation*

Hacker Skills

Once you've found a hacker, how do you know if they are any good? We asked Alastair Dant from the Guardian for his views on how to spot a good one:

They code the full stack
When dealing with deadlines, it's better to be a jack of all trades than a master of one. News apps require data wrangling, dynamic graphics, and derring-do.

They see the whole picture
Holistic thinking favors narrative value over technical detail. I'd rather hear one note played with feeling than unceasing virtuosity in obscure scales. Find out how happy someone is to work alongside a designer.

They tell a good story
Narrative presentation requires arranging things in space and time. Find out what project they're most proud of and ask them to walk you through how it was built; this will reveal as much about their ability to communicate as their technical understanding.

They talk things through
Building things fast requires mixed teams working towards common goals. Each participant should respect their fellows and be willing to negotiate. Unforeseen obstacles often require rapid re-planning and collective compromise.

They teach themselves
Technology moves fast. It's a struggle to keep up with. Having met good developers from all sorts of backgrounds, the most common trait is a willingness to learn new stuff on demand.

— *Lucy Chambers, Open Knowledge Foundation, interviewing Alastair Dant, Lead Interactive Technologist, the Guardian*

How To Find Your Dream Developer

The productivity difference between a good and a great developer is not linear—it's exponential. Hiring well is extremely important. Unfortunately, hiring well is also very difficult. It's hard enough to vet candidates if you are not an experienced technical manager. Add to that the salaries that news organizations can afford to pay, and you've got quite a challenge.

At Tribune, we recruit with two angles: an emotional appeal and a technical appeal. The emotional appeal is this: journalism is essential to a functioning democracy. Work here and you can change the world. Technically, we promote how much you'll learn. Our projects are small, fast, and iterative. Every project is a new set of tools, a new language, a new topic (fire safety, the pension system), that you must learn. The newsroom is a crucible. I've never managed a team that has learned so much, so fast, as our team.

As for where to look, we've had great luck finding great hackers in the open government community. The Sunlight Labs mailing list is where do-gooder nerds with crappy day jobs hang out at night. Another potential resource is Code for America. Every year, a group of fellows emerges from CfA, looking for their next big project. And as a bonus, CfA has a rigorous interview process; they've already done the vetting for you. Nowadays, programming-interested journalists are also emerging from journalism schools. They're green, but they've got tons of potential.

Lastly, it's not enough to just hire developers. You need technical management. A lone-gun developer (especially fresh from journalism school, with no industry experience) is going to make many bad decisions. Even the best programmer, when left to her own devices, will choose technically interesting work over doing what's most important to your audience.

Call this hire a news applications editor, a project manager, whatever. Just like writers, programmers need editors, mentorship, and somebody to wrangle them towards making software on deadline.

— *Brian Boyer, Chicago Tribune*

Harnessing External Expertise Through Hackathons

In March 2010, Utrecht-based digital culture organzation SETUP put on an event called Hacking Journalism (*http://setup.nl/content/hacking-journalism*). The event was organized to encourage greater collaboration between developers and journalists.

"We organize hackathons to make cool applications, but we can't recognize interesting stories in data. What we build has no social relevance," said the programmers. "We recognize the importance of data journalism, but we don't have all the technical skills to build the things we want," said the journalists.

Figure 2-10. Journalists and developers at RegioHack (photo by Heinze Havinga)

Working for a regional newspaper, there was no money or incentive to hire a programmer for the newsroom. Data journalism was still an unknown quantity for Dutch newspapers at that time.

The hackathon model was perfect; a relaxed environment for collaboration, with plenty of pizza and energy drinks. RegioHack (*http://www.regiohack.nl/*) was a hackathon organized by my employer, the regional newspaper De Stentor (*http://www.destentor .nl/*), our sister publication TC Tubantia (*http://www.tctubantia.nl/*), and Saxion Hogescholen Enschede (*http://saxion.nl/*), who provided the location for the event.

The setup was as follows: everyone could enlist for a 30-hour hackathon. We provided the food and drink. We aimed for 30 participants, which we divided into 6 groups. These groups would focus on different topics, such as crime, health, transport, safety, aging, and power. For us, the three main objectives for this event were as follows:

Find stories
> For us, data journalism is something new and unknown. The only way we can prove its use is through well crafted stories. We planned to produce at least three data stories.

Connect people

We, the journalists, don't know how data journalism is done and we don't pretend to. By putting journalists, students, and programmers in one room for 30 hours, we want them to share knowledge and insights.

Host a social event

Newspapers don't organize a lot of social events, let alone hackathons. We wanted to experience how such an event can yield results. In fact, the event could have been tense: 30 hours with strangers, lots of jargon, bashing your head against basic questions, and working out of your comfort zone. By making it a social event (remember the pizza and energy drinks?), we wanted to create an environment in which journalists and programmers could feel comfortable and collaborate effectively.

Before the event, TC Tubantia had an interview with the widow of a policeman who had written a book on her husband's working years. She also had a document with all registered murders in the eastern part of the Netherlands, maintained by her husband since 1945. Normally, we would publish this document on our website. This time, we made a dashboard using the Tableau software (*http://bit.ly/tableau-dashboard*). We also blogged (*http://bit.ly/regiohack-blog*) about how this came together on our RegioHack site.

During the hackathon, one project group came up with the subject of development of schools and the aging of our region. By making a visualization of future projections (*http://bit.ly/tableau-workbook*), we understood which cities would get in trouble after a few years of decline in enrollments. With this insight, we made an article on how this would affect schools in our region.

We also started a very ambitious project called De Tweehonderd van Twente (in English, The Two Hundred of Twente) to determine who had the most power in our region and build a database of the most influential people. Through a Google-ish calculation—who has the most ties with powerful organizations—a list of influential people will be composed. This could lead to a series of articles, but it's also a powerful tool for journalists. Who has connections with who? You can ask questions to this database and use it in your daily routine. Also, this database has cultural value. Artists already asked if they could use this database when finished, in order to make interactive art installations.

After RegioHack, we noticed that journalists considered data journalism a viable addition to traditional journalism. My colleagues continued to use and build on the techniques learned on that day to create more ambitious and technical projects, such as a database of the administrative costs of housing. With this data, I made an interactive map in Fusion Tables (*http://bit.ly/stentor-map*). We asked our readers to play around with the data and crowdsourced results at *http://bit.ly/scratchbook-crowdsourcing*, for example. After a lot of questions on how we made a map in Fusion Tables, I also recorded a video tutorial (*http://bit.ly/vermanen-video*).

Figure 2-11. New communities around data journalism (photo by Heinze Havinga)

What did we learn? We learned a lot, but we also came along a lot of obstacles. We recognized these four:

Where to begin: question or data?

Almost all projects stalled when searching for information. Most of the time, they began with a journalistic question. But then? What data is available? Where can you find it? And when you find this data, can you answer your question with it? Journalists usually know where they can find information when doing research for an article. With data journalism, most journalists don't know what information is available.

Little technical knowledge

Data journalism is quite a technical discipline. Sometimes you have to scrape, other times you'll have to do some programming to visualize your results. For excellent data journalism, you'll need two aspects: the journalistic insight of an experienced journalist and the technical know-how of a digital all-rounder. During RegioHack, this was not a common presence.

Is it news?

Participants mostly used one dataset to discover news, instead of searching interconnections between different sources. The reason for this is that you need some statistical knowledge to verify news from data journalism.

What's the routine?

> What everything above comes down to is that there's no routine. The participants have some skills under their belt, but don't know how and when to use them. One journalist compared it with baking a cake. "We have all the ingredients: flour, eggs, milk, etcetera. Now we throw it all in a bag, shake it, and hope a cake comes out." Indeed, we have all the ingredients, but don't know what the recipe is.

What now? Our first experiences with data journalism could help other journalists or programmers aspiring to enter the same field of work, and we are working to produce a report.

We are also considering how to continue RegioHack in a hackathon form. We found it fun, educational, and productive and a great introduction to data journalism.

But for data journalism to work, we have to integrate it in the newsroom. Journalists have to think in data, in addition to quotes, press releases, council meetings, and so on. By doing RegioHack, we proved to our audience that data journalism isn't just hype. We can write better informed and more distinctive articles, while presenting our readers with different articles in print and online.

— *Jerry Vermanen, NU.nl*

Following the Money: Data Journalism and Cross-Border Collaboration

Investigative journalists and citizens interested in uncovering organized crime and corruption that affect the lives of billions worldwide, with each passing day, have unprecedented access to information. Huge volumes of data are made available online by governments and other organizations, and it seems that much needed information is more and more in everyone's grasp. However, at the same time, corrupt officials in governments and organized crime groups are doing their best to conceal information in order to hide their misdeeds. They make efforts to keep people in the dark while conducting ugly deals that cause disruptions at all society levels and lead to conflict, famine, or other crises.

It is the duty of investigative journalists to expose such wrongdoings, and by doing so, disable corrupt and criminal mechanisms.

There are three main guidelines that, if followed, can lead to good, thorough journalism when investigating major acts of corruption and crime even in the most austere of environments:

Think outside your country

> In many instances, it is much easier to get information from abroad than from within the country where the investigative journalist operates. Information gathered from abroad via foreign information databases or by using other countries'

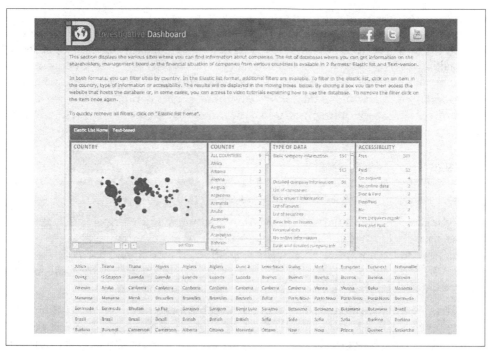

Figure 2-12. The Investigative Dashboard (OCCRP)

access to information laws might be just what you need to put the investigative puzzle together. On top of that, criminals and corrupt officials don't keep their money in the place they have stolen it from. They would rather deposit it in foreign banks or invest in other countries. Crime is global. Databases that assist the investigative journalist in tracking the money worldwide can be found in many places on the Internet. For example, the Investigative Dashboard (*http://www.investigati vedashboard.org/category/wwd/*) enables journalists to follow the money across borders.

Make use of existing investigative journalism networks

Investigative journalists all over the world are grouped in orgranzations such as The Organized Crime and Corruption Reporting Project (*http://www.reportingproject .net/*), The African Forum for Investigative Reporting (*http://www.fairreporters .org/*), The Arab Reporters for Investigative Journalism (*http://arij.net/*), and The Global investigative Journalism Network (*http://www.gijn.org/*). Journalists can also make use of professional journalism platforms such as IJNet, where global journalism related information is exchanged on a daily basis. Many of the reporters grouped in networks work on similar issues and confront similar situations, so it makes a lot of sense to exchange information and methods. Emailing lists or social network groups are attached to these networks, so it is quite easy to get in touch with fellow journalists and to ask for information or advice. Investigative story ideas can also be gathered from such forums and emailing lists.

Make use of technology and collaborate with hackers

Software helps investigative journalists access and process information. Various types of software assist the investigator in cutting through the noise, in digging and making sense of large volumes of data, and in finding the right documents needed to break the story. There are many ready-made software programs that can be used as tools for analyzing, gathering, or interpreting information—and more importantly, investigative journalists need to be aware that there are scores of computer programmers ready to help if asked. These programmers or hackers know how to obtain and handle information, and they can assist a great deal with the investigative effort. These programmers, some of them members of global open data movements, can become invaluable allies in the fight against crime and corruption, able to assist journalists in gathering and analyzing information.

A good example of an interface between programmers and citizens is ScraperWiki (*https://scraperwiki.com/*), a site where journalists can ask programmers for help with extracting data from websites. Investigative Dashboard maintains a list of ready-made tools (*http://bit.ly/dashboard-resources*) that could help journalists gather, shape, and analyze data.

The usefulness of the aforementioned guidelines has been visible in many instances. One good example is the work of Khadija Ismayilova, a very experienced Azeri investigative reporter who works in an austere environment when it comes to information access. Ms. Ismayilova has to overcome obstacles on a daily basis in order to offer the Azeri public good and reliable information. In June of 2011, Khadija Ismayilova, an investigative reporter with Radio Free Europe/Radio Liberty's (RFE/RL) Baku-based office reported that the daughters of the Azeri president, Ilham Aliyev, secretly run a fast-rising telecom company, Azerfon (*http://bit.ly/rferl-azerfon*) through offshore companies based in Panama. The company boasts nearly 1.7 million subscribers, covers 80 percent of the country's territory, and was (at the time) Azerbaijan's only provider of 3G services. Ismayilova spent three years trying to find out who the owners of the telecom company were, but the government refused to disclose shareholder information and lied numerous times about the company's ownership. They even claimed that the company was owned by the Germany-based Siemens AG, a claim that has been flatly denied by that corporation. The Azeri reporter managed to find out that Azerfon was owned by a few Panama-based private companies. This seemed to be a dead end to her reporting until she got help from outside. In early 2011, Ms. Ismayilova learned through the Investigative Dashboard that Panama-based companies can be tracked down through an application (*http://ohuiginn.net/panama/*) developed by programmer and activist Dan O'Huiginn. With this tool, she finally managed to uncover the fact that the president's two daughters were involved with the telecom company through the Panama-based businesses.

In fact, O'Huiginn created a tool that helped journalists from all over the world to report on corruption—Panama, a very well-known offshore haven, has been widely used by several corrupt officials as a place to hide stolen money (from cronies of the former Egyptian president, Hosni Mubarak to dirty officials in the Balkans or in Latin America). What the programmer-activist has done is called web scraping; a method that allows the extraction and reshaping of information so that it can be used by investigators. O'Huiginn scraped the Panama registry of companies (*http://www.registro -publico.gob.pa/*) because this registry, although open, only allowed searches if the investigative reporter knew the name of the commercial company he or she was looking for. This limited the possibilities of investigation, as reporters usually look for names of persons in order to track down their assets. He extracted the data and created a new website where name-based searches are also possible. The new website allowed investigative reporters in many countries to fish for information, to run names of officials in governments and Parliaments, and to check if they secretly owned corporations in Panama (just as the family of the Azerbaijan president did).

There are other advantages to using the guidelines highlighted above, besides better access to information. One of them has to do with minimizing harm and ensuring better protection for investigative reporters who work in hostile environments. This is due to the fact that when working in a network, the journalist is not alone; the investigative reporter works with colleagues in other countries, so it is harder for criminals to pinpoint who is responsible for their wrongdoings being exposed. As a result, retaliation by governments and corrupt officials is much harder to achieve.

Another thing to keep in mind is that information that doesn't seem very valuable in a geographical area might be crucially important in another. The exchange of information over investigative networks can lead to breaking very important stories. For example, the information that a Romanian was caught in Colombia with 1 kilogram of cocaine is most probably not front page news in Bogota, but could be very important to the Romanian public if a local reporter manages to find out that the person who was caught with the narcotics is working for the government in Bucharest.

Efficient investigative reporting is the result of cooperation between investigative journalists, programmers, and others who want to use data to contribute to create a cleaner, fairer, and more just global society.

— *Paul Radu, Organized Crime and Corruption Reporting Project*

Our Stories Come As Code

OpenDataCity (*http://www.opendatacity.de/*) was founded towards the end of 2010. There was pretty much nothing that you could call data journalism happening in Germany at this time.

Why did we do this? Many times we heard people working for newspapers and broadcasters say: "No, we are not ready to start a dedicated data journalism unit in our newsroom. But we would be happy to outsource this to someone else."

As far as we know, we are the only company specializing exclusively in data journalism in Germany. There are currently three of us: two of us with a journalism background and one with a deep understanding of code and visualization. We work with a handful of freelance hackers, designers, and journalists.

In the last twelve months we have undertaken four data journalism projects with newspapers, and have offered training and consultancy to media workers, scientists, and journalism schools. The first app we did was TAZ, an interactive tool on airport noise (*http://bit.ly/taz-airport-noise*) around the the newly built airport in Berlin. Our next notable project was an application about data retention (*http://bit.ly/zeit-tele phone*) of the mobile phone usage of a German politician with ZEIT Online. For this, we won a Grimme Online Award (*http://bit.ly/grimme-award*) and a Lead Award in Germany, and an Online Journalism Award from the Online Journalism Association (*http://bit.ly/online-news-award*) in the US. At the time of writing, we have several projects in the pipeline, ranging from simpler interactive infographics up to designing and developing a kind of data journalism middleware.

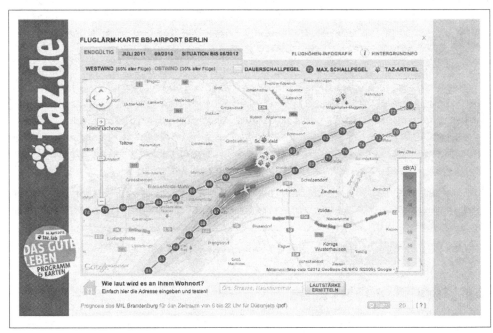

Figure 2-13. Airport noise map (Taz.de)

Of course, winning prizes helps build a reputation. But when we talk to the publishers, who have to approve the projects, our argument for investing into data journalism is not about winning prizes. Rather it is about getting attention over a longer period of time in a sustainable way. That is, building things for their long term impact, not for the scoop, which is often forgotten after a few days.

Here are three arguments that we have used to encourage publishers to undertake longer term projects:

Data projects don't date
> Depending on their design, new material can be added to data journalism apps. And they are not just for the users, but can be used internally for reporting and analysis. If you're worried that this means that your competitors will also benefit from your investment, you could keep some features or some data for internal use only.

You can build on your past work
> When undertaking a data project, you will often create bits of code that can be reused or updated. The next project might take half the time, because you know much better what to do (and what not to), and you have bits and pieces you can build on.

Data journalism pays for itself
> Data-driven projects are cheaper than traditional marketing campaigns. Online news outlets will often invest in things like Search Engine Optimization (SEO) and Search Engine Marketing (SEM). A executed data project will normally generate a lot of clicks and buzz, and may go viral. Publishers will typically pay less for this than trying to generate the same attention by clicks and links through SEM.

Our work is not very different from other new media agencies: providing applications or services for news outlets. But maybe we differ in that we think of ourselves first and foremost as journalists. In our eyes, the products we deliver are articles or stories, albeit ones which are provided not in words and pictures, audio or video, but in code. When we are talking about data journalism, we have to talk about technology, software, devices, and how to tell a story with them.

To give an example, we just finished working on an application that pulls in realtime data via a scraper from the German railway website, thus enabling us to develop an interactive Train Monitor for Süddeutsche Zeitung (*http://zugmonitor.sueddeutsche .de/*), showing the delays of long-distance trains in real time. The application data is updated every minute or so, and we are providing an API for it, too. We started doing this several months ago, and have so far collected a huge dataset that grows every hour. By now it amounts to hundreds of thousands of rows of data. The project enables the user to explore this realtime data, and to do research in the archive of previous months. In the end, the story we are telling will be significantly defined by the individual action of the users.

In traditional journalism, due to the linear character of written or broadcasted media, we have to think about a beginning, the end, the story arc, and the length and angle of our piece. With data journalism things are different. There is a beginning, yes. People come to the website and get a first impression of the interface. But then they are on their own. Maybe they stay for a minute, or half an hour.

Our job as data journalists is to provide the framework or environment for this. As well as the coding and data management bits, we have to think of clever ways to design experiences. The User Experience (UX) derives mostly from the (Graphical) User Interface (GUI). In the end, this is the part which will make or break a project. You could have the best code working in the background handling an exciting dataset. But if the front end sucks, nobody will care about it.

There is still a lot to learn about and to experiment with. But luckily there is the games industry, which has been innovating with respect to digital narratives, ecosystems, and interfaces for several decades now. So when developing data journalism applications, we should closely watch how game design works and how stories are told in games. Why are casual games like Tetris such fun? And what makes the open worlds of sandbox games like Grand Theft Auto or Skyrim rock?

We think that data journalism is here to stay. In a few years, data journalism workflows will be quite naturally embedded in newsrooms, because news websites will have to change. The amount of data that is publicly available will keep on increasing. But luckily, new technologies will continue to enable us to find new ways of telling stories. Some of the stories will be driven by data, and many applications and services will have a journalistic character. The interesting question is which strategy newsrooms will develop to foster this process. Are they going to build up teams of data journalists integrated into their newsroom? Will there be R&D departments, a bit like in-house start-ups? Or will parts of the work be outsourced to specialized companies? We are still right at the beginning and only time will tell.

— *Lorenz Matzat, OpenDataCity*

Kaas & Mulvad: Semi-Finished Content for Stakeholder Groups

Stakeholder media is an emerging sector, largely overlooked by media theorists, which could potentially have a tremendous impact either through online networks or by providing content to news media. It can be defined as (usually online) media controlled by organizational or institutional stakeholders, which is used to advance certain interests and communities. NGOs typically create such media; so do consumer groups, professional associations, labor unions, and so on. The key limit on its ability to influence public opinion or other stakeholders is often that it lacks the capacity to undertake discovery of important information, even more so than the downsized news media. Kaas & Mulvad, a for-profit Danish corporation, is one of the first investigative media enterprises that provides expert capacity to these stakeholder outlets.

The firm originated in 2007 as a spinoff of the non-profit Danish Institute for Computer-Assisted Reporting (Dicar), which sold investigative reports to media and trained journalists in data analysis. Its founders, Tommy Kaas and Nils Mulvad, were previously reporters in the news industry. Their new firm offers what they call "data plus journalistic insight" (content that remains semi-finished, requiring further editing or rewriting) mainly to stakeholder media, which finalize the content into news releases or stories and distribute it through both news media and their own outlets (such as websites). Direct clients include government institutions, PR firms, labor unions, and NGOs such as EU Transparency and the World Wildlife Fund. The NGO work includes monitoring farm and fishery subsidies, and regular updates on EU lobbyist activities generated through "scraping" of pertinent websites. Indirect clients include foundations that fund NGO projects. The firm also works with the news industry; a tabloid newspaper purchased their celebrity monitoring service, for example.

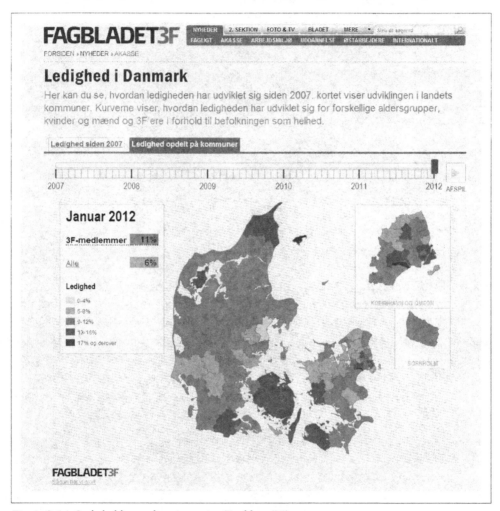

Figure 2-14. Stakeholder media companies (Fagblaget3F)

Data journalism projects in their portfolio include:

Unemployment Map for 3F (http://bit.ly/3F-unemployment)
A data visualization with key figures about unemployment in Denmark undertaken for 3F, which is the union for unskilled labor in Denmark.

Living Conditions for 3F (http://bit.ly/3F-living)
Another project for 3F shows how different living conditions are in different parts of Denmark. The map uses 24 different indicators.

Debt for "Ugebrevet A4" (http://bit.ly/3F-debt-index)
A project that calculates a "debt index" and visualizes the differences in private economy.

Dangerous Facilities in Denmark (http://bit.ly/3F-dangerous-facilities)
A project which maps and analyzes the proximity of dangerous facilities to kindergartens and other daycare institutions, undertaken for "Børn&Unge," a magazine published by BUPL, the Danish Union of Early Childhood and Youth Educators.

Corporate Responsibility Data for Vestas (http://data.vestas.com)
Data visualization on five areas of CR-data for the Danish wind turbine company, Vestas, with auto-generated text. Automatically updated on a quarterly basis with 400 web pages from world scale data down to the single production unit.

Name Map for Experian (http://xpoint.experian.dk/navnekort)
Type in your last name and look at the distribution of this name around different geographical areas in Denmark.

Smiley Map for Ekstra Bladet (http://ekstrabladet.dk/kup/fodevarer)
Every day Kaas & Mulvad extract all the bad food inspections and map all the latest for the Danish tabloid Ekstra Bladet (see halfway down the website for the map).

Kaas & Mulvad are not the first journalists to work with stakeholder media. Greenpeace, for example, routinely engages journalists as collaborators for its reports. But we know of no other firm whose offerings to stakeholder media are data-driven; it is much more typical for journalists to work with NGOs as reporters, editors, or writers. The current focus in computer-assisted news media is on search and discovery (think of WikiLeaks); here again, Kaas & Mulvad innovate by focusing on data analysis. Their approach requires not only programming skills, but also an understanding of what kind of information can make a story with impact. It can safely be said that anyone who wishes to imitate their service would probably have to acquire those two skill sets through partnership, because individuals rarely possess both.

Processes: Innovative IT Plus Analysis

The firm undertakes about 100 projects per year, ranging in duration from a few hours to a few months. It also continuously invests in projects that expand its capacity and offerings. The celebrity monitoring service was one such experiment. Another involved scraping the Internet for news of home foreclosures and creating maps of the events. The partners say that their first criteria for projects is whether they enjoy the work and learn from it; markets are sought after a new service is defined. They make it clear that in the news industry, they found it difficult to develop new methods and new business.

Mulvad comments that:

> We have no editors or bosses to decide which projects we can do, which software or hardware we can buy. We can buy the tools according to project needs, like the best solutions for text scraping and mining. Our goal is to be cutting edge in these areas. We try to get customers who are willing to pay, or if the project is fun we do it for a lower charge.

Value Created: Personal and Firm Brands and Revenue

Turnover in 2009 was approximately 2.5 million Danish kroner, or €336,000. The firm also sustains the partners' reputations as cutting edge journalists, which maintains demand for their teaching and speaking services. Their public appearances, in turn, support the firm's brand.

Key Insights of This Example

- The news industry's crisis of declining capacity is also a crisis of under-utilization of capacity. Kaas and Mulvad had to leave the news industry to do work they valued, and that pays. Nothing prevented a news organization from capturing that value.

- In at least some markets, there exists a profitable market for "semi-finished" content that can serve the interests of stakeholder groups.

- However, this opportunity raises the issue of how much control journalists can exercise over the presentation and use of their work by third parties. We recall that this issue already exists within the news industry (where editors can impose changes on a journalist's product), and it has existed within other media industries (such as the film industry, where conflicts between directors and studios over "final cuts" are hardly rare). It is not a particular moral hazard of stakeholder media, but it will not disappear, either. More attention is needed to the ethics of this growing reality and market.

- From a revenue standpoint, a single product or service is not enough. Successful watchdog enterprises would do better to take a portfolio approach, in which consulting, teaching, speaking, and other services bring in extra revenue and support the watchdog brand.

— Edited excerpt from Mark Lee Hunter and Luk N. Van Wassenhove, "Disruptive News Technologies: Stakeholder Media and the Future of Watchdog Journalism Business Models". INSEAD Working Paper, 2010

Business Models for Data Journalism

Amidst all the interest and hope regarding data-driven journalism, there is one question that newsrooms are always curious about: what are the business models?

While we must be careful about making predictions, a look at the recent history and current state of the media industry can give us some insight. Today there are many news organizations who have gained by adopting new approaches.

Terms like "data journalism" and the newest buzzword, "data science," may sound like they describe something new, but this is not strictly true. Instead these new labels are just ways of characterizing a shift that has been gaining strength over decades.

Many journalists seem to be unaware of the size of the revenue that is already generated through data collection, data analytics, and visualization. This is the business of information refinement. With data tools and technologies, it is increasingly possible to shed light on highly complex issues, be this international finance, debt, demography, education, and so on. The term "business intelligence" describes a variety of IT concepts that aim to provide a clear view on what is happening in commercial corporations. The big and profitable companies of our time, including McDonalds, Zara, and H&M, rely on constant data tracking to turn out a profit. And it works pretty well for them.

What is changing right now is that the tools developed for this space are now becoming available for other domains, including the media. And there are journalists who get it. Take Tableau, a company that provides a suite of visualization tools. Or the "Big Data" movement, where technology companies use (often open source) software packages to dig through piles of data, extracting insights in milliseconds.

These technologies can now be applied to journalism. Teams at the Guardian and The New York Times are constantly pushing the boundaries in this emerging field. And what we are currently seeing is just the tip of the iceberg.

But how does this generate money for journalism? The big, worldwide market that is currently opening up is all about transformation of publicly available data into something our that we can process: making data visible and making it human. We want to be able to relate to the big numbers we hear every day in the news—what the millions and billions mean for each of us.

There are a number of very profitable data-driven media companies, who have simply applied this principle earlier than others. They enjoy healthy growth rates and sometimes impressive profits. One example is Bloomberg. The company operates about 300,000 terminals and delivers financial data to its users. If you are in the money business, this is a power tool. Each terminal comes with a color-coded keyboard and up to 30,000 options to look up, compare, analyze, and help you to decide what to do next. This core business generates an estimated $6.3 billion (US) per year—at least as estimated in a 2008 piece by The New York Times (*http://nyti.ms/IQcRgY*). As a result,

Bloomberg has been hiring journalists left, right and center, they bought the venerable but loss-making "Business Week," and so on.

Another example is the Canadian media conglomerate today known as Thomson Reuters. They started with one newspaper, bought up a number of well-known titles in the UK, and then decided two decades ago to leave the newspaper business. Instead, they have grown based on information services, aiming to provide a deeper perspective for clients in a number of industries. If you worry about how to make money with specialized information, my advice would be to just read about the company's history on Wikipedia (*http://en.wikipedia.org/wiki/The_Thomson_Corporation*).

And look at the Economist. The magazine has built an excellent, influential brand on its media side. At the same time, the "Economist Intelligence Unit" is now more like a consultancy, reporting about relevant trends and forecasts for almost any country in the world. They are employing hundreds of journalists and claim to serve about 1.5 million customers worldwide.

And there are many niche data-driven services that could serve as inspiration: eMarketer in the US, providing comparisons, charts, and advice for anybody interested in internet marketing; Stiftung Warentest in Germany, an institution looking into the quality of products and services; Statista, again from Germany, a start-up helping to visualize publicly available information.

Around the world, there is currently a wave of startups in this sector, naturally covering a wide range of areas; for example, Timetric, which aims to "reinvent business research," OpenCorporates, Kasabi, Infochimps, and Data Market. Many of these are arguably experiments, but together they can be taken as an important sign of change.

Then there is the public media, which in terms of data-driven journalism, is a sleeping giant. In Germany, €7.2 billion per year is flowing into this sector. Journalism is a special product: if done well, it is not just about making money, but serves an important role in society. Once it is clear that data journalism can provide better, more reliable insights more easily, some of this money could be used for new jobs in newsrooms.

With data journalism, it is not just about being first, but about being a trusted source of information. In this multichannel world, attention can be generated in abundance, but *trust* is an increasingly scarce resource. Data journalists can help to collate, synthesize, and present diverse and often difficult sources of information in a way that gives their audience real insights into complex issues. Rather than just recycling press releases and retelling stories they've heard elsewhere, data journalists can give readers a clear, comprehensible, and preferably customizable perspective with interactive graphics and direct access to primary sources. Not trivial, but certainly valuable.

So what is the best approach for aspiring data journalists to explore this field and convince management to support innovative projects?

The first step should be to look for immediate opportunities close to home: low-hanging fruit. For example, you might already have collections of structured texts and data that you could use. A prime example of this is the "Homicide database" of the Los Angeles Times. Here, data and visualizations are the core, not an afterthought. The editors collect all the crimes they find and only then write articles based on this. Over time, such collections are becoming better, deeper, and more valuable.

This might not work the first time. But it will over time. One very hopeful indicator here is that the Texas Tribune and ProPublica, which are both arguably post-print media companies, reported that funding for their non-profit journalism organizations exceeded their goals much earlier than planned.

Becoming proficient in all things data—whether as a generalist or as a specialist focused on one aspect of the data food chain—provides a valuable perspective for people who believe in journalism. As one well-known publisher in Germany recently said in an interview, "There is this new group who call themselves data journalists. And they are not willing to work for peanuts anymore."

— *Mirko Lorenz, Deutsche Welle*

CHAPTER 3

Case Studies

In this section we take a more in-depth, behind-the-scenes look at several data journalism projects—from apps developed in a day to nine-month investigations. We learn about how data sources have been used to augment and improve coverage of everything from elections to spending, riots to corruption, the performance of schools to the price of water. As well as larger media organizations such as the BBC, the Chicago Tribune, the Guardian, the Financial Times, Helsingin Sanomat, La Nación, Wall Street Journal, and the Zeit Online, we learn from smaller initiatives such as California Watch,

Hack/HackersBuenos Aires, ProPublica, and a group of local Brazilian citizen-journalists called Friends of Januária.

The Opportunity Gap

The Opportunity Gap (*http://projects.propublica.org/schools*) used never-before-released U.S. Department of Education civil rights data and showed that some states, like Florida, have levelled the field and offer rich and poor students roughly equal access to high-level courses, while other states, like Kansas, Maryland, and Oklahoma, offer less opportunity in districts with poorer families.

Figure 3-1. The Opportunity Gap project (ProPublica)

The data included every public school in a district with 3,000 students or more. More than three-quarters of all public-school children were represented. A reporter in our newsroom obtained the data and our Computer-Assisted Reporting Director cleaned it very extensively.

It was roughly a three-month project. Altogether, six people worked on the story and news application: two editors, a reporter, a CAR person, and two developers. Most of us weren't working on it exclusively throughout that period.

The project really required our combined skills: deep domain knowledge, an understanding of data best practices, design and coding skills, and so on. More importantly it required an ability to find the story in the data. It also took editing, not only for the story that went with it, but for the news app itself.

For the data cleaning and analysis we used mostly Excel and cleaning scripts, as well as MS Access. The news app was written in Ruby on Rails and uses JavaScript pretty extensively.

In addition to an overview story, our coverage included an interactive news application, which let readers understand and find examples within this large national dataset that related to them. Using our news app, a reader could find their local school—say, for example, Central High School in Newark, N.J. (*http://goo.gl/HJVCf*)—and immediately see how well the school does in a wide variety of areas. Then they could hit a button that says "Compare to High and Low Poverty Schools" (*http://goo.gl/WrAIi*), and immediately see other high schools, their relative poverty, and the extent to which they offer higher math, Advanced Placement, and other important courses. In our example, Central High is bookended by Millburn Sr. High. The Opportunity Gap shows how only 1% of Milburn students get Free or Reduced Price lunch but 72% of them are taking at least one AP course. In the other extreme, International High has 85% of its students getting Free/Reduced Price lunch and only 1% taking AP courses.

Through this example a reader can use something they know—a local high school—to understand something they don't know: the distribution of educational access, and the extent to which poverty is a predictor of that access.

We also integrated the app with Facebook, so readers could log into Facebook and our app would automatically let them know about schools that might interest them.

Traffic to all of our news apps is excellent, and we're particularly proud of the way this app tells a complex story; more to the point, it helps readers tell their own particular story for themselves.

As with many projects that start with government data, the data needed a lot of cleaning. For instance, while there are only around 30 possible Advanced Placement courses, some schools reported having hundreds of them. This took lots of manual checking and phone calls to schools for confirmation and corrections.

We also worked really hard at making sure the app told a "far" story and a "near" story. That is, the app needed to present the reader with a broad, abstract national picture; a way to compare how states did relative to each other on educational access. But given that abstraction sometimes leaves readers confused as to what the data means to them, we also wanted readers to be able to find their own local school and compare it to high- and low-poverty schools in their area.

If I were to advise aspiring data journalists interested in taking on this kind of project, I'd say you have to know the material and be inquisitive! All of the rules that apply to other kinds of journalism apply here. You have to get the facts right, make sure you tell the story well, and—crucially—make sure your news app doesn't disagree with a story you're writing. If it does, one of the two might be wrong.

Also, if you want to learn to code, the most important thing is to start. You might like learning through classes or through books or videos, but make sure you have a really good idea for a project and a deadline by which you have to complete it. If there's a story in your head that can only come out as a news app, then not knowing how to program won't stop you!

— *Scott Klein, ProPublica*

A Nine Month Investigation into European Structural Funds

In 2010, the Financial Times (*http://www.ft.com/intl/eu-funds*) and the Bureau of Investigative Journalism (BIJ) (*http://bit.ly/bureau-billions*) joined forces to investigate European Structural Funds. The intention was to review who the beneficiaries of European Structural Funds are and check whether the money was put to good use. At €347 billion over seven years, Structural Funds is the second largest subsidy program in the EU. The program has existed for decades, but apart from broad, generalized overviews, there was little transparency about who the beneficiaries are. As part of a rule change in the current funding round, authorities are obliged to make public a list of beneficiaries, including project description and amount of EU and national funding received.

Figure 3-2. EU Structural Funds investigation (Financial Times and The Bureau of Investigative Journalism)

The project team was made up of up to 12 journalists and one full-time coder collaborating for nine months. Data gathering alone took several months.

The project resulted in five days of coverage in the Financial Times and the BIJ, a BBC radio documentary, and several TV documentaries.

Before you tackle a project of this level of effort, you have to be certain that the findings are original, and that you will end up with good stories nobody else has.

The process was broken up into a number of distinct steps.

1. Identify who keeps the data and how it is kept

The European Commission's Directorate General for the Regions have a portal (*http: //bit.ly/ec-portal*) to the websites of regional authorities that publish the data. We believed that the Commission would have an overarching database of project data that we could either access directly, or which we could obtain through a Freedom of Information request. No such database exists to the level of detail we required. We quickly realized that many of the links the Commission provided were faulty and that most of the authorities published the data in PDF format, rather than analysis-friendly formats such as CSV or XML.

A team of up to 12 people worked to identify the latest data and collate the links into one spreadsheet we used for collaboration. Since the data fields were not uniform (for example, headers were in different languages, some datasets used different currencies, and some included breakdowns of EU and National Funding) we needed to be as precise as possible in translating and describing the data fields available in each dataset.

2. Download and prepare the data

The next step consisted of downloading all the spreadsheets, PDFs, and, in some cases, web scraping the original data.

Each dataset had to then be standardized. Our biggest task was extracting data out of PDFs, some hundreds of pages long. Much of this was done using UnPDF and ABBYY FineReader, which allow data to be extracted to formats such as CSV or Excel.

It also involved checking and double-checking that the PDF extraction tools had captured the data correctly. This was done using filtering, sorting, and summing up totals (to ensure it corresponded with what was printed on the PDFs).

3. Create a database

The team's coder set up a SQL database. Each of the prepared files was then used as a building block for the overall SQL database. A once-a-day process would upload all the individual data files into one large SQL database, which could be queried on the fly through its front end via keywords.

4. Double-checking and analysis

The team analyzed the data in two main ways:

Via the database front end
> This entailed typing particular keywords of interest (e.g., "tobacco," "hotel," "company A" into the search engine. With help of Google Translate, which was plugged into the search functionality of our database, those keywords would be translated into 21 languages and would return appropriate results. These could be downloaded and reporters could do further research on the individual projects of interest.

By macro-analysis using the whole database
> Occasionally, we would download a full dataset, which could then be analyzed (for example, using keywords, or aggregating data by country, region, type of expenditure, number of projects by beneficiary, etc.)

Our story lines were informed by both these methods, but also through on-the-ground and desk research.

Double-checking the integrity of the data (by aggregating and checking against what authorities said had been allocated) took a substantial amount of time. One of the main problems was that authorities would for the most part only divulge the amount of "EU and national funding". Under EU rules, each program is allowed to fund a certain percentage of the total cost using EU funding. The level of EU funding is determined, at program level, by the so-called co-financing rate. Each program (e.g., regional competitiveness) is made up of numerous projects. At the project levels, technically one project could receive 100 percent EU funding, and another none at all, as long as grouped together, the amount of EU funding at the program level is not more than the approved co-financing rate.

This meant that we needed to check each EU amount of funding we cited in our stories with the beneficiary company in question.

— *Cynthia O'Murchu, Financial Times*

The Eurozone Meltdown

So we're covering the Eurozone meltdown (*http://on.wsj.com/tYM82O*). Every bit of it. The drama as governments clash and life savings are lost; the reaction from world leaders, austerity measures, and protests against austerity measures. Every day in the Wall Street Journal, there are charts on jobs loss, declining GDP, plunging world markets. It is incremental. It is numbing.

The Page One editors call a meeting to discuss ideas for year-end coverage and as we leave the meeting, I find myself wondering: what must it be like to be living through this?

Is this like 2008 when I was laid off and dark news was incessant? We talked about jobs and work and money every night at dinner, nearly forgetting how it might upset my daughter. And weekends, they were the worst. I tried to deny the fear that seemed to have a permanent grip at the back of my neck and the anxiety tightening my rib cage. Is this what was it like right now to be a family in Greece? In Spain?

I turned back and followed Mike Allen, the Page One editor, into his office and pitched the idea of telling the crisis through families in the Eurozone by looking first at the data, finding demographic profiles to understand what made up a family and then surfacing that along with pictures and interviews, audio of the generations. We'd use beautiful portraiture, the voices—and the data.

Back at my desk, I wrote a précis and drew a logo.

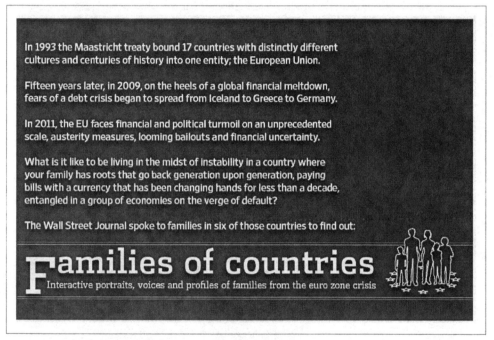

In 1993 the Maastricht treaty bound 17 countries with distinctly different cultures and centuries of history into one entity; the European Union.

Fifteen years later, in 2009, on the heels of a global financial meltdown, fears of a debt crisis began to spread from Iceland to Greece to Germany.

In 2011, the EU faces financial and political turmoil on an unprecedented scale, austerity measures, looming bailouts and financial uncertainty.

What is it like to be living in the midst of instability in a country where your family has roots that go back generation upon generation, paying bills with a currency that has been changing hands for less than a decade, entangled in a group of economies on the verge of default?

The Wall Street Journal spoke to families in six of those countries to find out:

Families of countries
Interactive portraits, voices and profiles of families from the euro zone crisis

Figure 3-3. The Eurozone Meltdown: precis (Wall Street Journal)

For the next three weeks I chased numbers: metrics on marriage, mortality, family size, and health spending. I read up on living arrangements and divorce rates, looked at surveys on well-being and savings rates. I browsed national statistics divisions, called the UN population bureau, the IMF, Eurostat, and the OECD until I found an economist who had spent his career tracking families. He led me to a scholar on family composition. She pointed me to white papers on my topic.

With my editor, Sam Enriquez, we narrowed down the countries. We gathered a team to discuss the visual approach and which reporters could deliver words, audio and story. Matt Craig, the Page One photo editor, set to work finding the shooters. Matt Murray, the Deputy Managing Editor for world coverage, sent a memo to the bureau chiefs requesting help from the reporters. (This was crucial: sign-off from the top.)

But first the data. Mornings I'd export data into spreadsheets and make charts to see trends: savings shrinking, pensions disappearing, mothers returning to work, health spending, along with government debt and unemployment. Afternoons I'd look at those data in clusters, putting the countries against each other to find stories.

I did this for a week before I got lost in the weeds and started to doubt myself. Maybe this was the wrong approach. Maybe it wasn't about countries, but it was about fathers and mothers, and children and grandparents. The data grew.

And shrank. Sometimes I spent hours gathering information only to find out that it told me, well, nothing. That I had dug up the entirely wrong set of numbers. Sometimes the data were just too old.

ITALY_onlychildren.xlsx			
Distribution of households by number of children, 2007 (2)			
	1 child	2	3 4+
Sweden	43.3	40.6	12.8	3.:
Finland	42.7	39.2	13.5	4.(
Denmark	41.3	43.4	12.5	2.t
Netherlands	38.8	42.7	14.1	4.«
France	45.3	39.9	11.7	3.:
Germany	48.6	39.5	9	:
Austria	50.1	37.2	10.2	2.«
Belgium	44.5	36.8	13.7	:
Luxembourg	44.8	46	8.1	1.:
Ireland	43.8	35.2	16	:
Italy	55.2	37.9	6.1	0.t
Spain	55.2	39.9	3.9	0.‹
Portugal	61.4	33.7	4	:
Greece	46.4	47.9	4.3	1.:
Cyprus	42.5	46.8	8.5	2.:
Hungary	49.5	36.9	10.5	3.:
Estonia	58	32.9	7.5	1.:
Latvia	62.8	29.5	5.8	1.‹
Lithuania	59.7	31.4	6.8	2.:
Slovenia	49.7	41.5	7.2	1.(
Slovakia	53.7	36	8.3	:
Poland	53.5	35.2	8.6	2.:
EU-25	49.5	38.9	9	2.t
EU-15	48.7	39.5	9.2	2.t
nnc	c3 c	3c	0 3	3 .

Figure 3-4. Judging the usefulness of a dataset can be a very time-consuming task (Sarah Slobin)

And then the data grew again as I realized I still had questions, and I didn't understand the families.

I needed to see it, to shape it. So I made a quick series of graphics in Illustrator, and began to arrange and edit them.

As the charts emerged, so did a cohesive picture of the families.

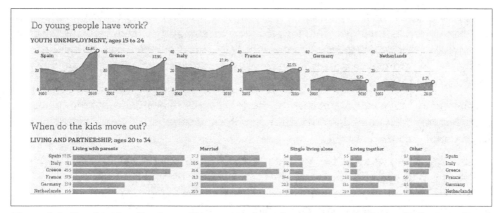

Figure 3-5. Graphic visualization: making sense of trends and patterns hidden in the datasets (Sarah Slobin)

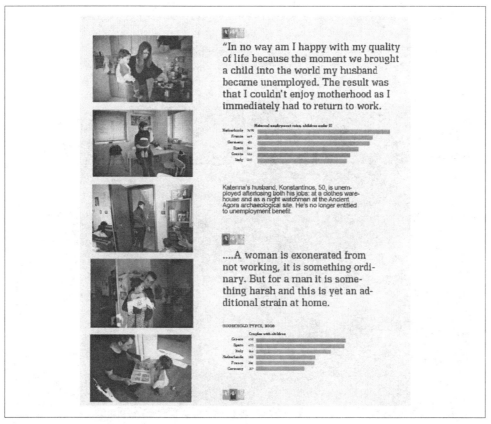

Figure 3-6. Numbers are people: the value of data lies in the individual stories they represent (Wall Street Journal)

We launched. I called each reporter. I sent them the charts, the broad pitch and an open invitation to find stories that they felt were meaningful, that would bring the crisis closer to our readers. We needed a small family in Amsterdam, and larger ones in Spain and Italy. We wanted to hear from multiple generations to see how personal history shaped responses.

From here on in, I would be up early to check my email to be mindful of the time-zone gap. The reporters came back with lovely subjects, summaries, and surprises that I hadn't anticipated.

For photography, we knew we wanted portraits of the generations. Matt's vision was to have his photographers follow each family member through a day in their lives. He chose visual journalists who had covered the world, covered news and even covered war. Matt wanted each shoot to end at the dinner table. Sam suggested we include the menus.

From here it was a question of waiting to see what story the photos told. Waiting to see what the families said. We designed the look of the interactive. I stole a palette from a Tintin novel, we worked through the interaction. And when it was all together and we had storyboards, we added back in some (not much but some) of the original charts. Just enough to punctuate each story, just enough to harden the themes. The data became a pause in the story, a way to switch gears.

Figure 3-7. Life in the Euro Zone (Wall Street Journal)

In the end, the data were the people; they were the photographs and the stories. They were what was framing each narrative and driving the tension between the countries.

By the time we published, right before the New Year as we were all contemplating what was on the horizon, I knew all the family members by name. I still wonder how they are now. And if this doesn't seem like a data project, that's fine by me. Because those moments that are documented in Life in the Eurozone, these stories of sitting down for a meal and talking about work and life with your family was something we were able to share with our readers. Understanding the data is what made it possible.

— *Sarah Slobin, Wall Street Journal*

Covering the Public Purse with OpenSpending.org

In 2007, Jonathan came to the Open Knowledge Foundation with a one page proposal for a project called *Where Does My Money Go?* (*http://www.wheredoesmymoneygo.org/*), which aimed to make it easier for UK citizens to understand how public funds are spent. This was intended to be a proof-of-concept for a bigger project to visually represent public information, based on the pioneering work of Otto and Marie Neurath's Isotype Institute in the 1940s.

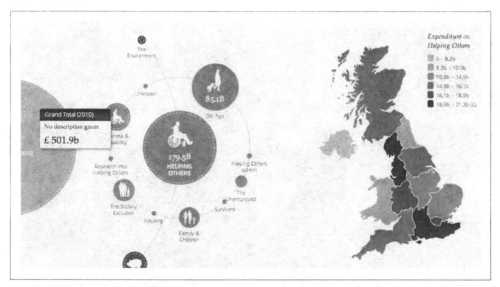

Figure 3-8. Where Does My Money Go? (Open Knowledge Foundation)

The *Where Does My Money Go?* project enabled users to explore public data from a wide variety of sources using intuitive open source tools. We won an award to help to develop a prototype of the project, and later received funding from Channel 4's 4IP to turn this into a fully fledged web application. Information design guru David McCandless (from Information is Beautiful; *http://www.informationisbeautiful.net/*) created several different views of the data that helped people relate to the big numbers—including the "Country and Regional Analysis," which shows how money is disbursed in different parts of the country, and "Daily Bread" (*http://wheredoesmymoneygo.org/dailybread.html*), which shows citizens a breakdown of their tax contributions per day in pounds and pence.

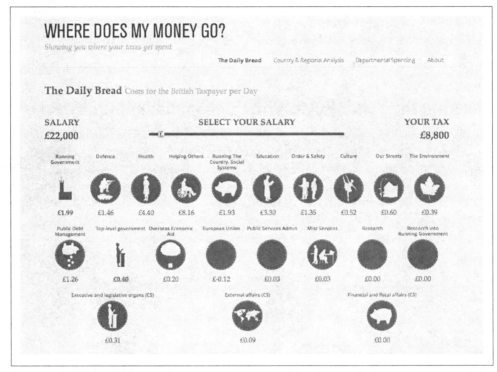

Figure 3-9. The Where Does My Money Go? Daily Bread tax calculator (Open Knowledge Foundation)

Around that time, the holy grail for the project was the cunningly acronymed Combined Online Information System (*http://data.gov.uk/dataset/coins*) (or COINS) data, which was the most comprehensive and detailed database of UK government finance available. Working with Lisa Evans (before she joined the Guardian Datablog team), Julian Todd and Francis Irving (now of Scraperwiki fame), Martin Rosenbaum (BBC), and others, we filed numerous requests for the data—many of them unsuccessful (the saga is partially documented by Lisa in the sidebar "Using FOI to Understand Spending" on page 120).

When the data was finally released in mid-2010, it was widely considered a coup for transparency advocates. We were given advance access to the data to load it into our web application, and we received a significant attention from the press when this fact was made public. On the day of the release, we had dozens of journalists showing up on our IRC channel to discuss and ask about the release, as well as to enquire about how to open and explore it (the files were tens of gigabytes in size). While some pundits claimed the massive release was so complicated it was effectively obscurity through transparency (*http://bit.ly/archive-silicon*), lots of brave journalists got stuck in the data to give their readers an unprecedented picture of how public funds are spent. The Guardian live-blogged (*http://bit.ly/guardian-coins*) about the release and numerous other media outlets covered it, and gave analyses of findings from the data.

It wasn't long before we started to get requests and enquiries about running similar projects in other countries around the world. Shortly after launching OffenerHaushalt (*http://offenerhaushalt.de*)—a version of the project for the German state budget created by Friedrich Lindenberg—we launched OpenSpending (*http://openspending.org/*), an international version of the project, which aimed to help users map public spending from around the world a bit like OpenStreetMap helped them to map geographical features. We implemented new designs with help from the talented Gregor Aisch, partially based on David McCandless's original designs.

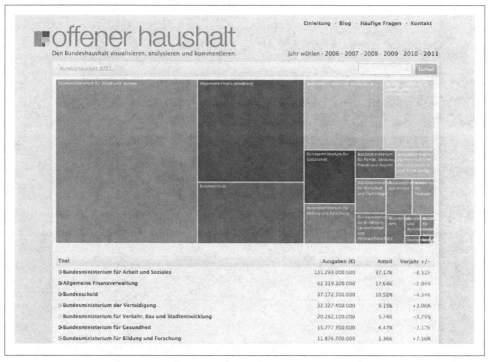

Figure 3-10. OffenerHaushalt, the German version of Where Does My Money Go? (Open Knowledge Foundation)

With the OpenSpending project, we have worked extensively with journalists to acquire, represent, interpret, and present spending data to the public. OpenSpending is first and foremost an enormous, searchable database of public spending—both high-level budget information and transaction-level actual expenditure. On top of this are built a series of out-of-the-box visualizations such as treemaps and bubbletrees. Anyone can load in their local council data and produce visualizations from it.

While initially we thought there would be a greater demand for some of our more sophisticated visualizations, after speaking to news organizations we realized that there were more basic needs that needed to be satisfied first, such as the the ability to embed dynamic tables of data in their blogposts. Keen to encourage news organizations to give the public access to the data alongside their stories, we built a widget for this too.

Our first big release was around the time of the first International Journalism Festival in Perugia. A group of developers, journalists and civil servants collaborated to load Italian data into the OpenSpending platform, which gave a rich view of how spending was broken down amongst central, regional, and local administrations. It was covered in Il Fatto Quotidiano (*http://bit.ly/ilfatto-spending*), Il Post (*http://bit.ly/ilpost-spend ing*), La Stampa (*http://bit.ly/lastampa-spending*), Repubblica (*http://bit.ly/repubblica -spending*), and Wired Italia (*http://bit.ly/wired-italy-spending*), as well as in the Guardian (*http://bit.ly/guardian-italy-spending*).

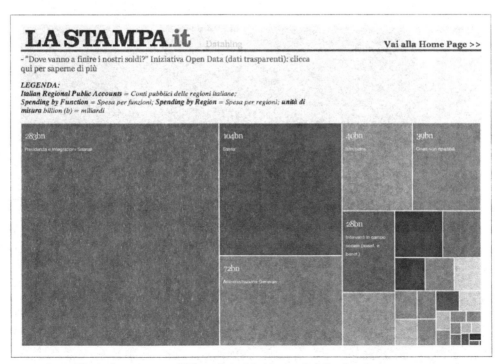

Figure 3-11. The Italian version of Where Does My Money Go? (La Stampa)

In 2011 we worked with Publish What You Fund (*http://www.publishwhatyoufund.org/*) and the Overseas Development Institute (*http://www.odi.org.uk/*) to map aid funding to Uganda from 2003-2006. This was new because for the first time you could see aid funding flows alongside the national budget—enabling you to see to what extent the priorities of donors aligned with the priorities of governments. There were some interesting conclusions—for example, both counter HIV programs and family planning emerged as almost entirely funded by external donors. This was covered in the Guardian (*http://bit.ly/guardian-uganda-viz*).

We've also been working with NGOs and advocacy groups to cross-reference spending data with other sources of information. For example, Privacy International approached us with a big list of surveillance technology companies and a list of agencies attending a well-known international surveillance trade show, known colloquially as the 'wire-tappers ball'. By systematically cross-referencing company names with spending datasets, it was possible to identify which companies had government contracts—which could then be followed up with FOI requests. This was covered by the Guardian (*http://bit.ly/guardian-surveillance*).

We're currently working to increase fiscal literacy among journalists and the public as part of a project called Spending Stories (*http://bit.ly/ss-faq*), which lets users link public spending data to public spending related stories to see the numbers behind the news, and the news around the numbers.

Through our work in this area, we've learned that:

- Journalists are often not used to working with raw data, and many don't consider it a necessary foundation for their reporting. Sourcing stories from raw information is still a relatively new idea.

- Analyzing and understanding data is a time-intensive process, even with the necessary skills. Fitting this into a short-lived news cycle is hard, so data journalism is often used in longer-term, investigative projects.

- Data released by governments is often incomplete or outdated. Very often, public databases cannot be used for investigative purposes without the addition of more specific pieces of information requested through FOI.

- Advocacy groups, scholars, and researchers often have more time and resources to conduct more extensive data-driven research than journalists. It can be very fruitful to team up with them, and to work in teams.

— *Lucy Chambers and Jonathan Gray, Open Knowledge Foundation*

Finnish Parliamentary Elections and Campaign Funding

In recent months there have been ongoing trials related to the election campaign funding of the Finnish general elections of 2007.

After the elections in 2007, the press found out that the laws on publicizing campaign funding had no effect on politicians. Basically, campaign funding has been used to buy favors from politicians, who have then failed to declare their funding as mandated by Finnish law.

After these incidents, the laws became stricter. After the general election in March 2011, Helsingin Sanomat decided to carefully explore all the available data on campaign funding. The new law stipulates that election funding must be declared, and only donations below 1,500 euros may be anonymous.

1. Find data and developers

Helsingin Sanomat has organized HS Open hackathons since March 2011. We invite Finnish coders, journalists, and graphic designers to the basement of our building. Participants are divided into groups of three, and they are encouraged to develop applications and visualizations. We have had about 60 participants in each of our three events so far. We decided that campaign funding data should be the focus of HS Open #2, May 2011.

The National Audit Office of Finland is the authority that keeps records of campaign funding. That was the easy part. Chief Information Officer Jaakko Hamunen built a website that provides real-time access to their campaign funding database. The Audit Office made this in just two months after our request.

The Vaalirahoitus.fi (*http://www.vaalirahoitus.fi/*) website will provide the public and the press with information on campaign funding for every election from now on.

2. Brainstorm for ideas

The participants of HS Open 2 came up with twenty different prototypes about what to do with the data. You can find all the prototypes on our website (*http://bit.ly/hs -prototype*) (text in Finnish).

A bioinformatics researcher called Janne Peltola noted that campaign funding data looked like the gene data they research, in terms of containing many interdependencies. In bioinformatics there is an open source tool called Cytoscape (*http://www.cytoscape .org/*) that is used to map these interdependencies. So we ran the data through Cytoscape, and got a very interesting prototype.

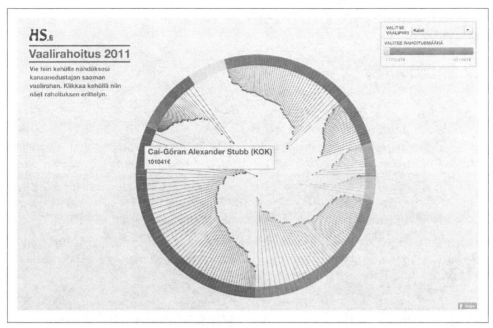

Figure 3-12. Election financing (Helsingin Sanomat)

3. Implement the idea on paper and on the Web

The law on campaign funding states that elected members of parliament must declare their funding two months after the elections. In practice this meant that we got the real data in mid-June. In HS Open, we had data only from MPs who had filed before the deadline.

There was also a problem with the data format. The National Audit Office provided the data as two CSV files. One contained the total budget of campaigns, the other listed all the donors. We had to combine these two, creating a file that contained three columns: donor, receiver, and amount. If the politicians had used their own money, in our data format it looked like Politician A donated X euros to Politician A. Counterintuitive perhaps, but it worked for Cytoscape.

When the data was cleaned and reformatted, we just ran it through Cytoscape. Then our graphics department made a full-page graphic out of it.

Finally we created a beautiful visualization on our website (*http://www.vaaliraha .com/*). This was not a network analysis graphic. We wanted to give people an easy way to explore how much campaign funding there is and who gives it. The first view shows the distribution of funding between MPs. When you click on one MP, you get the breakdown of his or her funding. You can also vote on whether this particular donor is good or not. The visualization was made by Juha Rouvinen and Jukka Kokko, from an ad agency called Satumaa.

The web version of campaign funding visualization uses the same data as the network analysis.

4. Publish the data

Of course, the National Audit Office already publishes the data, so there was no need to republish. But, as we had cleaned up the data and given it a better structure, we decided to publish it. We give out our data with a Creative Commons Attribution licence (*http://creativecommons.org/licenses/by/3.0/*). Subsequently several independent developers have made visualizations of the data, some of which we have published.

The tools we used for the project were Excel and Google Refine for data cleaning and analysis; Cytoscape for network analysis; and Illustrator and Flash for the visualizations. The Flash should have been HTML5, but we ran out of time.

What did we learn? Perhaps the most important lesson was that data structures can be very hard. If the original data is not in suitable format, recalculating and converting it will take a lot of time.

Electoral Hack in Realtime (Hacks/Hackers Buenos Aires)

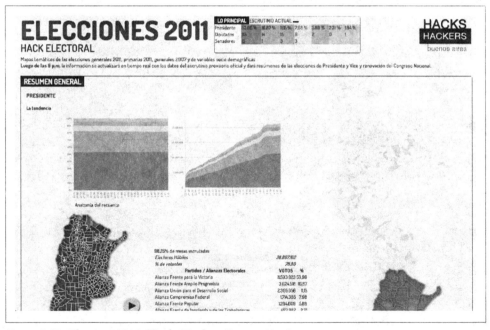

Figure 3-13. Elections 2011 (Hacks/Hackers Buenos Aires)

Electoral Hack (*http://elecciones.hhba.info*) is a political analysis project that visualizes data from the provisional ballot results of the October 2011 elections in Argentina. The system also features information from previous elections and socio-demographic statistics from across the country. The project was updated in real time with information from the provisional ballot count of the national elections of 2011 in Argentina, and gave summaries of election results. It was an initiative of Hacks/Hackers Buenos Aires with the political analyst Andy Tow, and was a collaborative effort of journalists, developers, designers, analysts, political scientists, and others from the local chapter of Hacks/Hackers.

What Data Did We Use?

All data came from official sources: the National Electoral Bureau provided access to data of the provisional count by Indra; the Department of the Interior provided information about elected posts and candidates from different political parties; a university project (*http://yoquierosaber.org/*) provided biographical information and the policy platforms of each presidential ticket; while socio-demographic information came from the 2001 National Census of Population and Housing (INDEC), the 2010 Census (INDEC), and the Ministry of Health.

How Was It Developed?

The application was generated during the 2011 Election Hackathon by Hacks/Hackers Buenos Aires the day before the election on October 23, 2011. The hackathon saw the participation of 30 volunteers with a variety of different backgrounds. Electoral Hack was developed as an open platform that could be improved over time. For the technology, we used Google Fusion Tables, Google Maps, and vector graphics libraries.

We worked on the construction of polygons for displaying geographic mapping and electoral demographics. Combining polygons in GIS software and geometries from public tables in Google Fusion Tables, we generated tables with keys corresponding to the electoral database of the Ministry of Interior, Indra, and sociodemographic data from INDEC. From this, we created visualizations in Google Maps.

Using the Google Maps API, we published several thematic maps representing the spatial distribution of voting with different tones of color, where the intensity of color represented the percentage of votes for the various presidential tickets in different administrative departments and polling stations, with particular emphasis on major urban centers: the City of Buenos Aires, the 24 districts of Greater Buenos Aires, the City of Cordoba, and Rosario.

We used the same technique to generate thematic maps of previous elections, namely the presidential primaries of 2011 and the election of 2007, as well as of the distribution of sociodemographic data, such as for poverty, child mortality, and living conditions, allowing for analysis and comparison. The project also showed the spatial distribution of the differences in percentage of votes obtained by each ticket in the general election of October compared to the August primary election.

Later, using partial data from the provisional ballot counts, we created an animated map depicting the anatomy of the count, in which the progress of the vote count is shown from the closing of the local polls until the following morning.

Pros

- We set out to find and represent data and we were able to do that. We had the UNICEF's database of child sociodemographics (*http://infoargentina.unicef.org .ar/*) at hand, as well as the database of candidates created by the yoquierosaber.org group of Torcuato Di Tella University. During the hackathon we gathered a large volume of additional data that we did not end up including.

- It was clear that the journalistic and programming work was enriched by scholarship. Without the contributions of Andy Tow and Hilario Moreno Campos, the project would have been impossible to achieve.

Cons

- The sociodemographic data we could use was not up to date (most was from the 2001 census), and it was not very granular. For example, it did not include detail about local average GDP, main economic activity, education level, number of schools, doctors per capita, and lots of other things that it would have been great to have.

- Originally the system was intended as a tool that could be used to combine and display any arbitrary data, so that journalists could easily display data that interested them on the Web. But we had to leave this for another time.

- As the project was built by volunteers in a short time frame, it was impossible to do everything that we wanted to do. Nevertheless, we made a lot of progress in the right direction.

- For the same reason, all the collaborative work of 30 people ended up condensed into a single programmer when the data offered by the government began to appear, and we ran into some problems importing data in real time. These were solved within hours.

Implications

The Electoral Hack platform had a big impact in the media, with television, radio, print and online coverage. Maps from the project were used by several media platforms during the elections and in subsequent days. As the days went by, the maps and visualizations were updated, increasing traffic even more. On Election Day, the site created that very day received about 20 thousand unique visitors and its maps were reproduced on the cover page of the newspaper Página/12 for two consecutive days, as well as in articles in La Nación. Some maps appeared in the print edition of the newspaper Clarín.

It was the first time that an interactive display of real-time maps had been used in the history of Argentine journalism. In the central maps one could clearly see the overwhelming victory of Cristina Fernandez de Kirchner by 54 percent of the vote, broken up by color saturation. It also served to help users understand specific cases where local candidates had landslide victories in the provinces.

— *Mariano Blejman, Mariana Berruezo, Sergio Sorín, Andy Tow, and Martín Sarsale from Hacks/Hackers Buenos Aires*

Data in the News: WikiLeaks

It began with one of the investigative reporting team asking, "You're good with spreadsheets, aren't you?" And this was one hell of a spreadsheet: 92,201 rows of data, each one containing a detailed breakdown of a military event in Afghanistan. This was the WikiLeaks war logs (*http://bit.ly/guardian-warlogs*). Part one, that is. There were to be two more episodes to follow: Iraq and the cables. The official term was SIGACTS: the US military Significant Actions Database.

The Afghanistan war logs—shared with The New York Times and Der Spiegel—was data journalism in action. What we wanted to do was enable our team of specialist reporters to get great human stories from the information—and we wanted to analyze it to get the big picture, to show how the war really is going.

It was central to what we would do quite early on that we would not publish the full database. WikiLeaks was already going to do that and we wanted to make sure that we didn't reveal the names of informants or unnecessarily endanger NATO troops. At the same time, we needed to make the data easier to use for our team of investigative reporters led by David Leigh and Nick Davies (who had negotiated releasing the data with Julian Assange). We also wanted to make it simpler to access key information, out there in the real world, as clear and open as we could make it.

The data came to us as a huge Excel file; over 92,201 rows of data, some with nothing in it at all or poorly formatted. It didn't help reporters trying to trawl through the data for stories and was too big to run meaningful reports on.

Our team built a simple internal database using SQL. Reporters could now search stories for key words or events. Suddenly the dataset became accessible and generating stories became easier.

The data was well structured: each event had the following key data: time, date, a description, casualty figures, and—crucially—detailed latitude and longitude.

We also started filtering the data to help us tell one of the key stories of the war: the rise in IED (improvised explosive device) attacks, homemade roadside bombs which are unpredictable and difficult to fight. This dataset was still massive, but easier to manage. There were around 7,500 IED explosions or ambushes (an ambush is where the attack is combined with, for example, small arms fire or rocket grenades) between

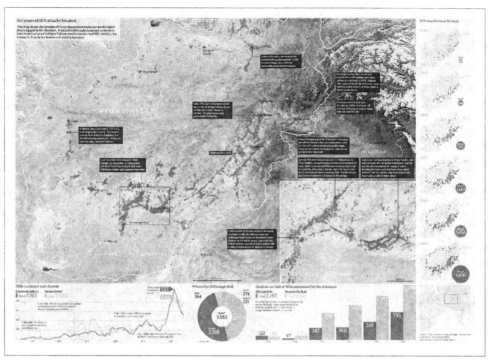

Figure 3-14. The WikiLeaks war logs (the Guardian)

2004 and 2009. There were another 8,000 IEDs which were found and cleared. We wanted to see how they changed over time—and how they compared. This data allowed us to see that the south, where British and Canadian troops were based then, was the worst-hit area—which backed up what our reporters who had covered the war knew.

The Iraq war logs release in October 2010 dumped another 391,000 records of the Iraq war into the public arena.

This was in a different league to the Afghanistan leak; there's a good case for saying this made the war the most documented in history. Every minor detail was now there for us to analyze and break down. But one factor stands out: the sheer volume of deaths, most of which are civilians.

As with Afghanistan, the Guardian decided not to republish the entire database, largely because we couldn't be sure the summary field didn't contain confidential details of informants and so on.

But we did allow our users to download a spreadsheet containing the records of every incident where somebody died, nearly 60,000 in all. We removed the summary field so it was just the basic data: the military heading, numbers of deaths, and the geographic breakdown.

We also took all these incidents where someone had died and put it on a map using Google Fusion tables (*http://bit.ly/guardian-iraq-map*). It was not perfect, but a start in trying to map the patterns of destruction that had ravaged Iraq.

December 2010 saw the release of the cables. This was in another league altogether, a huge dataset of official documents: 251,287 dispatches, from more than 250 worldwide US embassies and consulates. It's a unique picture of US diplomatic language—including over 50,000 documents covering the current Obama administration. But what did the data include?

The cables themselves came via the huge Secret Internet Protocol Router Network, or SIPRNet. SIPRNet is the worldwide US military Internet system, kept separate from the ordinary civilian Internet and run by the Department of Defense in Washington. Since the attacks of September 2001, there had been a move in the US to link up archives of government information, in the hope that key intelligence no longer gets trapped in information silos or "stovepipes." An increasing number of US embassies have become linked to SIPRNet over the past decade, so that military and diplomatic information can be shared. By 2002, 125 embassies were on SIPRNet: by 2005, the number had risen to 180, and by now the vast majority of US missions worldwide are linked to the system—which is why the bulk of these cables are from 2008 and 2009. As David Leigh wrote:

> An embassy dispatch marked SIPDIS is automatically downloaded onto its embassy classified website. From there, it can be accessed not only by anyone in the state department, but also by anyone in the US military who has a security clearance up to the "Secret" level, a password, and a computer connected to SIPRNet.

...which astonishingly covers over 3 million people. There are several layers of data in here; all the way up to *SECRET NOFORN,* which means that they are designed never be shown to non-US citizens. Instead, they are supposed to be read by officials in Washington up to the level of Secretary of State Hillary Clinton. The cables are normally drafted by the local ambassador or subordinates. The "Top Secret" and above foreign intelligence documents cannot be accessed from SIPRNet.

Unlike the previous releases, this was predominantly text, not quantified or with identical data. This is what was included:

A source
    The embassy or body which sent it.

A list of recipients
    Normally cables were sent to a number of other embassies and bodies.

A subject field
    A summary of the cable.

Tags
    Each cable was tagged with a number of keyword abbreviations.

Body text

The cable itself. We opted not to publish these in full for obvious security reasons.

One interesting nuance of this story is how the cables have almost created leaks on demand. They led the news for weeks upon being published; now, whenever a story comes up about some corrupt regime or international scandal, access to the cables gives us access to new stories.

Analysis of the cables is an enormous task which may never be entirely finished.

— *This is an edited version of a chapter first published in Facts are Sacred: The Power of Data by Simon Rogers, the Guardian (published on Kindle)*

Mapa76 Hackathon

We opened the Buenos Aires chapter of Hacks/Hackers (*http://www.meetup.com/Hack sHackersBA/*) in April 2011. We hosted two initial meetups to publicize the idea of greater collaboration between journalists and software developers, with between 120 and 150 people at each event. For a third meeting we had a 30-hour hackathon with eight people at a digital journalism conference in the city of Rosario, 300 kilometers from Buenos Aires.

A recurring theme in these meetings was the desire to scrape large volumes of data from the Web, and then to represent it visually. To help with this, a project called Mapa76.info was born, which helps users to extract data and then to display it using maps and timelines. Not an easy task.

Figure 3-15. Mapa76 (Hacks/Hackers Buenos Aires)

Why Mapa76? On March 24, 1976 there was a coup in Argentina, which lasted until 1983. In that period, there were an estimated 30,000 disappeared people, thousands of deaths, and 500 children born in captivity appropriated for the military dictatorship. Over 30 years later, the number of people in Argentina convicted of crimes against humanity committed during the dictatorship amounts to 262 people (September 2011). Currently there are 14 ongoing trials and 7 with definite starting dates. There are 802 people in various open court cases.

These prosecutions generate large volumes of data that are difficult for researchers, journalists, human rights organizations, judges, prosecutors, and others to process. Data is produced in a distributed manner and investigators often don't take advantage of software tools to assist them with interpreting it. Ultimately this means that facts are often overlooked and hypotheses are often limited. Mapa76 is an investigative tool providing open access to this information for journalistic, legal, juridical, and historical purposes.

To prepare for the hackathon, we created a platform which developers and journalists could use to collaborate on the day of the event. Martin Sarsale developed some basic algorithms to extract structured data from simple text documents. Some libraries were also used from DocumentCloud.org project, but not many. The platform would automatically analyze and extract names, dates and places from the texts—and would enable users to explore key facts about different cases (e.g., date of birth, place of arrest, alleged place of disappearance, and so on).

Our goal was to provide a platform for the automatic extraction of data on the judgments of the military dictatorship in Argentina. We wanted a way to automatically (or at least semi-automatically) display key data related to cases from 1976-1983 based on written evidence, arguments and judgments. The extracted data (names, places and dates) are collected, stored, and can be analyzed and refined by the researcher, as well as being explored using maps, timelines, and network analysis tools.

The project will allow journalists and investigators, prosecutors and witnesses to follow the story of a person's life, including the course of their captivity and subsequent disappearance or release. Where information is absent, users can comb through a vast number of documents for information that could be of possible relevance to the case.

For the hackathon, we made a public announcement through Hacks/Hackers Buenos Aires (*http://www.meetup.com/HacksHackersBA/*), which then had around 200 members (at the time of writing, there are around 540). We also contacted many human rights associations. The meeting was attended by about forty people, including journalists, advocacy organizations, developers and designers.

During the hackathon, we identified tasks that different types of participants could pursue independently to help things run smoothly. For example, we asked designers to work on an interface that combined maps and timelines, we asked developers to look into ways of extracting structured data and algorithms to disambiguate names, and we asked journalists to look into what happened with specific people, to compare different versions of stories, and to comb through documents to tell stories about particular cases.

Probably the main problem we had after the hackathon was that our project was very ambitious, our short-term objectives were demanding, and it is hard to coordinate a loose-knit network of volunteers. Nearly everyone involved with the project had a busy day job and many also participated in other events and projects. Hacks/Hackers Buenos Aires had 9 meetings in 2011.

The project is currently under active development. There is a core team of four people working with over a dozen collaborators. We have a public mailing list (*http://groups .google.com/group/mapa76-dev/*) and code repository (*https://github.com/mapa76/*) through which anyone can get involved with the project.

— *Mariano Blejman, Hacks/Hackers Buenos Aires*

The Guardian Datablog's Coverage of the UK Riots

During the summer of 2011, the UK was hit by a wave of riots. At the time, politicians suggested that these actions were categorically not linked to poverty and those who did the looting were simply criminals. Moreover, the Prime Minister, along with leading conservative politicians, blamed social media for causing the riots, suggesting that incitement had taken place on these platforms and that riots were organized using Facebook, Twitter, and Blackberry Messenger (BBM). There were calls to temporarily shut social media down. Because the government did not launch an inquiry into why the riots happened, the Guardian, in collaboration with the London School of Economics, set up the groundbreaking Reading the Riots (*http://www.guardian.co.uk/uk/series/ reading-the-riots*) project to address these issues.

The newspaper extensively used data journalism to enable the public to better understand who was doing the looting and why. What is more, they also worked with another team of academics, led by Professor Rob Procter at the University of Manchester, to better understand the role of social media, which the Guardian itself had extensively used in its reporting during the riots. The Reading the Riots team was led by Paul Lewis, the Guardian's Special Projects Editor. During the riots Paul reported on the front line in cities across England (most notably via his Twitter account, @paullewis). This second team worked on 2.6 million riot tweets donated by Twitter. The main aim of this social media work was to see how rumors circulate on Twitter, the function different users/actors have in propagating and spreading information flows, to see whether the platform was used to incite, and to examine other forms of organization.

In terms of the use of data journalism and data visualizations, it is useful to distinguish between two key periods: the period of the riots themselves and the ways in which data helped tell stories as the riots unfolded; and then a second period of much more intense research with two sets of academic teams working with the Guardian, to collect data, analyze it, and write in-depth reports on the findings. The results from the first phase of the Reading the Riots project were published during a week of extensive coverage in

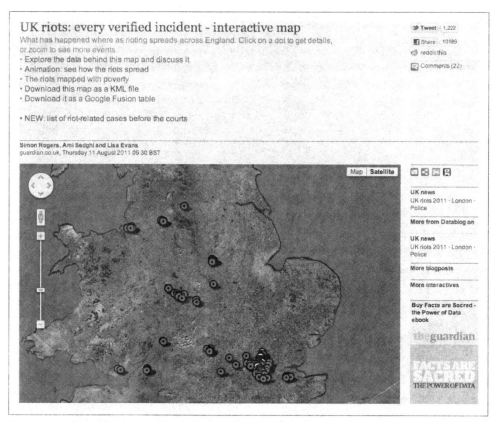

Figure 3-16. The UK Riots: every verified incident (the Guardian)

early December 2011. Below are some key examples of how data journalism was used during both periods.

Phase One: The Riots As They Happened

By using simple maps, the Guardian data team showed the locations of confirmed riots spots (*http://bit.ly/guardian-riots-map*) and through mashing up deprivation data with where the riots took place (*http://bit.ly/guardian-riots-poverty*), started debunking the main political narrative that there was no link to poverty. Both of these examples used off-the-shelf mapping tools, and in the second example, combine location data with another dataset to start making other connections and links.

In relation to the use of social media during the riots (in this case, Twitter), the newspaper created a visualization of riot-related hashtags used during this period (*http://bit .ly/guardian-riots-twitter*), which highlighted that Twitter was mainly used to respond to the riots rather than to organize people to go looting, with *#riotcleanup*, the spontaneous campaign to clean up the streets after the rioting, showing the most significant spike during the riot period.

Phase Two: Reading the Riots

When the paper reported its findings from months of intensive research and working closely with two academic teams, two visualizations stand out and have been widely discussed. The first one, a short video (*http://bit.ly/guardian-riots-commute*), shows the results of combining the known places where people rioted with their home address and showing a so-called "riot commute." Here the paper worked with transport mapping specialist, ITO World, to model the most likely route traveled by the rioters as they made their way to various locations to go looting, highlighting different patterns for different cities, with some traveling long distances.

The second one deals with the ways in which rumors spread on Twitter. In discussion with the academic team, seven rumors were agreed on for analysis. The academic team then collected all data related to each rumor and devised a coding schedule that coded the tweet according to four main codes: people simply repeating the rumor (making a claim), rejecting it (making a counter claim), questioning it (query), or simply commenting (comment). All tweets were coded in triplicate and the results were visualized (*http://bit.ly/guardian-riots*) by the Guardian Interactive Team. The Guardian team has written about how they built the visualization (*http://bit.ly/guardian-riots-twitter-interactive*).

What is so striking about this visualization is that it powerfully shows what is very difficult to describe and that is the viral nature of rumors and the ways in which their life cycle plays out over time. The role of the mainstream media is evident in some of these rumors (for example, outright debunking them, or indeed confirming them quickly as news), as is the corrective nature of Twitter itself in terms of dealing with such rumors. This visualization not only greatly aided the storytelling, but also gave a real insight into how rumors work on Twitter, which provides useful information for dealing with future events.

What is clear from the last example is the powerful synergy between the newspaper and an academic team capable of an in-depth analysis of 2.6 million riot tweets. Although the academic team built a set of bespoke tools to do their analysis, they are now working to make these widely available to anyone who wishes to use them (*http://www.analysingsocialmedia.org/*) in due course, providing a workbench for their analysis. Combined with the how-to description provided by the Guardian team, it will provide a useful case study of how such social media analysis and visualization can be used by others to tell such important stories.

— *Farida Vis, University of Leicester*

Illinois School Report Cards

Each year, the Illinois State Board of Education releases school "report cards," data on the demographics and performance of all the public schools Illinois. It's a massive dataset—this year's drop was ~9,500 *columns* wide. The problem with that much data is choosing what to present. (As with any software project, the hard part is not *building* the software, but building the *right* software.)

We worked with the reporters and editor from the education team to choose the interesting data. (There's a lot of data out there that seems interesting but which a reporter will tell you is actually flawed or misleading.)

We also surveyed and interviewed folks with school-age kids in our newsroom. We did this because of an empathy gap—nobody on the news apps team has school-age kids. Along the way, we learned much about our users and much about the usability (or lack thereof!) of the previous version of our schools site.

Figure 3-17. 2011 Illinois school report cards (Chicago Tribune)

We aimed to design for a couple of specific users and use cases:

- Parents with a child in school who want to know how their school measures up
- Parents who're trying to sort out where to live, since school quality often has a major impact on that decision.

The first time around, the schools site was about a six-week, two-developer project. Our 2011 update was a four-week, two-developer project. (There were actually three people actively working on the recent project, but none were full-time, so it adds up to about two.)

A key piece of this project was information design. Although we present far less data than is available, it's still a *lot* of data, and making it digestible was a challenge. Luckily, we got to borrow someone from our graphics desk—a designer who specializes in presenting complicated information. He taught us much about chart design and, in general, guided us to a presentation that is readable, but does not underestimate the reader's ability or desire to understand the numbers.

The site was built in Python and Django. The data is housed in MongoDB—the schools data is heterogeneous and hierarchical, making it a poor fit for a relational database. (Otherwise we probably would have used PostgreSQL.)

We experimented for the first time with Twitter's Bootstrap user interface framework on this project, and were happy with the results. The charts are drawn with Flot.

The app is also home to the many stories about school performance that we've written. It acts as sort of a portal in that way; when there's a new school performance story, we put it at the top of the app, alongside lists of schools relevant to the story. (And when a new story hits, readers of www.chicagotribune.com are directed to the app, not the story.)

Early reports are that readers love the schools app. The feedback we've received has been largely positive (or at least constructive!), and page views are through the roof. As a bonus, this data will remain interesting for a full year, so although we expect the hits to trail off as the schools stories fade from the homepage, our past experience is that readers have sought out this application year-round.

A few key ideas we took away from this project are:

- The graphics desk is your friend. They're good at making complex information digestible.

- Ask the newsroom for help. This is the second project for which we've conducted a newsroom-wide survey and interviews, and it's a great way to get the opinion of thoughtful people who, like our audience, are diverse in background and generally uncomfortable with computers.

- Show your work! Much of our feedback has been requests for the data that the application used. We've made a lot of the data publicly available via an API, and we will shortly release the stuff that we didn't think to include initially.

— *Brian Boyer, Chicago Tribune*

Hospital Billing

Investigative reporters at CaliforniaWatch (*http://californiawatch.org/*) received tips that a large chain of hospitals in California might be systematically gaming the federal Medicare program that pays for the costs of medical treatments of Americans aged 65 or older. The particular scam that was alleged is called *upcoding*, which means reporting

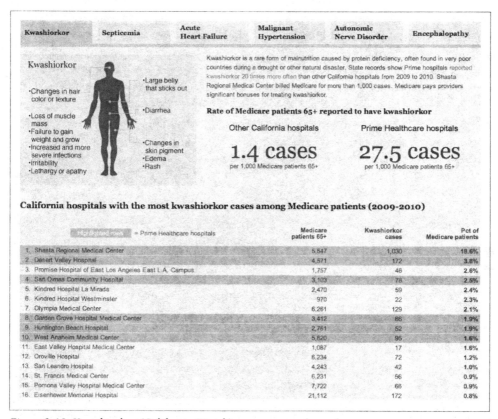

| Kwashiorkor | Septicemia | Acute Heart Failure | Malignant Hypertension | Autonomic Nerve Disorder | Encephalopathy |

Kwashiorkor

•Changes in hair color or texture

•Loss of muscle mass
•Failure to gain weight and grow
•Increased and more severe infections
•Irritability
•Lethargy or apathy

•Large belly that sticks out

•Diarrhea

•Changes in skin pigment
•Edema
•Rash

Kwashiorkor is a rare form of malnutrition caused by protein deficiency, often found in very poor countries during a drought or other natural disaster. State records show Prime hospitals reported kwashiorkor 20 times more often than other California hospitals from 2009 to 2010. Shasta Regional Medical Center billed Medicare for more than 1,000 cases. Medicare pays providers significant bonuses for treating kwashiorkor.

Rate of Medicare patients 65+ reported to have kwashiorkor

Other California hospitals	Prime Healthcare hospitals
1.4 cases	**27.5 cases**
per 1,000 Medicare patients 65+	per 1,000 Medicare patients 65+

California hospitals with the most kwashiorkor cases among Medicare patients (2009-2010)

	Medicare patients 65+	Kwashiorkor cases	Pct of Medicare patients
1. Shasta Regional Medical Center	5,547	1,030	18.6%
2. Desert Valley Hospital	4,571	172	3.8%
3. Promise Hospital of East Los Angeles East L.A. Campus	1,757	46	2.6%
4. San Dimas Community Hospital	3,103	78	2.5%
5. Kindred Hospital La Mirada	2,470	59	2.4%
6. Kindred Hospital Westminster	970	22	2.3%
7. Olympia Medical Center	6,261	129	2.1%
8. Garden Grove Hospital Medical Center	3,412	66	1.9%
9. Huntington Beach Hospital	2,761	52	1.9%
10. West Anaheim Medical Center	5,820	95	1.6%
11. East Valley Hospital Medical Center	1,087	17	1.6%
12. Oroville Hospital	6,234	72	1.2%
13. San Leandro Hospital	4,243	42	1.0%
14. St. Francis Medical Center	6,231	56	0.9%
15. Pomona Valley Hospital Medical Center	7,722	66	0.9%
16. Eisenhower Memorial Hospital	21,112	172	0.8%

(Highlighted rows = Prime Healthcare hospitals)

Figure 3-18. Kwashiorkor (California Watch)

patients having more complicated conditions—worth higher reimbursement—than actually existed. But a key source was a union that was fighting with the hospital chain's management, and the CaliforniaWatch team knew that independent verification was necessary for the story to have credibility.

Luckily, California's department of health has public records that give very detailed information about each case treated in all the state's hospitals. The 128 variables include up to 25 diagnosis codes from the "International Statistical Classification of Diseases and Related Health Problems" manual (commonly known as ICD-9) published by the World Health Organization. While patients aren't identified by name in the data, other variables tell the age of the patient, how the costs are paid, and which hospital treated him. The reporters realized that with these records, they could see if the hospitals owned by the chain were reporting certain unusual conditions at significantly higher rates than were being seen at other hospitals.

The datasets were large; nearly 4 million records per year. The reporters wanted to study six years worth of records in order to see how patterns changed over time. They ordered the data from the state agency; it arrived on CD-ROMs that were easily copied into a desktop computer. The reporter doing the actual data analysis used a system called SAS (*http://www.sas.com/*) to work with the data. SAS is very powerful (allowing analysis of many millions of records) and is used by many government agencies, including the California health department, but it is expensive—the same kind of analysis could have been done using any of a variety of other database tools, such as Microsoft Access or the open-source MySQL (*http://www.mysql.com/*).

With the data in hand and the programs written to study it, finding suspicious patterns was relatively simple. For example, one allegation was that the chain was reporting various degrees of malnutrition at much higher rates than were seen at other hospitals. Using SAS, the data analyst extracted frequency tables that showed the numbers of malnutrition cases being reported each year by each of California's more than 300 acute care hospitals. The raw frequency tables then were imported into Microsoft Excel for closer inspection of the patterns for each hospital; Excel's ability to sort, filter and calculate rates from the raw numbers made seeing the patterns easy.

Particularly striking were reports of a condition called Kwashiorkor, a protein deficiency syndrome that is almost exclusively seen in starving infants in famine-afflicted developing countries. Yet the chain was reporting its hospitals were diagnosing Kwashiorkor among elderly Californians at rates as much as 70 times higher than the state average of all hospitals (*http://bit.ly/californiawatch-malnutrition*).

For other stories, the analysis used similar techniques to examine the reported rates of conditions like septicemia, encephalopathy, malignant hypertension, and autonomic nerve disorder (*http://bit.ly/californiawatch-rare*). And another analysis looked at allegations that the chain was admitting from its emergency rooms into hospital care unusually high percentages of Medicare patients (*http://bit.ly/californiawatch-chains*), whose source of payment for hospital care is more certain than is the case for many other emergency room patients.

To summarize, stories like these become possible when you use data to produce evidence to test independently allegations being made by sources who may have their own agendas. These stories also are a good example of the necessity for strong public records laws; the reason the government requires hospitals to report this data is so that these kinds of analyses can be done, whether by government, academics, investigators, or even citizen journalists. The subject of these stories is important because it examines whether millions of dollars of public money is being spent properly.

— *Steve Doig, Walter Cronkite School of Journalism, Arizona State University*

Care Home Crisis

A Financial Times investigation (*http://on.ft.com/care-home-crisis*) into the private care home industry exposed how some private equity investors turned elderly care into a profit machine and highlighted the deadly human costs of a business model that favored investment returns over good care.

The analysis was timely, because the financial problems of Southern Cross, then the country's largest care home operator, were coming to a head. The government had for decades promoted a privatization drive in the care sector and continued to tout the private sector for its astute business practices.

Our inquiry began with analyzing data we obtained from the UK regulator in charge of inspecting care homes. The information was public, but it required a lot of persistence to get the data in a form that was usable.

The data included ratings (now defunct) on individual homes' performance and a breakdown of whether they were private, government-owned, or non-profit. The Care Quality Commission (CQC), up to June 2010, rated care homes on quality (0 stars = poor, to 3 stars = excellent).

The first step required extensive data cleaning, as the data provided by the Care Quality Commission for example contained categorizations that were not uniform. This was primarily done using Excel. We also determined—through desk and phone research—whether particular homes were owned by private-equity groups. Before the financial crisis, the care home sector was a magnet for private equity and property investors, but several—such as Southern Cross—had begun to face serious financial difficulties. We wanted to establish what effect, if any, private equity ownership had on quality of care.

A relatively straightforward set of Excel calculations enabled us to establish that the non-profit and government-run homes, on average, performed significantly better than the private sector. Some private equity-owned care home groups performed well over average, and others well below average.

Paired with on-the-ground reporting, case studies of neglect, an in-depth look at the failures in regulatory policies, as well as other data on levels of pay, turnover rates, etc., our analysis was able to paint a picture of the true state of elderly care.

Some tips:

- Make sure you keep notes on how you manipulate the original data.
- Keep a copy of the original data and never change the original.
- Check and double-check the data. Do the analysis several times (if need be, from scratch).
- If you mention particular companies or individuals, give them a right to reply.

— *Cynthia O'Murchu, Financial Times*

The Tell-All Telephone

Most people's understanding of what can actually be done with the data provided by our mobile phones is theoretical; there were few real-world examples. That is why Malte Spitz from the German Green party decided to publish his own data. To access the information, he had to file a suit against telecommunications giant Deutsche Telekom.

The data, contained in a massive Excel document, was the basis for Zeit Online's accompanying interactive map. Each of the 35,831 rows of the spreadsheet represent an instance when Spitz's mobile phone transferred information over a half-year period.

Seen individually, the pieces of data are mostly harmless. But taken together they provide what investigators call a profile: a clear picture of a person's habits and preferences, and indeed, of her life. This profile reveals when Spitz walked down the street, when he took a train, when he was in a plane. It shows that he mainly works in Berlin and which cities he visited. It shows when he was awake and when he slept.

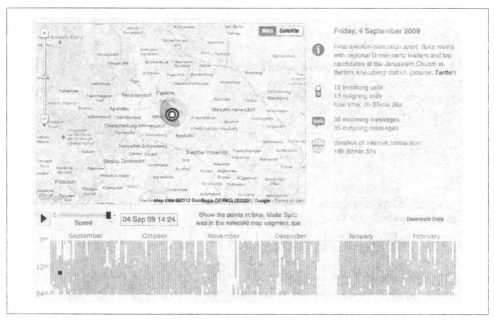

Figure 3-19. The Tell-All Telephone (Zeit Online)

Deutsche Telekom's dataset already kept one part of Spitz's data record private, namely, whom he called and who called him. That kind of information could not only infringe on the privacy of many other people in his life, it would also—even if the numbers were encrypted—reveal much too much about Spitz (but government agents in the real world would have access to this information).

We asked Lorenz Matzat and Michael Kreil from OpenDataCity to explore the data and find a solution for the visual presentation. "At first we used tools like Excel and Fusion Tables to understand the data ourselves. Then we started to develop a map interface to allow the audience to interact with the data in a non-linear way," said Matzat. To illustrate just how much detail from someone's life can be mined from this stored data, finally this was augmented with publicly accessible information about his whereabouts (Twitter, blog entries, party information like public calendar entries from his website). It is the kind of process that any good investigator would likely use to profile a person under observation. Together with Zeit Online's in-house graphics and R&D team they finalized a great interface to navigate: by pushing the play button, you'll set off on a trip through Malte Spitz's life.

After a very successful launch of the project in Germany, we noticed that we were having very high traffic from outside Germany and decided to create an English version of the app. After earning the German Grimme Online Award, the project was honored with an ONA Award in September 2011, the first time for a German news website.

All of the data is available in a Google Docs spreadsheet (*http://bit.ly/zeitonline-data*). Read the story on Zeit Online (*http://www.zeit.de/datenschutz/malte-spitz-data-reten tion*).

— *Sascha Venohr, Zeit Online*

Which Car Model? MOT Failure Rates

In January 2010, the BBC obtained data about the MOT pass and fail rates for different makes and models of cars. This is the test that assesses whether a car is safe and road-worthy; any car over three years old has to have an MOT test annually.

We obtained the data under freedom of information following an extended battle with VOSA, the Department for Transport agency that oversees the MOT system. VOSA turned down our FOI request for these figures on the grounds that it would breach commercial confidentiality. It argued that it could be *commercially damaging* to vehicle manufacturers with high failure rates. However, we then appealed to the Information Commissioner, who ruled that disclosure of the information would be in the public interest. VOSA then released the data, 18 months after we asked for it.

We analyzed the figures, focusing on the most popular models and comparing cars of the same age. This showed wide discrepancies. For example, among three year-old cars, 28% of Renault Méganes failed their MOT, in contrast to only 11% of Toyota Corollas. The figures were reported on television, radio, and online.

The data was given to us as a 1,200 page PDF document, which we then had to convert into a spreadsheet to do the analysis. As well as reporting our conclusions, we published this Excel spreadsheet (with over 14,000 lines of data) on the BBC News website along with our story (*http://bbc.in/mot-failure-rates*). This gave everyone else access to the data in a usable form.

The result was that others then used this data for their own analyses, which we did not have time to do in the rush to get the story out quickly (and which in some cases would have stretched our technical capabilities at the time). This included examining the failure rates for cars of other ages, comparing the records of manufacturers rather than individual models, and creating searchable databases for looking up the results of individuals models. We added links to these sites to our online news story, so our readers could get the benefit of this work.

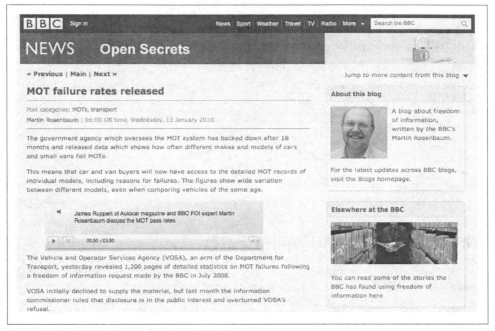

Figure 3-20. MOT failure rates released (BBC)

This illustrated some advantages of releasing the raw data to accompany a data-driven story. There may be exceptions (for example, if you are planning to use the data for other follow-up stories later and want to keep it to yourself in the meantime), but on the whole publishing the data has several important benefits:

- Your job is to find things out and tell people about them. If you've gone to the trouble of obtaining all the data, it's part of your job to pass it on.

- Other people may spot points of significant interest which you've missed, or simply details that matter to them even if they weren't important enough to feature in your story.

- Others can build on your work with further, more detailed analysis of the data, or different techniques for presenting or visualizing the figures, using their own ideas or technical skills that may probe the data productively in alternative ways.

- It's part of incorporating accountability and transparency into the journalistic process. Others can understand your methods and check your work if they want to.

— *Martin Rosenbaum, BBC*

Bus Subsidies in Argentina

Since 2002, subsidies for the public bus transportation system in Argentina have been growing exponentially, breaking a new record every year. But in 2011, after winning the elections, Argentina's new government announced cuts in subsidies for public services starting December of the same year. At the same time the national government decided to transfer the administration of the local bus lines and metro lines to the City of Buenos Aires government. As the transfer of subsidies to this local government hasn't been clarified and there was a lack of sufficient local funds to guarantee the safety of the transportation system, the government of the City of Buenos Aires rejected this decision.

As this was happening, I and my colleagues at La Nación were meeting for the first time to discuss how to start our own data journalism operation. Our Financial Section Editor suggested that the subsidies data published by the Secretaría de Transporte (the Department of Transportation; *http://www.transporte.gov.ar/*) would be a good challenge to start with, as it was very difficult to make sense of due to the format and the terminology.

The poor conditions of the public transportation system impact the life of more than 5,800,000 passengers every day. Delays, strikes, vehicle breakdowns, or even accidents are often happening. We thus decided to look into where the subsidies for the public transportation system in Argentina go and make this data easily accessible to all Argentinian citizens by means of a "Transport Subsidies Explorer," which is currently in the making.

We started with calculating how much bus companies receive every month from the government. To do this, we looked at the data published on the website of the Department of Transportation (*http://www.transporte.gov.ar/content/subsidios-sistau/*), where more than 400 PDFs containing monthly cash payments to more than 1,300 companies since 2006 were published.

We teamed up with a senior programmer to develop a scraper in order to automate the regular download and conversion of these PDFs into Excel and Database files. We are using the resulting dataset with more than 285,000 records for our investigations and visualizations, in both print and online. Additionally, we are making this data available in machine-readable format for every Argentinian to reuse and share.

The next step was to identify how much the monthly maintenance of a public transport vehicle costed the government on average. To find this out we went to another government website, that of the Comisión Nacional de Regulación del Transporte (CNRT, or The National Commission for the Regulation of Transport; *http://www.cnrt.gov.ar/index2.htm*), responsible for regulating transportation in Argentina. On this website, we found a list of bus companies that owned 9000 vehicles altogether. We developed a normalizer to allow us to reconcile bus company names and cross-reference the two datasets.

To proceed, we needed the registration number of each vehicle. On the CNRT website, we found a list of vehicles per bus line per company with their license plates. Vehicle registration numbers in Argentina are composed of letters and numbers that correspond to the vehicle's age. For example, my car has the registration number IDF234, and the

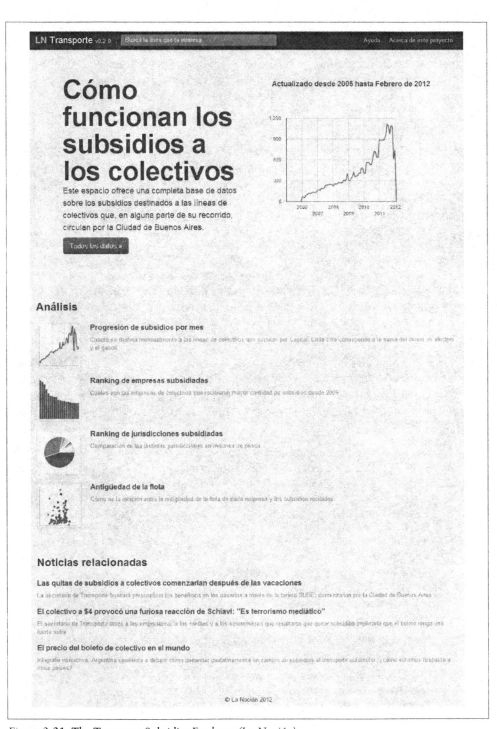

Figure 3-21. The Transport Subsidies Explorer (La Nación)

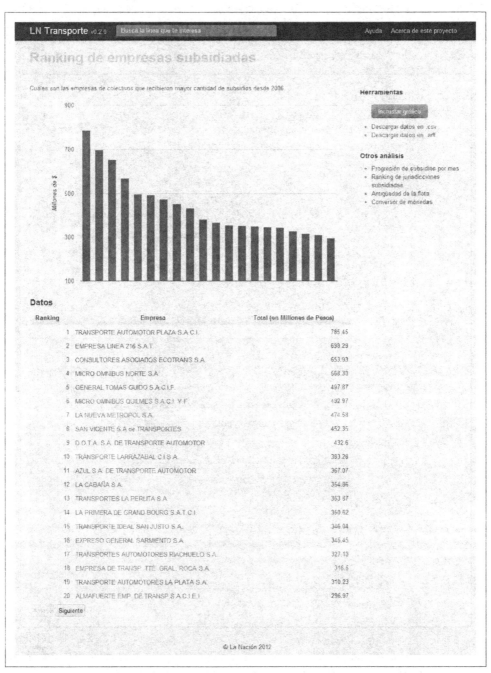

Figure 3-22. Ranking subsidized transport companies (La Nación)

"I" corresponds to March-April 2011. We reverse engineered the license plates for buses belonging to all listed companies to find the average age of buses per company, in order to show how much money goes to each company and compare the amounts based on the average age of their vehicles.

In the middle of this process, the content of the government-released PDFs containing the data we needed mysteriously changed, although the URLs and names of the files remained the same. Some PDFs were now missing the vertical "totals," making it impossible to cross-check totals across all the entire investigated time period, 2002-2011.

We took this case to a hackathon organized by Hacks/Hackers in Boston, where developer Matt Perry generously created what we call the "PDF Spy." This application won the "Most Intriguing" category in that event. The PDF Spy (*http://gristlabs.com/2011/09/24/pdfspy/*) points at a web page full of PDFs and checks if the content within the PDFs has changed. "Never be fooled by 'government transparency' again," writes Matt Perry.

Who Worked on the Project?

A team of seven journalists, programmers and an interactive designer were working on this investigation for 13 months.

The skills we needed for this project were:

- Journalists with knowledge of how the subsidies for the public transportation system work and what the risks were; knowledge of the bus companies market.
- A programmer skilled in Web scraping, parsing and normalizing data, and extracting data from PDFs into Excel spreadsheets.
- A statistician for conducting the data analysis and the different calculations.
- A designer for producing the interactive data visualizations.

What Tools Did We Use?

We used VBasic for applications, Excel Macros, Tableau Public, and the Junar Open Data Platform, as well as Ruby on Rails, the Google charts API, and Mysql for the Subsidies Explorer.

The project had a great impact. We've had tens of thousands of views and the investigation was featured on the front page of La Nación's print edition.

The success of this first data journalism project helped us internally to make the case for establishing a data operation that would cover investigative reporting and provide service to the public. This resulted in Data.lanacion.com.ar, a platform where we publish data on various topics of public interest in machine-readable format.

— *Angélica Peralta Ramos, La Nación (Argentina)*

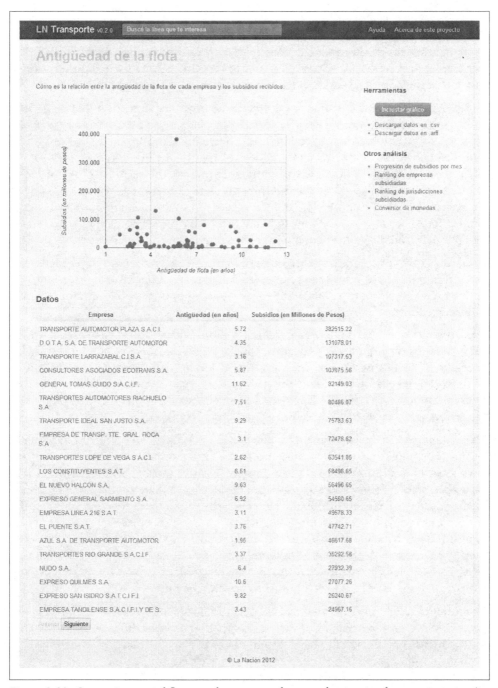

Figure 3-23. Comparing age of fleets to the amount of money they receive from government (La Nación)

Citizen Data Reporters

Large newsrooms are not the only ones that can work on data-powered stories. The same skills that are useful for data journalists can also help citizens reporters access data about their locality, and turn them into stories.

This was the primary motivation of the citizen media project Friends of Januária (*http: //amigosdejanuaria.wordpress.com/*), in Brazil, which received a grant from Rising Voices (*http://rising.globalvoicesonline.org/*), the outreach arm of Global Voices Online (*http://globalvoicesonline.org/*), and additional support from the organization Article 19 (*http://www.article19.org/*). Between September and October 2011, a group of young residents of a small town located in north of the state of Minas Gerais, which is one of the poorest regions of Brazil, were trained in basic journalism techniques and budget monitoring. They also learned how to make Freedom of Information requests and access publicly available information from official databases on the Internet.

Januária, a town of approximately 65,000 residents, is also renowned for the failure of its local politicians. In three four-year terms, it had seven different mayors. Almost all of them were removed from office due to wrongdoing in their public administrations, including charges of corruption.

Small towns like Januária often fail to attract attention from the Brazilian media, which tends to focus on larger cities and state capitals. However, there is an opportunity for residents of small towns to become a potential ally in the monitoring of the public administration because they know the daily challenges facing their local communities better than anyone. With the Internet as another important ally, residents can now better access information such as budget and other local data.

After taking part in twelve workshops, some of the new citizen reporters from Januária began to demonstrate how this concept of accessing publicly available data in small towns can be put into practice. For example, Soraia Amorim, a 22 year-old citizen journalist, wrote a story about the number of doctors that are on the city payroll according to Federal Government data. However, she found that the official number did not correspond with the situation in the town. To write this piece, Soraia had access to health data, which is available online at the website of the SUS (Sistema Único de Saúde or Unique Health System) (*http://bit.ly/tabnet-datasus*), a federal program that provides free medical assistance to the Brazilian population. According to SUS data, Januária should have 71 doctors in various health specialities.

The number of doctors indicated by SUS data did not match what Soraia knew about doctors in the area: residents were always complaining about the lack of doctors and some patients had to travel to neighboring towns to see one. Later, she interviewed a woman that had recently been in a motorcycle accident and could not find medical assistance at Januária's hospital because no doctor was available. She also talked to the town's Health Secretary, who admitted that there were less doctors in town than the number published by SUS.

Figure 3-24. The Friends of Januária citizen media project teaches key skills to citizens to turn them into data journalists

These initial findings raise many questions about reasons for this difference between the official information published online and the town's reality. One of them is that the federal data may be wrong, which would mean that there is an important lack of health information in Brazil. Another possibility may be that Januária is incorrectly reporting the information to SUS. Both of these possibilities should lead to a deeper investigation to find the definitive answer. However, Soraia's story is an important part of this chain because it highlights an inconsistency and may also encourage others to look more closely at this issue.

"I used to live in the countryside, and finished high school with a lot of difficulty," says Soraia. "When people asked me what I wanted to do with my life, I always told them that I wanted to be a journalist. But I imagined that it was almost impossible due to the world I lived in." After taking part in the Friends of Januária training, Soraia believes that access to data is an important tool to change the reality of her town. "I feel able to help to change my town, my country, the world," she adds.

Another citizen journalist from the project is 20 year-old Alysson Montiériton, who also used data for an article. It was during the project's first class, when the citizen reporters walked around the city to look for subjects that could become stories, that

Alysson decided to write about a broken traffic light located in a very important inter-section, which had remained broken since the beginning of the year. After learning how to look for data on the Internet, he searched for the number of vehicles that exists in town and the amount of taxes paid by those who own cars. He wrote:

> The situation in Januária gets worse because of the high number of vehicles in town. According to IBGE (the most important statistics research institute in Brazil), Januária had 13,771 vehicles (among which 7,979 were motorcycles) in 2010. ... The town's res-idents believe that the delay in fixing the traffic light is not a result of lack of resources. According to the Treasury Secretary of Minas Gerais state, the town received 470 thou-sand reais in vehicle taxes in 2010.

By having access to data, Alysson was able to show that Januária has many vehicles (almost one for every five residents), and that a broken traffic light could put a lot of people in danger. Furthermore, he was able to tell his audience the amount of funds received by the town from taxes paid by vehicle owners and, based on that, to question whether this money would not be enough to repair the traffic light to provide safe conditions to drivers and pedestrians.

Although the two stories written by Soraia and Alysson are very simple, they show that data can be used by citizen reporters. You don't need to be in a large newsroom with a lot of specialists to use data in your articles. After twelve workshops, Soraia and Alysson, neither of whom have a background in journalism, were able to work on data-powered stories and write interesting pieces about their local situation. In addition, their articles show that data itself can be useful even on a small scale. In other words, that there is also valuable information in small datasets and tables—not only in huge databases.

— *Amanda Rossi, Friends of Januária*

The Big Board for Election Results

Election results provide great visual storytelling opportunities for any news organiza-tion, but for many years this was an opportunity missed for us. In 2008, we and the graphics desk set out to change that.

We wanted to find a way to display results that told a story and didn't feel like just a jumble of numbers in a table or on a map. In previous elections, that's exactly what we did (*http://nyti.ms/senate-1*; *http://nyti.ms/senate-2*; *http://nyti.ms/senate-3*).

Not that there is necessarily anything wrong with a big bag of numbers, or what I call the "CNN model" of tables, tables, and more tables. It works because it gives the reader pretty much exactly what she wants to know: who won?

And the danger in messing with something that isn't fundamentally broken is signifi-cant. By doing something radically different and stepping away from what people ex-pect, we could have made things more confusing, not less.

In the end, it was Shan Carter of the graphics desk who came up with the right answer, what we eventually ended up calling the "big board" (*http://nyti.ms/board-elections*). When I saw the mockups for the first time, it was quite literally a head-slap moment.

It was exactly right.

President

Big Board   Map   Electoral Explorer   Obama: Victory Speech   McCain: Concession Speech   Exit Polls

SHARE   E-MAIL

365 ☑ **Obama** Electoral Votes Projected Winner

0 uncalled

173 **McCain** Electoral Votes

Popular vote: 59,862,698   273 needed to win   Popular vote: 55,218,442

■■ WIN   LEAD

Obama was expected to win easily				Obama was expected to win narrowly				Battleground states				McCain was expected to win narrowly				McCain was expected to win easily			
E.V.		Obama	McCain %Rpt.	E.V.		Obama	McCain %Rpt.	E.V.		Obama	McCain %Rpt.	E.V.		Obama	McCain %Rpt.	E.V.		Obama	McCain %Rpt.
65	Calif.	61% 37% 100%		9	Colo.	54% 45% 100%		27	Fla.	51% 48% 100%		15	Ga.	47% 52% 99%		9	Ala.	39% 60% 99%
7	Conn.	61% 38% 100%		7	Iowa	54% 45% 100%		11	Ind.	50% 49% 99%		3	Mont.	47% 50% 100%		3	Alaska	38% 60% 100%
3	Del.	62% 37% 100%		10	Minn.	54% 44% 100%		11	Mo.	49% 49% 100%		3	N.D.	45% 53% 100%		10	Ariz.	45% 54% 100%
3	D.C.	93% 7% 100%		5	Nev.	55% 43% 100%		15	N.C.	50% 50% 100%		5	W.Va.	43% 56% 100%		6	Ark.	39% 59% 100%
4	Hawaii	72% 27% 100%		4	N.H.	54% 45% 100%		20	Ohio	51% 47% 100%						4	Idaho	36% 62% 100%
21	Ill.	62% 37% 100%		5	N.M.	57% 42% 100%										6	Kan.	41% 57% 100%
4	Me.	58% 41% 100%		21	Pa.	55% 44% 100%										8	Ky.	41% 57% 100%
10	Md.	62% 37% 100%		13	Va.	53% 46% 100%										9	La.	40% 59% 100%
12	Mass.	62% 36% 100%		13	Wis.	56% 42% 100%										6	Miss.	43% 56% 100%
17	Mich.	57% 41% 100%														5*	Neb.	42% 57% 100%
15	N.J.	57% 42% 99%														7	Okla.	34% 66% 100%
31	N.Y.	62% 37% 99%														8	S.C.	45% 54% 100%
7	Ore.	57% 41% 97%														3	S.D.	45% 53% 100%
4	R.I.	63% 35% 100%														11	Tenn.	42% 57% 100%
3	Vt.	68% 31% 100%														34	Tex.	44% 55% 100%
11	Wash.	57% 41% 93%														5	Utah	35% 62% 100%
																3	Wyo.	33% 65% 100%

Figure 3-25. The big board for election results (New York Times)

What makes this a great piece of visual journalism? To begin with, the reader's eye is immediately drawn to the big bar showing the electoral college votes at the top, what we might in the journalism context call the *lede*. It tells the reader exactly what she wants to know, and it does so quickly, simply and without any visual noise.

Next, the reader is drawn to is the five-column grouping of states below, organized by how likely The Times felt a given state was to go for one candidate or the other. There in the middle column is what we might call in the journalism context our *nut graph*, where we explain why Obama won. The interactive makes that crystal clear: Obama took all the states he was expected to and four of the five toss-up states.

To me, this five-column construct is an example of how visual journalism differs from other forms of design. Ideally, a great piece of visual journalism will be both beautiful and informative. But when deciding between story or aesthetics, the journalist must err on the side of story. And while this layout may not be the way a pure designer might choose to present the data, it does tell the story very, very well.

And finally, like any good web interactive, this one invites the reader to go deeper still. There are details like state-by-state vote percentages, the number of electoral votes and percent reporting deliberately played down so as not to compete with the main points of the story.

All of this makes the "big board" a great piece of visual journalism that maps almost perfectly to the tried-and-true inverted pyramid.

— *Aron Pilhofer, New York Times*

Crowdsourcing the Price of Water

Since March 2011, information about the price of tap water throughout France is gathered through a crowdsourcing experiment. In just 4 months, over 5,000 people fed up with corporate control of the water market took the time to look for their water utility bill, scan it, and upload it on Prix de l'Eau ("price of water"; *http://www.prixdeleau .fr/*) project. The result is an unprecedented investigation that brought together geeks, NGO, and traditional media to improve transparency around water projects.

Figure 3-26. The Price of Water (Fondation France Liberté)

The French water utility market consists in over 10,000 customers (cities buying water to distribute to their taxpayers) and just a handful of utility companies. The balance of power on this oligopoly is distorted in favor of the corporations, which sometimes charge different prices to neighboring towns!

The French NGO France Libertés has been dealing with water issues worldwide for the past 25 years. It now focuses on improving transparency on the French market and empowering citizens and mayors, who negotiate water utility deals. The French government decided to tackle the problem 2 years ago with a nationwide census of water price and quality. So far, only 3% of the data has been collected. To go faster, France Libertés (*http://www.france-libertes.org/*) wanted to get citizens directly involved.

Together with the OWNI team, I designed a crowdsourcing interface where users would scan their water utility bill and enter the price they paid for tap water on *http://www.prixdeleau.fr/*. In the past 4 months, 8,500 signed up and over 5,000 bills have been uploaded and validated.

While this does not allow for a perfect assessment of the market situation, it showed stakeholders such as national water-overseeing bodies that there was a genuine, grassroots concern about the price of tap water. They were skeptical at first about transparency, but changed their minds over the course of the operation, progressively joining France Libertés in its fight against opacity and corporate malpractice. What can media organizations learn from this?

Partner with NGOs
> NGOs need large amount of data to design policy papers. They will be more willing to pay for a data collection operation than a newspaper executive.

Users can provide raw data
> Crowdsourcing works best when users do a data collection or data-refining task.

Ask for the source
> We pondered whether to ask users for a scan of the original bill, thinking it would deter some of them (especially as our target audience was older than average). While it might have put off some, it increased the credibility of the data.

Set up a validation mechanism
> We designed a point system and a peer-review mechanism (*http://www.prixdeleau.fr/valider*) to vet user contributions. This proved too convoluted for users, who had little incentive to make repeated visits to the website. It was used by the France Libertés team, however, whose 10 or so employees did feel motivated by the points system.

Keep it simple
> We built an automated mailing mechanism so that users could file a Freedom of Information request regarding water pricing in just a few clicks. Though innovative and well-designed, this feature did not provide substantial ROI (only 100 requests have been sent).

Target your audience
> France Libertés partnered with consumers' rights news magazine *60 Millions de Consommateurs*, who got their community involved in a big way. It was the perfect match for such an operation.

Choose your key performance indicators carefully

The project gathered only 45,000 visitors in 4 months, equivalent to 15 minutes worth of traffic on *http://www.nytimes.com/*. What's really important is that 1 in 5 signed up and 1 in 10 took the time to scan and upload his or her utility bill.

— *Nicolas Kayser-Bril, Journalism++*

CHAPTER 4

Getting Data

So, you're all ready to get started on your first data journalism project. What now? First of all you need some data. This section looks at where you can get it from. We learn how to find data on the web, how to request it using freedom of information laws, how to use "screen-scraping" to gather data from unstructured sources, and how to use "crowd-sourcing" to collect your own datasets from your readers. Finally we look at what the law says about republishing datasets, and how to use simple legal tools to let others reuse your data.

A Five Minute Field Guide

Looking for data on a particular topic or issue? Not sure what exists or where to find it? Don't know where to start? In this section we look at how to get started with finding public data sources on the web.

Streamlining Your Search

While they may not always be easy to find, many databases on the web are indexed by search engines, whether the publisher intended this or not. Here are a few tips:

- When searching for data, make sure that you include both search terms relating to the content of the data you're trying to find, as well as some information on the format or source that you would expect it to be in. Google and other search engines allow you to search by file type. For example, you can look only for spreadsheets (by appending your search with "filetype:XLS filetype:CSV"), geodata ("filetype:shp"), or database extracts ("filetype:MDB, filetype:SQL, filetype:DB"). If you're so inclined, you can even look for PDFs ("filetype:pdf").

- You can also search by part of a URL. Googling for "inurl:downloads filetype:xls" will try to find all Excel files that have "downloads" in their web address (if you find a single download, it's often worth just checking what other results exist for the same folder on the web server). You can also limit your search to only those results on a single domain name, by searching for "site:agency.gov", for example.

- Another popular trick is not to search for content directly, but for places where bulk data may be available. For example, "site:agency.gov Directory Listing" may give you some listings generated by the web server with easy access to raw files, while "site:agency.gov Database Download" will look for intentionally created listings.

Going Straight to the Source

The first trick I use in getting hold of data that is held by a public entity is to try to go directly to the data holder, not the public affairs person, not through an FOIA. I could craft an FOIA or public records request of course, but it will start the wheels turning slowly. It's likely that I'll get a response back that the data is not in the format I requested, or (as has happened in some cases) that the governmental body uses a proprietary software and can't extract the data in the format I requested. But, if I first successfully reach the person who handles data for that organization, I can ask questions about what data they keep on the subject and how they keep it. I can find out the format. I can speak data-language and find out what I need to know to successfully request the data. The roadblocks to this approach? Often, it's hard to reach these people. The Public Information Officer (PIO) will want me to deal with them. I've found in those cases, it's best to try to then set up a conference call, or even better, an in-person meeting with the PIO, the data guru, and me. And I can set it up in a way that makes it hard for them to say no. "I don't want to create work for them," I say. "I don't want to create an unnecessarily burdensome or overly broad request, so a meeting will help me understand exactly what they have and how I can best request exactly what is needed."

If this method does not work, my fallback is to ask first for their record layout and data dictionary in a request. Then, I actually request the data. I sometimes will also ask first how they keep the data, and in what system. That way, I can research the ways the data can be exported in advance of writing my request.

Lastly, my best success story comes from when I was working at a small newspaper in Montana. I needed some county data, which I was told could not be exported out of the mainframe. I did a little research, and offered to come in and help. I worked with the data person, we built a short script, and printed the data to a floppy disk (this was a long time ago). I had my data, and the county now was equipped to provide data to anyone who requested it. They didn't intend for that to happen, but they needed to extract the data sometimes too and didn't fully understand their system, so we all helped each other.

— *Cheryl Philips, The Seattle Times*

Browse Data Sites and Services

Over the last few years, a number of dedicated data portals, data hubs, and other data sites have appeared on the web. These are a good place to get acquainted with the kinds of data that is out there. For starters you might like to take a look at:

Official data portals
> The government's willingness to release a given dataset will vary from country to country. A growing number of countries are launching data portals (inspired by the U.S.'s data.gov and the U.K.'s data.gov.uk) to promote the civic and commer-

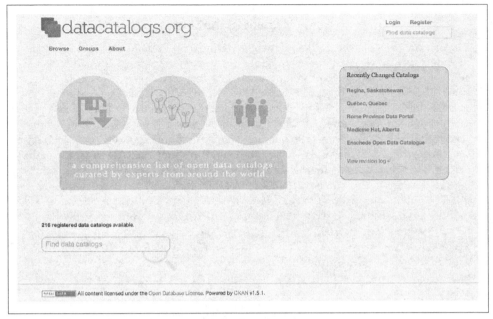

Figure 4-1. datacatalogs.org (Open Knowledge Foundation)

cial reuse of government information. An up-to-date, global index of such sites can be found at *http://datacatalogs.org/*. Another handy site is the Guardian World Government Data (*http://www.guardian.co.uk/world-government-data*), a meta search engine that includes many international government data catalogues.

The Data Hub (http://thedatahub.org/)
A community-driven resource run by the Open Knowledge Foundation that makes it easy to find, share, and reuse openly available sources of data, especially in ways that are machine-automated.

ScraperWiki (https://scraperwiki.com/)
An online tool to make the process of extracting "useful bits of data easier so they can be reused in other apps, or rummaged through by journalists and researchers." Most of the scrapers and their databases are public and can be reused.

World Bank (http://data.worldbank.org/) and United Nations (http://data.un.org/) data portals
These services provide high-level indicators for all countries, often for many years in the past.

Buzzdata (http://buzzdata.com/), Infochimps (http://www.infochimps.com/), and Data-Market (http://datamarket.com/)
Emerging startups that aim to build communities around data sharing and resale.

DataCouch (http://datacouch.com/)
A place to upload, refine, share, and visualize your data.

Freebase (http://www.freebase.com/)

>   An interesting Google subsidiary that provides "an entity graph of people, places and things, built by a community that loves open data."

Research data

>   There are numerous national and disciplinary aggregators of research data, such as the UK Data Archive (*http://www.data-archive.ac.uk/*). While there will be lots of data that is free at the point of access, there will also be much data that requires a subscription, or which cannot be reused or redistributed without asking permission first.

Getting Data from Paper Archives

Right after Wikileak's release of US military documents in Afghanistan and Iraq, we decided to adapt the concept to celebrate the 50th anniversary of the Algerian War by publishing the Algerian War Diaries. We set out to collect and digitize the archives of the French Army in Algeria. These are available in the War Ministry archive in Paris, albeit in a paper format. We sent out journalists and students to take photographs of the documents. We tried scanning them using a Canon P-150 portable scanner, but it didn't work mainly because much of the archives are stapled.

In the end, about 10,000 pages were collected in a few weeks. We ran a text recognition software on them (ABBYY FineReader), which produced poor results. What's more, the ministry arbitrarily denied access to the most interesting boxes of archives. Above all, the ministry forbids anyone from republishing documents that can be freely photographed on location, so we decided that it wasn't worth the risk and the project was put on hold.

— *Nicolas Kayser-Bril, Journalism++*

Ask a Forum

Search for existing answers or ask a question at Get The Data (*http://getthedata.org/*) or Quora (*http://www.quora.com/*). GetTheData is Q&A site where you can ask your data-related questions, including where to find data relating to a particular issue, how to query or retrieve a particular data source, what tools to use to explore a dataset in a visual way, how to cleanse data, or get it into a format you can work with.

Ask a Mailing List

Mailing lists combine the wisdom of a whole community on a particular topic. For data journalists, the Data-Driven Journalism List (*http://bit.ly/ddj-list*) and the NICAR-L (*http://bit.ly/nicar-subscribe/*) lists are excellent starting points. Both of these lists are filled with data journalists and Computer-Assisted Reporting (CAR) geeks, who work on all kinds of projects. Chances are that someone may have done a story like yours, and may have an idea of where to start, if not a link to the data itself. You could also try Project Wombat (*http://project-wombat.org/*; "a discussion list for difficult reference questions"), the Open Knowledge Foundation's many mailing lists (*http://lists.okfn.org/mailman/listinfo*), mailing lists at theInfo (*http://theinfo.org/*), or searching for mailing lists on the topic or in the region that you are interested in.

Join Hacks/Hackers

Hacks/Hackers (*http://hackshackers.com/*) is a rapidly expanding international grassroots journalism organization with dozens of chapters and thousands of members across four continents. Its mission is to create a network of journalists ("hacks") and technologists ("hackers") who rethink the future of news and information. With such a broad network, you stand a strong chance of someone knowing where to look for the thing you seek.

Ask an Expert

Professors, public servants, and industry folks often know where to look. Call them. Email them. Accost them at events. Show up at their office. Ask nicely. "I'm doing a story on X. Where would I find this? Do you know who has this?"

Learn About Government IT

Understanding the technical and administrative context in which governments maintain their information is often helpful when trying to access data. Whether it's CORDIS, COINS, or THOMAS, big-acronym databases often become most useful once you understand a bit about their intended purpose.

Find government organizational charts and look for departments/units with a cross-cutting function (e.g., reporting, IT services), then explore their websites. A lot of data is kept in multiple departments and while for one, a particular database may be their crown jewels, another may give it to you freely.

Look out for dynamic infographics on government sites. These are often powered by structured data sources/APIs that can be used independently (e.g., flight tracking applets, weather forecast Java apps).

Trawling Through Phone Logs

A few months ago, I wanted to parse (then-presidential candidate) Texas Gov. Rick Perry's phone logs. It was the result of a long-awaited state public-records request. The data essentially came in the form of 120-plus pages of fax-quality documents. It was an endeavor that required data entry and cleanup, followed by a WhitePages.com API to reverse lookup the phone numbers.

Mashing together names with state and federal (FEC) election data, we found that Perry reached out to campaign and super PAC donors from state work phones (*http://bo.st/perry-phone*), a frowned-upon practice that raised questions about ties between him and a "super PAC" working in his favor.

— *Jack Gillum, Associated Press*

Search Again

When you know more about what you are looking for, search again using phrases and improbable sets of words you've spotted since last time. You may have a bit more luck with search engines!

Write an FOI Request

If you believe that a government body has the data you need, a Freedom of Information request may be your best tool. See the next section for more information on how to file one.

— *Brian Boyer (Chicago Tribune), John Keefe (WNYC), Friedrich Lindenberg (Open Knowledge Foundation), Jane Park (Creative Commons), Chrys Wu (Hacks/Hackers)*

When The Law Fails

After reading a scholarly article (*http://bit.ly/hygiene-inspections*) explaining that publishing the outcome of hygiene inspections in restaurants reduced the number of food-related illnesses in Los Angeles, I asked the Parisian hygiene services for the list of inspections. Following the procedure set out by the French FOIA, I waited 30 days for their refusal to answer, then went to the Access to Public Data Commission (CADA in French), which rules on the legitimacy of FOI requests. CADA upheld my demand and ordered the administration to release the data. The administration subsequently asked for two months extra time, and CADA accepted that. Two months later, the administration still hadn't done anything.

I tried to get some big-name (and big-pocketed) open data advocates to go to court (which is a €5000 affair and a sure win with CADA support), but they were afraid to compromise their relations with official open data programs. This example is one among several where the French administration simply ignores the law and the official initiatives do nothing to support grassroots demands for data.

— *Nicolas Kayser-Bril, Journalism++*

Your Right to Data

Before you make a Freedom of Information (FOI) request, you should check to see if the data you are looking for is already available—or has already been requested by others. The previous chapter has some suggestions for where you might look. If you've looked around and still can't get hold of the data you need, then you may wish to file a formal request. Here are some tips that may help to make your request more effective:

Plan ahead to save time
> Think about submitting a formal access request whenever you set out to look for information. It's better not to wait until you have exhausted all other possibilities. You will save time by submitting a request at the beginning of your research and carrying out other investigations in parallel. Be prepared for delay: sometimes public bodies take a while to process requests, so it is better to expect this.

Check the rules about fees
> Before you start submitting a request, check the rules about fees for either submitting requests or receiving information. That way, if a public official suddenly asks you for money, you will know what your rights are. You can ask for electronic documents to avoid copying and posting costs, mention in your request that you would prefer the information in electronic format. That way you will avoid paying a fee, unless of course the information is not available electronically, although these days, it's usually possible to scan documents which are not already digitalized and then to send them as an attachment by email.

Know your rights
> Find out what your rights are before you begin, so you know where you stand and what the public authorities are and are not obliged to do. For example, most freedom of information laws provide a time limit for authorities to reply to you. Globally, the range in most laws is from a few days to one month. Make sure that you know what this is before you set out, and make a note of when you submit your request.

Governments are not obliged to process data for you, but should give you all the data they have, and if it is data that they should have in order to perform their legal competencies, they should certainly produce it for you.

Say that you know your rights
> Usually the law does not require that you mention the access to information law or freedom of information act, but this is recommended because it shows you know your legal rights and is likely to encourage correct processing of the requests according to the law. We note that for requests to the EU, it's important to mention that it's an access to documents request and it's best to make a specific mention of Regulation 1049/2001.

Keep it simple

In all countries, it is better to start with a simple request for information and then to add more questions once you get the initial information. That way you don't run the risk of the public institution applying an extension because it is a "complex request."

Keep it focused

A request for information only held by one part of a public authority will probably be answered more quickly than one which requires a search across the entire authority. A request which involves the authority in consulting third parties (e.g., a private company which supplied the information, another government which is affected by it) can take a particularly long time. Be persistent.

Think inside the filing cabinet

Try to find out what data is collated. For example, if you get a blank copy of the form the police fill out after traffic accidents, you can then see what information they do or do not record about car crashes.

Be specific

Before you submit your request, think: is it in any way ambiguous? This is especially important if you are planning to compare data from different public authorities. For example, if you ask for figures for *the past three years*, some authorities will send you information for the past three calendar years and others for the past three financial years, which you won't be able to directly compare. If you decide to hide your real request in a more general one, then you should make your request broad enough so that it captures the information you want but not so broad as to be unclear or discourage a response. Specific and clear requests tend to get faster and better answers.

Submit multiple requests

If you are unsure where to submit your request, there is nothing to stop you submitting the request with two, three, or more bodies at the same time. In some cases, the various bodies will give you different answers, but this can actually be helpful in giving you a fuller picture of the information available on the subject you are investigating.

Submit international requests

Increasingly, requests can be submitted electronically, so it doesn't matter where you live. Alternatively, if you do not live in the country where you want to submit the request, you can sometimes send the request to the embassy and they should transfer it to the competent public body. You will need to check with the relevant embassy first if they are ready to do this—sometimes the embassy staff will not have been trained in the right to information and if this seems to be the case, it's safer to submit the request directly to the relevant public body.

Do a test run

If you are planning to send the same request to many public authorities, start by sending an initial draft of the request to a few authorities as a pilot exercise. This will show you whether you are using the right terminology to obtain the material you want and whether answering your questions is feasible, so that you can then revise the request if necessary before sending it to everyone.

Anticipate the exceptions

If you think that exceptions might be applied to your request, then, when preparing your questions, separate the question about the potentially sensitive information from the other information that common sense would say should not fall under an exception. Then split your question in two and submit the two requests separately.

Ask for access to the files

If you live near where the information is held (e.g., in the capital where the documents are kept), you can also ask to inspect original documents. This can be helpful when researching information that might be held in a large number of documents that you'd like to have a look through. Such inspection should be free of charge and should be arranged at a time that is reasonable and convenient for you.

Keep a record!

Make your request in writing and save a copy or a record of it so that in the future you are able to demonstrate that your request was sent, in case you need to make an appeal against failure to answer. This also gives you evidence of submitting the request if you are planning to do a story on it.

Make it public

Speed up answers by making it public that you submitted a request: if you write or broadcast a story that the request has been submitted, it can put pressure on the public institution to process and respond to the request. You can update the information as and when you get a response to the request—or if the deadline passes and there is no response, you can make this into a news story as well. Doing this has the additional benefit of educating members of the public about the right of access to information and how it works in practice.

 There are also several excellent services which you can use to make your request, and any subsequent responses, publicly viewable on the web, such as What Do They Know? (*http://www.whatdotheyknow.com/*) for UK public bodies, Frag den Staat (*https://fragdenstaat.de/*) for German public bodies, and Ask the EU (*http://www.asktheeu.org/*) for EU institutions. The Alaveteli (*http://www.alaveteli.org/*) project is helping to bring similar services to dozens of countries around the world.

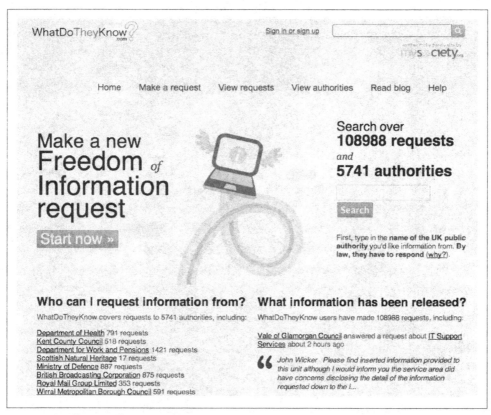

Figure 4-2. What Do They Know? (My Society)

Involve colleagues

If your colleagues are skeptical about the value of access to information requests, one of the best ways to convince them is to write a story based on information you obtained using an access to information law. Mentioning in the final article or broadcast piece that you used the law is also recommended as a way of enforcing its value and raising public awareness of the right.

Ask for raw data

If you want to analyze, explore, or manipulate data using a computer, then you should explicitly ask for data in an electronic, machine-readable format. You may wish to clarify this by specifying, for example, that you require budgetary information in a format "suitable for analysis with accounting software." You may also wish to explicitly ask for information in disaggregated or granular form. You can read more about this point in this report (*http://bit.ly/access-report*).

Asking about organizations exempt from FOI laws

You may wish to find out about NGOs, private companies, religious organizations, and/or other organizations that are not required to release documents under FOI laws. However, it is possible to find information about them by asking public bodies, which are covered by FOI laws. For example, you could ask a government department or ministry if they have funded or dealt with a specific private company or NGO and request supporting documents. If you need further help with making your FOI request, you can also consult the Legal Leaks toolkit for journalists (*http://www.legalleaks.info/toolkit.html*)

— *Helen Darbishire (Access Info Europe), Djordje Padejski (Knight Journalism Fellow, Stanford University), Martin Rosenbaum (BBC), and Fabrizio Scrollini (London School of Economics and Political Science)*

Using FOI to Understand Spending

I've used FOI in couple of different ways to help cover COINS, the UK Government's biggest database of spending, budget and financial information. At the beginning of 2010, there was talk from George Osborne that if he became chancellor, he would release the COINS database to facilitate greater transparency in the Treasury. At this time it seemed a good idea to investigate the data in and structure of COINS so I sent a few FOI requests, one for the schema of the database (*http://bit.ly/wdtk-coins-1*), one for the guidance Treasury workers receive when they work with COINS (*http://bit.ly/wdtk-coins-2*), and one for the Treasury contract with the database provider (*http://bit.ly/wdtk-coins-3*). All of which resulted in publication of useful data. I also requested all the spending codes in the database, which was also published (*http://bit.ly/wdtk-coins-4*). All of this helped to understand COINS when George Osborne became chancellor in May 2010 and published COINS in June 2010. The COINS data was used in a number of websites encouraging the public to investigate the data—including OpenSpending.org (*http://openspending.org/*) and the Guardian's Coins Data Explorer (*http://coins.guardian.co.uk/coins-explorer/search*).

After further investigation it seemed that a large part of the database was missing: the Whole of Government Accounts (WGA) which is 1,500 sets of accounts for public funded bodies. I used FOI to request the 2008/09 WGA data (*http://bit.ly/wdtk-coins-5*) but to no avail. I also asked for the report from the audit office for WGA—which I hoped would explain the reasons the WGA was not in a suitable state to be released. That was also refused (*http://bit.ly/wdtk-coins-6*).

In December 2011, the WGA was released in the COINS data. However I wanted to make sure there was enough guidance to create the complete set of accounts for each of the 1,500 bodies included in the WGA exercise. This brings me on to the second way I used FOI: to ensure the data released under the UK transparency agenda is well-explained and contains what it should. I put in a FOI request for the full set of accounts for every public body included in WGA (*http://bit.ly/wdtk-coins-7*).

— *Lisa Evans, the Guardian*

Wobbing Works. Use It!

Using freedom of information legislation—or wobbing, as it is sometimes called—is an excellent tool. But it requires method and, often, persistence. Here are three examples illustrating the strengths and challenges of wobbing from my work as an investigative journalist.

Case Study 1: Farm Subsidy

Every year, EU pays almost €60 billion to farmers and the farming industry. Every year. This has been going on since late 1950s and the political narrative was that the subsidies help our poorest farmers. However a first FOI breakthrough in Denmark in 2004 indicated that this was just a narrative. The small farmers were struggling, as they so often complained about in private and in public, and in reality most of the money went to a few large landowners and to the agricultural industry. So obviously I wanted to know: is there a pattern across Europe?

In the summer of 2004, I asked the European Commission for the data. Every year in February, the Commission receives data from the member states. The data shows who applies for EU funding, how much beneficiaries get, and whether they get it for farming their land, developing their region, or for exporting milk powder. At that time, the Commission received the figures as CSV files on a CD. A lot of data, but in principle easy to work with. If you could get it out, that is.

In 2004 the Commission refused to release the data; the key argument was that the data was uploaded into a database and couldn't be retrieved without a lot of work. An argument that the European Ombudsmand called *maladministration*. You can find all documents in this case on the wobbing.eu website (*http://bit.ly/eu-wobbing*). Back in 2004, we did not have the time to be legal foodies. We wanted the data.

So we teamed up with partners throughout Europe to get the data country by country. English, Swedish, and Dutch colleagues got the data in 2005. Finland, Poland, Portugal, regions of Spain, Slovenia, and other countries opened up too. Even in wob-difficult Germany I got a breakthrough and received some data in the province of North Rhine-Westfalia in 2007. I had to go to court to get the data—but it resulted in some nice articles in the Stern and Stern online news magazine (*http://bit.ly/stern-wobbing*).

Was it a coincidence that Denmark and the UK were the first to open up their data? Not necessarily. Looking at the bigger political picture, the farm subsidies at the time had to be seen in the context of the WTO negotiations where subsidies were under pressure. Denmark and the UK are amongst the more liberal countries in Europe, so there may well have been political winds blowing into the direction of transparency in those countries.

The story did not stop there; for more episodes and for the data, see *http://farmsubsidy .org/*.

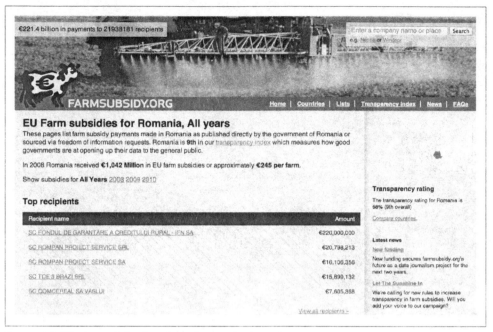

Figure 4-3. The Farm Subsidy website (Farmsubsidy.org)

Lesson: go wob-shopping. We have a fabulous diversity of freedom of information laws in Europe, and different countries have different political interests at different times. This can be used to your advantage.

Know Your Rights

When you are publishing data, should you worry about copyright and other rights in data? While you should always clear all of this with your legal team, as a rule of thumb: if it is published by government, you should neither ask forgiveness nor permission; if it is published by an organization that doesn't make money selling data, you shouldn't have to worry too much; if it is published by a organization that does make money from selling data, then you should definitely ask permission.

— *Simon Rogers, the Guardian*

Case Study 2: Side Effects

We are all guinea pigs when it comes to taking medicine. Drugs can have side effects. We all know this: we balance potential benefits with potential risks, and we make a decision. Unfortunately, this is not often an informed decision.

When teenagers take a pill against pimples, they hope for smooth skin, not for a bad mood. Yet exactly this happened with one drug, where the youngsters became depressed and even suicidal after taking it. The danger of this particular side effect—an obvious story for journalists—was not easily available.

There is data about side effects. The producers regularly have to deliver information to the health authorities about observed side effects. They are held by national or European authorities once a drug is allowed on the market.

The initial breakthrough again came at the national level in Denmark. During a cross-border research by a Danish-Dutch-Belgian team, the Netherlands opened up too. Another example of wob-shopping: it greatly helped our case to point out to the Dutch authorities that the data was accessible in Denmark.

But the story was true: in Europe there were suicidal young people and sadly also suicides in several countries as a result of the drug. Journalists, researchers, and the family of a young victim were all pushing hard to get access to this information. The European Ombudsman helped to push for the transparency at the European Medicines Agency, and it looks as if he succeeded (*http://bit.ly/eu-ombudsman*). So now the task is upon journalists to get out data and analyze the material thoroughly. Are we all guinea pigs, as one researcher put it, or are the control mechanisms sound?

Lessons: don't take no for an answer when it's about transparency. Be persistent and follow a story over time. Things may well change and allow better reporting based upon better access at a later point.

Case Study 3: Smuggling Death

Recent history can be utterly painful for entire populations, particularly after wars and in times of transition. So how can journalists obtain hard data to investigate, when—for example—last decade's war profiteers are now in power? This was the task that a team of Slovenian, Croatian and Bosnian journalists set out to pursue.

The team set out to investigate arms trades in former Yugoslavia during the UN embargo in the early 1990s. The basis of the work was documents from parliamentary inquiries into this subject. In order to document the routes of the shipment and understand the structure of the trading, transports had to be traced by vessel number in ports and license plates of trucks.

Slovenian parliamentary commissions have held inquiries into the question of profiteering from the Balkan wars, but have never reached a conclusion. Yet there was an extremely valuable trail of declassified documents and data, including 6,000 pages which the Slovene team obtained through a freedom of information request.

In this case the data had to be extracted from the documents and sorted in databases. By augmenting the data with further data, analysis, and research, they were able to map numerous routes of the illegal weapon trade (*http://bit.ly/kaasogmulvad-smuggling*).

The team succeeded and the results are unique (*http://bit.ly/journalismfund-smug gling1*) and have already won the team their first award. Most importantly, the story matters for the entire region and may well be picked up by journalists in other countries through which the deadly cargo has passed.

Lessons: get out good raw material even if you find it in unexpected places and combine it with existing publicly accessible data.

— *Brigitte Alfter, Journalismfund.eu*

FOI with Friends

Many Balkan countries have issues with government corruption. Corruption is often even higher when it comes to accountability of the local governments in those countries. For several months a group of Serbian journalists around the Belgrade-based Centre for Investigative Reporting (*http://www.cins.org.rs/*) have been questioning different types of FOI documents from over 30 local municipalities in 2009. Prior to that, almost nothing was accessible to the public. The idea was to get the original government records and to put the data in spreadsheets, to run basic checks and comparisons among the municipalities and to get maximum and minimum figures. Basic indicators were budget numbers, regular and special expenses, salaries of officials, travel expenses, numbers of employees, cell phone expenses, per diems, public procurement figures, and so on. It was the first time that reporters had asked for such information.

The result was a comprehensive database that unravels numerous phony representations, malfeasances, and corruption cases. A list of the highest-paid mayors indicated that a few of them were receiving more money than the Serbian president. Many other officials were overpaid, with many receiving enormous travel repayments and per diems. Our hard-earned public procurement data helped to highlight an official mess. More than 150 stories came out of the database and many of them were picked up by the local and national media in Serbia.

We learned that comparing the records with the comparable data from similar government entities can display deviations and shed light on probable corruption. Exaggerated and unusual expenses can be detected only by comparison.

— *Djordje Padejski, Knight Journalism Fellow, Stanford University*

Getting Data from the Web

You've tried everything else, and you haven't managed to get your hands on the data you want. You've found the data on the Web, but, alas—no download options are available and copy-paste has failed you. Fear not, there may still be a way to get the data out. For example you can:

- Get data from web-based APIs, such as interfaces provided by online databases and many modern web applications (including Twitter, Facebook, and many others). This is a fantastic way to access government or commercial data, as well as data from social media sites.

- Extract data from PDFs. This is very difficult, as PDF is a language for printers and does not retain much information on the structure of the data that is displayed within a document. Extracting information from PDFs is beyond the scope of this book, but there are some tools and tutorials that may help you do it.

- Screen scrape websites. During screen scraping, you're extracting structured content from a normal web page with the help of a scraping utility or by writing a small piece of code. While this method is very powerful and can be used in many places, it requires a bit of understanding about how the web works.

With all those great technical options, don't forget the simple options: often it is worth it to spend some time searching for a file with machine-readable data or to call the institution that is holding the data you want.

In this chapter we walk through a very basic example of scraping data from an HTML web page.

What Is Machine-Readable Data?

The goal for most of these methods is to get access to machine-readable data. Machine-readable data is created for processing by a computer, instead of the presentation to a human user. The structure of such data relates to contained information, and not the way it is displayed eventually. Examples of easily machine-readable formats include CSV, XML, JSON, and Excel files, while formats like Word documents, HTML pages, and PDF files are more concerned with the visual layout of the information. PDF, for example, is a language that talks directly to your printer; it's concerned with position of lines and dots on a page, rather than distinguishable characters.

Scraping Websites: What For?

Everyone has done this: you go to a website, see an interesting table and try to copy it over to Excel so you can add some numbers up or store it for later. Yet this often does not really work, or the information you want is spread across a large number of websites. Copying by hand can quickly become very tedious, so it makes sense to use a bit of code to do it.

The advantage of scraping is that you can do it with virtually any website, from weather forecasts to government spending, even if that site does not have an API for raw data access.

What You Can and Cannot Scrape

There are, of course, limits to what can be scraped. Some factors that make it harder to scrape a site include:

- Badly formatted HTML code with little or no structural information (e.g., older government websites).
- Authentication systems that are supposed to prevent automatic access (e.g., CAPTCHA codes and paywalls).
- Session-based systems that use browser cookies to keep track of what the user has been doing.
- A lack of complete item listings and possibilities for wildcard search.
- Blocking of bulk access by the server administrators.

Another set of limitations are legal barriers: some countries recognize database rights, which may limit your right to reuse information that has been published online. Sometimes, you can choose to ignore the license and do it anyway—depending on your jurisdiction, you may have special rights as a journalist. Scraping freely available government data should be fine, but you may wish to double-check before you publish. Commercial organizations—and certain NGOs—react with less tolerance and may try to claim that you're "sabotaging" their systems. Other information may infringe the privacy of individuals and thereby violate data privacy laws or professional ethics.

Patching, Scraping, Compiling, Cleaning

The challenge with huge swathes of UK data isn't getting it released—it's getting it into a usable format. Lots of data on hospitality, MPs' outside interests, lobbying and more is routinely published but in difficult-to-analyze ways.

For some information, there is only the hard slog: patching together dozens of Excel files, each containing just a dozen or so records, was the only way to make comprehensive lists of ministerial meetings. But for other information, web scraping proved incredibly helpful.

Using a service like ScraperWiki to ask coders to produce a scraper for information like the Register of MPs' interests did around half of our job for us: we had all MPs' information in one sheet, ready for the (lengthy) task of analysing and cleaning.

Services like this (or tools such as Outwit Hub) are a huge help to journalists trying to compile messy data who are unable to code themselves.

— *James Ball, the Guardian*

Tools That Help You Scrape

There are many programs that can be used to extract bulk information from a web site, including browser extensions and some web services. Depending on your browser, tools like Readability (*http://www.readability.com/*; which helps extract text from a page) or DownThemAll (*http://www.downthemall.net/*; which allows you to download many files at once) will help you automate some tedious tasks, while Chrome's Scraper extension (*http://bit.ly/chrome-scraper*) was explicitly built to extract tables from web sites. Developer extensions like FireBug (*http://getfirebug.com/*; for Firefox—the same thing is already included in Chrome, Safari, and IE) let you track exactly how a website is structured and what communications happen between your browser and the server.

ScraperWiki (*https://scraperwiki.com/*) is a website that allows you to code scrapers in a number of different programming languages, including Python, Ruby, and PHP. If you want to get started with scraping without the hassle of setting up a programming environment on your computer, this is the way to go. Other web services, such as Google Spreadsheets and Yahoo! Pipes, also allow you to perform some extraction from other websites.

How Does a Web Scraper Work?

Web scrapers are usually small pieces of code written in a programming language such as Python, Ruby, or PHP. Choosing the right language is largely a question of which community you have access to: if there is someone in your newsroom or city already working with one of these languages, then it makes sense to adopt the same language.

While some of the click-and-point scraping tools mentioned before may be helpful to get started, the real complexity involved in scraping a website is in addressing the right pages and the right elements within these pages to extract the desired information. These tasks aren't about programming, but understanding the structure of the website and database.

When displaying a website, your browser will almost always make use of two technologies: HTTP, to communicate with the server and to request specific resource, such as documents, images or videos; and HTML, the language in which websites are composed.

The Anatomy of a Web Page

Any HTML page is structured as a hierarchy of boxes (which are defined by HTML "tags"). A large box will contain many smaller ones—for example, a table that has many smaller divisions: rows and cells. There are many types of tags that perform different functions—some produce boxes—others tables, images, or links. Tags can also have additional properties (e.g., they can be unique identifiers) and can belong to groups called "classes" that make it possible to target and capture individual elements within a document. Selecting the appropriate elements this way and extracting their content is the key to writing a scraper.

Viewing the elements in a web page, everything can be broken up into boxes within boxes.

To scrape web pages, you'll need to learn a bit about the different types of elements that can be in an HTML document. For example, the `<table>` element wraps a whole table, which has `<tr>` (table row) elements for its rows, which in turn contain `<td>` (table data) for each cell. The most common element type you will encounter is `<div>`, which can basically mean any block of content. The easiest way to get a feel for these elements is by using the developer toolbar (*http://bit.ly/developer-toolbar*) in your browser: they will allow you to hover over any part of a web page and see what the underlying code is.

Tags work like book ends, marking the start and the end of a unit. For example `<em>` *signifies the start of an italicized or emphasized piece of text and* `</em>` signifies the end of that section. Easy.

An Example: Scraping Nuclear Incidents with Python

NEWS (*http://www-news.iaea.org/EventList.aspx*) is the International Atomic Energy Agency's (IAEA) portal on worldwide radiation incidents (and a strong contender for membership in the Weird Title Club!). The web page lists incidents in a simple, blog-like site that can be easily scraped.

Figure 4-4. The International Atomic Energy Agency's (IAEA) portal (news.iaea.org)

To start, create a new Python scraper on ScraperWiki (*https://scraperwiki.com/*) and you will be presented with a text area that is mostly empty, except for some scaffolding code. In another browser window, open the IAEA site (*http://www-news.iaea.org/Event List.aspx*) and open the developer toolbar in your browser. In the "Elements" view, try to find the HTML element for one of the news item titles. Your browser's developer toolbar helps you connect elements on the web page with the underlying HTML code.

Investigating this page will reveal that the titles are `<h4>` elements within a `<table>`. Each event is a `<tr>` row, which also contains a description and a date. If we want to extract the titles of all events, we should find a way to select each row in the table sequentially, while fetching all the text within the title elements.

In order to turn this process into code, we need to make ourselves aware of all the steps involved. To get a feeling for the kind of steps required, let's play a simple game: in your ScraperWiki window, try to write up individual instructions for yourself, for each thing you are going to do while writing this scraper, like steps in a recipe (prefix each line with a hash sign to tell Python that this not real computer code). For example:

```
# Look for all rows in the table
# Unicorn must not overflow on left side.
```

Try to be as precise as you can and don't assume that the program knows anything about the page you're attempting to scrape.

Once you've written down some pseudo-code, let's compare this to the essential code for our first scraper:

```
import scraperwiki
from lxml import html
```

In this first section, we're importing existing functionality from libraries—snippets of pre-written code. `scraperwiki` will give us the ability to download websites, while `lxml` is a tool for the structured analysis of HTML documents. Good news: if you are writing a Python scraper with ScraperWiki, these two lines will always be the same.

```
url = "http://www-news.iaea.org/EventList.aspx"
doc_text = scraperwiki.scrape(url)
doc = html.fromstring(doc_text)
```

Next, the code makes a name (variable): `url`, and assigns the URL of the IAEA page as its value. This tells the scraper that this thing exists and we want to pay attention to it. Note that the URL itself is in quotes as it is not part of the program code but a *string*, a sequence of characters.

We then use the `url` variable as input to a function, `scraperwiki.scrape`. A function will provide some defined job—in this case, it'll download a web page. When it's finished, it'll assign its output to another variable, `doc_text`. `doc_text` will now hold the actual text of the website; not the visual form you see in your browser, but the source code, including all the tags. Since this form is not very easy to parse, we'll use another function, `html.fromstring`, to generate a special representation where we can easily address elements, the so-called document object model (DOM).

```
for row in doc.cssselect("#tblEvents tr"):
    link_in_header = row.cssselect("h4 a").pop()
    event_title = link_in_header.text
    print event_title
```

In this final step, we use the DOM to find each row in our table and extract the event's title from its header. Two new concepts are used: the for loop and element selection (.cssselect). The for loop essentially does what its name implies; it will traverse a list of items, assigning each a temporary alias (row in this case) and then run any indented instructions for each item.

The other new concept, element selection, is making use of a special language to find elements in the document. CSS selectors are normally used to add layout information to HTML elements and can be used to precisely pick an element out of a page. In this case (line 6) we're selecting #tblEvents tr, which will match each <tr> within the table element with the ID tblEvents (the hash simply signifies ID). Note that this will return a list of <tr> elements.

That can be seen on the next line (line 7), where we're applying another selector to find any <a> (which is a hyperlink) within a <h4> (a title). Here we only want to look at a single element (there's just one title per row), so we have to pop it off the top of the list returned by our selector with the .pop() function.

Note that some elements in the DOM contain actual text (i.e., text that is not part of any markup language), which we can access using the [element].text syntax seen on line 8. Finally, in line 9, we're printing that text to the ScraperWiki console. If you hit run in your scraper, the smaller window should now start listing the event's names from the IAEA website.

Figure 4-5. A scraper in action (ScraperWiki)

You can now see a basic scraper operating: it downloads the web page, transforms it into the DOM form, and then allows you to pick and extract certain content. Given this skeleton, you can try and solve some of the remaining problems using the ScraperWiki and Python documentation:

- Can you find the address for the link in each event's title?
- Can you select the small box that contains the date and place by using its CSS class name and extract the element's text?
- ScraperWiki offers a small database to each scraper so you can store the results; copy the relevant example from their docs and adapt it so it will save the event titles, links and dates.
- The event list has many pages; can you scrape multiple pages to get historic events as well?

As you're trying to solve these challenges, have a look around ScraperWiki: there are many useful examples in the existing scrapers; quite often, the data is pretty exciting, too. This way, you don't need to start off your scraper from scratch: just choose one that is similar, fork it, and adapt it to your problem.

— *Friedrich Lindenberg, Open Knowledge Foundation*

Scraping a Public Database

Some French physicians are free to choose their own rates, so that one can pay between €70 and €500 for a 30-minute visit at an oncologist, for instance. This data regarding rates is legally public, but the administration provides only a hard-to-navigate online database. In order to have a good view of the doctors' rates for Le Monde, I decided to scrape the entire database.

That's where the fun began. The front-end search form was a Flash application that redirected to an HTML result page via a POST request. With help from Nicolas Kayser-Bril, it took us some time to figure out that the application used a third page as a "hidden" step between the search form and the result page. This page was actually used to store a cookie with values from the search form that was then accessed by the results page. It would have been hard to think of a more convoluted process, but the options of the cURL library in PHP make it easy to overcome the hurdles, once you know where they are! In the end, getting hold of the database was a 10-hour task, but it was worth it.

— *Alexandre Léchenet, Le Monde*

The Web as a Data Source

How can you find out more about something that only exists on the Internet? Whether you're looking at an email address, website, image, or Wikipedia article, in this chapter I'll take you through the tools that will tell you more about their backgrounds.

Web Tools

First, a few different services you can use to discover more about an entire site, rather than a particular page:

Whois

> If you go to *http://whois.domaintools.com/* (or just type whois *www.example.com* in Terminal.app on a Mac, with a URL in place of the placeholder here) you can get the basic registration information for any website. In recent years, some owners have chosen private registration, which hides their details from view, but in many cases you'll see a name, address, email, and phone number for the person who registered the site. You can also enter numerical IP addresses here and get data on the organization or individual that owns that server. This is especially handy when you're trying to track down more information on an abusive or malicious user of a service, since most websites record an IP address for everyone who accesses them.

Blekko

> The Blekko search engine (*http://blekko.com/*) offers an unusual amount of insight into the internal statistics it gathers on sites as it crawls the Web. If you type in a domain name followed by "/seo", you'll receive a page of information on that URL. The first tab in Figure 4-7 shows you which other sites are linking to the domain in popularity order. This can be extremely useful when you're trying to understand what coverage a site is receiving, and if you want to understand why it's ranking highly in Google's search results, since they're based on those inbound links. Figure 4-8 tells you which other websites are running from the same machine. It's common for scammers and spammers to astroturf their way towards legitimacy by building multiple sites that review and link to each other. They look like independent domains, and may even have different registration details, but they'll often actually live on the same server because that's a lot cheaper. These statistics give you an insight into the hidden business structure of the site you're researching.

Figure 4-6. The Blekko search engine (Blekko.com)

Inbound links: 6,050 from 302 domains:				
#	from host	host rank	links	last	actions
1	twitter.com	12,366.4	1		
2	www.guardian.co.uk	6,481.2	1		
3	www.forbes.com	3,699.8	1	41d ago	
4	www.newscientist.com	3,678.4	2		
5	code.google.com	3,461.1	1		
6	www.huffingtonpost.com	3,238.2	1		
7	news.cnet.com	3,185.8	2		
8	gizmodo.com	2,119.3	6	39d ago	

Figure 4-7. Understanding web popularity: who links to who? The other handy tab is "Crawl stats", especially the "Cohosted with" section. (Blekko.com)

Cohosted With:	host	whois	view
	thelongtail.com	whois	
	codinghorror.com	whois	
	longtail.com	whois	
	cityofsound.com	whois	
	hypebot.com	whois	
	therestisnoise.com	whois	
	stevenberlinjohnson.com	whois	
	planetout.com	whois	
	riehlworldview.com	whois	

Figure 4-8. Spotting web spammers and scammers (Blekko.com)

Compete.com

By surveying a cross-section of American consumers, *http://www.compete.com/* builds up detailed usage statistics for most websites, and makes some basic details freely available. Choose the Site Profile tab and enter a domain (Figure 4-9). You'll then see a graph of the site's traffic over the last year, together with figures for how many people visited, and how often (as in Figure 4-10). Since they're based on surveys, the numbers are only approximate, but I've found them reasonably accurate when I've been able to compare them against internal analytics. In particular, they seem to be a good source when comparing two sites, since while the absolute numbers may be off for both, it's still a good representation of their relative difference in popularity. They only survey US consumers though, so the data will be poor for predominantly international sites.

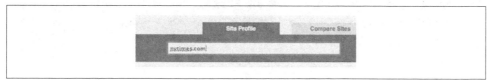

Figure 4-9. Compete.com's site profile service (Compete.com)

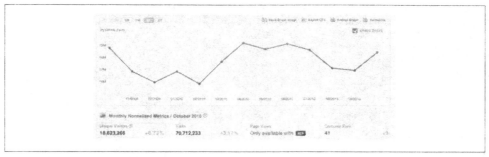

Figure 4-10. What's in vogue? What's in demand?: Hotspots on the web (Compete.com)

Google's Site Search

One feature that can be extremely useful when you're trying to explore all the content on a particular domain is the "site:" keyword. If you add "site:example.com" to your search phrase, Google will only return results from the site you've specified. You can even narrow it down further by including the prefix of the pages you're interested in, for example, "site:example.com/pages/", and you'll only see results that match that pattern. This can be extremely useful when you're trying to find information that domain owners may have made publicly available but aren't keen to publicize, so picking the right keywords can uncover some very revealing material.

Web Pages, Images, and Videos

Sometimes you're interested in the activity that's surrounding a particular story, rather than an entire website. The tools below give you different angles on how people are reading, responding to, copying, and sharing content on the web.

Bit.ly

I always turn to bit.ly (*http://bitly.com/*) when I want to know how people are sharing a particular link with each other. To use it, enter the URL you're interested in. Then click on the Info Page+ link. That takes you to the full statistics page (though you may need to choose "aggregate bit.ly link" first if you're signed in to the service). This will give you an idea of how popular the page is, including activity on Facebook and Twitter, and below that you'll see public conversations about the link provided by backtype.com. I find this combination of traffic data and conversations very helpful when I'm trying to understand why a site or page is popular, and who exactly its fans are. For example, it provided me with strong evidence that the prevailing narrative about grassroots sharing and Sarah Palin was wrong.

Twitter

As the micro-blogging service becomes more widely used, it becomes more useful as a gauge of how people are sharing and talking about individual pieces of content. It's deceptively simple to discover public conversations about a link. You just paste the URL you're interested in into the search box, and then possibly hit "more tweets" to see the full set of results.

Google's Cache

When a page becomes controversial, the publishers may take it down or alter it without acknowledgment. If you suspect you're running into the problem, the first place to turn is Google's cache of the page as it was when it did its last crawl. The frequency of crawls is constantly increasing, so you'll have the most luck if you try this within a few hours of the suspected changes. Enter the target URL in Google's search box, and then click the triple arrow on the right of the result for that page. A graphical preview should appear, and if you're lucky, there will be a small "Cache" link at the top of it. Click that to see Google's snapshot of the page. If that has trouble loading, you can switch over to the more primitive text-only page by clicking another link at the top of the full cache page. You'll want to take a screenshot or copy-paste any relevant content you do find, since it may be invalidated at any time by a subsequent crawl.

The Internet Archive's Wayback Machine

If you need to know how a particular page has changed over a longer time period, like months or years, the Internet Archive runs a service called The Wayback Machine (*http://archive.org/web/web.php*) that periodically takes snapshots of the most popular pages on the web. You go to the site, enter the link you want to research, and if it has any copies, it will show you a calendar so you can pick the time you'd like to examine. It will then present a version of the page roughly as it was at that point. It will often be missing styling or images, but it's usually enough to understand what the focus of that page's content was then.

View Source

It's a bit of a long shot, but developers often leave comments or other clues in the HTML code that underlies any page. It will be on different menus depending on your browser, but there's always a "View source" option that will let you browse the raw HTML. You don't need to understand what the machine-readable parts mean, just keep an eye out for the pieces of text that are often scattered amongst them. Even if they're just copyright notices or mentions of the author's names, these can often give important clues about the creation and purpose of the page.

TinEye

Sometimes you really want to know the source of an image, but without clear attribution text there's no obvious way to do this with traditional search engines like Google. TinEye (*http://www.tineye.com/*) offers a specialized "reverse image search" process, where you give it the image you have, and it finds other pictures on the web that look very similar. Because they use image recognition to do the matching, it even works when a copy has been cropped, distorted, or compressed. This can be extremely effective when you suspect that an image that's being passed off as original or new is being misrepresented, since it can lead back to the actual source.

YouTube
> If you click on the Statistics icon to the lower right of any video, you can get a rich set of information about its audience over time. While it's not complete, it is useful for understanding roughly who the viewers are, where they are coming from, and when.

Emails

If you have some emails that you're researching, you'll often want to know more details about the sender's identity and location. There isn't a good off-the-shelf tool available to help with this, but it can be very helpful to know the basics about the hidden headers included in every email message. These work like postmarks, and can reveal a surprising amount about the sender. In particular, they often include the IP address of the machine that the email was sent from, a lot like caller ID on a phone call. You can then run whois on that IP number to find out which organization owns that machine. If it turns out to be someone like Comcast or AT&T who provide connections to consumers, then you can visit MaxMind to get its approximate location.

To view these headers in Gmail, open the message and open the menu next to reply on the top right and choose "Show original".

You'll then see a new page revealing the hidden content. There will be a couple of dozen lines at the start that are words followed by a colon. The IP address you're after may be in one of these, but its name will depend on how the email was sent. If it was from Hotmail, it will be called `X-Originating-IP:`, but if it's from Outlook or Yahoo it will be in the first line starting with `Received:`.

Running the address through Whois tells me it's assigned to Virgin Media, an ISP in the UK, so I put it through MaxMind's geolocation service to discover it's coming from my home town of Cambridge. That means I can be reasonably confident this is actually my parents emailing me, not impostors!

Trends

If you're digging into a broad topic rather than a particular site or item, here's a couple of tools that can give you some insight:

Wikipedia Article Traffic
> If you're interested in knowing how public interest in a topic or person has varied over time, you can actually get day-by-day viewing figures for any page on Wikipedia at *http://stats.grok.se/*. This site is a bit rough and ready, but will let you

uncover the information you need with a bit of digging. Enter the name you're interested in to get a monthly view of the traffic on that page. That will bring up a graph showing how many times the page was viewed for each day in the month you specify. Unfortunately you can only see one month at a time, so you'll have to select a new month and search again to see longer-term changes.

Google Insights

You can get a clear view into the public's search habits using Insights from Google (*http://www.google.com/insights/search/*; Figure 4-11). Enter a couple of common search phrases, like "Justin Bieber vs Lady Gaga", and you'll see a graph of their relative number of searches over time. There's a lot of options for refining your view of the data, from narrower geographic areas, to more detail over time. The only disappointment is the lack of absolute values—you only get relative percentages, which can be hard to interpret.

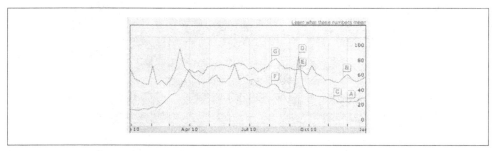

Figure 4-11. Google Insights (Google)

— Pete Warden, independent data analyst and developer

Crowdsourcing Data at the Guardian Datablog

Crowdsourcing, according to Wikipedia (*http://en.wikipedia.org/wiki/Crowdsourcing*), is "a distributed problem-solving and production process that involves outsourcing tasks to a network of people, also known as the crowd." The following is from an interview with Simon Rogers on how the Datablog used crowdsourcing to cover the MPs' expenses scandal, drug use, and the Sarah Palin papers:

Sometimes you will get a ton of files, statistics, or reports which it is impossible for one person to go through. Also you may get hold of material that is inaccessible or in a bad format and you aren't able to do much with it. This is where crowdsourcing can help.

One thing the Guardian has got is lots of readers, lots of pairs of eyes. If there is an interesting project where we need input, then we can ask them to help us. That is what we did with the MPs' Expenses (*http://mps-expenses.guardian.co.uk/*). We had 450,000 documents and very little time to do anything. So what better way than open up the task to our readership?

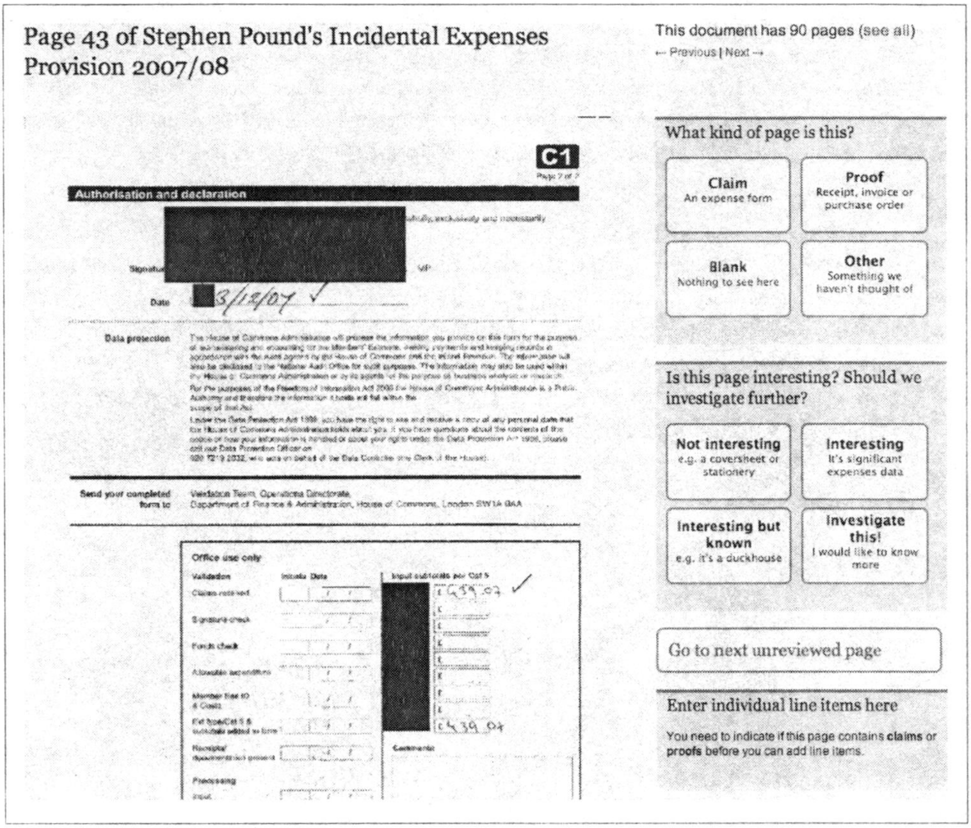

Page 43 of Stephen Pound's Incidental Expenses
Provision 2007/08

This document has 90 pages (see all)
← Previous | Next →

C1

Authorisation and declaration

Date 3/12/07

Data protection

What kind of page is this?

Claim
An expense form

Proof
Receipt, invoice or purchase order

Blank
Nothing to see here

Other
Something we haven't thought of

Is this page interesting? Should we investigate further?

Not interesting
e.g. a coversheet or stationery

Interesting
It's significant expenses data

Interesting but known
e.g. it's a duckhouse

Investigate this!
I would like to know more

Go to next unreviewed page

Enter individual line items here

You need to indicate if this page contains claims or proofs before you can add line items.

Figure 4-12. A redacted copy of Stephen Pound's incidental expenses (the Guardian)

The MPs' Expenses project generated lots of tip-offs. We got more stories than data. The project was remarkably successful in terms of traffic. People really liked it.

We are currently doing something with MixMag on drug use (*http://bit.ly/guardian -drugs*), which has been phenomenal as well. It looks like it is going to be bigger than the British crime survey in terms of how many people come back to it, which is brilliant.

What both of these projects have in common is that they are about issues that people really care about, so they are willing to spend time on them. A lot of the crowdsourcing we have done relies on help from obsessives. With the MPs' expenses, we had a massive amount of traffic at the beginning and it really died down. But we still have people that are obsessively going through every page looking for anomalies and stories. One person has done 30,000 pages. They know a lot of stuff.

We also used crowdsourcing with the Sarah Palin papers (*http://bit.ly/guardian-palin -papers*). Again this was a great help in scouring the raw information for stories.

In terms of generating stories crowdsourcing has worked really well for us. People really liked it and it made the Guardian look good. But in terms of generating data, we haven't used crowdsourcing so much.

Some of the crowdsourcing projects that we've done that have worked really well have been more like old-fashioned surveys. When you are asking people about their experience, about their lives, about what they've done, they work very well because people aren't as likely to make that up. They will say what they feel. When we asked people to kind of do our job for us, you have to find a framework for people to produce the data in a way you can trust them.

Regarding the reliability of data, I think the approach that Old Weather (*http://www .oldweather.org/*) have got is really good. They get ten people to do each entry, which is a good way to ensure accuracy. With the MPs' expenses, we tried to minimize the risk of MPs going online and editing their own records to make themselves look better. But you can't permanently guard against this. You can only really look out for certain URLs or if it's coming from the SW1 area of London. So that's a bit trickier. The data we were getting out was not always reliable. Even though stories were great, it wasn't producing raw numbers that we could confidently use.

If I were to give advice to aspiring data journalists who want to use crowdsourcing to collect data, I would encourage them do this on something that people really care about, and will continue to care about when it stops making front page headlines. Also if you make something more like a game, this can really help to engage people. When we did the expenses story a second time, it was much more like a game with individual tasks for people to do. It really helped to give people specific tasks. That made a big difference because I think if you just present people with the mountain of information to go through and say "go through this," it can make for hard and rather unrewarding work. So I think making it fun is really important.

— *Marianne Bouchart, Data Journalism Blog, interviewing Simon Rogers, the Guardian*

How the Datablog Used Crowdsourcing to Cover Olympic Ticketing

I think the crowdsourcing project that got the biggest response was a piece on the Olympic ticket ballot (*http://bit.ly/guardian-olympics*). Thousands of people in the UK tried to get tickets for the 2012 Olympics and there was a lot of fury that people hadn't received them. People had ordered hundreds of pounds worth and were told that they'd get nothing. But no one really knew if it was just some people complaining quite loudly while actually most people were happy. So we tried to work out a way to find out.

We decided the best thing we could really do, with the absence of any good data on the topic, was to ask people. And we thought we'd have to treat it as a light thing because it wasn't a balanced sample.

How many Olympic tickets did you get? Here's our readers' results

We asked how you had fared in the London 2012 ticket ballot. Here's our analysis of the information you gave us

Tweet 21
Share 84
reddit this
Comments (144)

Posted by
James Ball
Friday 3 June 2011 11.04 BST
guardian.co.uk
Article history

A larger | smaller

Sport
Olympic tickets · Olympic Games 2012

More from London 2012 Olympics blog on

Sport
Olympic tickets · Olympic Games 2012

More blogposts

The London 2012 Olympic stadium: will you be there? Will anyone you know?
Photograph: Handout/Getty Images

How much money did London 2012 ticket buyers have to put on the line to stand even a 50:50 chance of getting at least one ticket? If the results submitted by Guardian readers are to be believed, at least £1,000.

Earlier this week, we asked readers of the Guardian London 2012 blog to let us know how their ticket-purchasing attempts had fared. By the end of the day – when this analysis was carried out – we'd had more than 5,000 responses.

Figure 4-13. How many Olympic tickets did you get?: the readers' results (the Guardian)

We created a Google form and asked very specific questions (*http://bit.ly/guardian -olympics2*). It was actually a long form: it asked how much in value people had ordered their tickets, how much their card had been debited for, which events they went for, this kind of thing.

We put it up as a small picture on the front of the site and it was shared around really rapidly. I think this is one of the key things; you can't just think "What do I want to know for my story?", you have to think "What do people want to tell me right now?" And it's only when you tap into what people want to talk about that crowdsourcing is going to be successful. The volume of responses for this project, which is one of our first attempts at crowdsourcing, was huge. We had a thousand responses in less than an hour and seven thousand by the end of that day.

So obviously, we took presenting the results a bit more seriously at this point. Initially, we had no idea how well it would do. So we added some caveats: Guardian readers may be more wealthy than other people, people who got less than they expected might be more willing to talk to us, and so on.

We didn't know how much value the results would have. We ended up having a good seven thousand records to base our piece on, and we found that about half the people who'd asked for tickets had got nothing. We ran all of this stuff and because so many people had taken part the day before, there was a lot of interest in the results.

A few weeks later, the official summary report came out, and our numbers were shockingly close. They were almost exactly spot-on. I think partly through luck, but also because we got just so many people to respond.

If you start asking your readers about something like this on a comments thread, you will be limited in what you can do with the results. So you have to start by thinking, "What is the best tool for what I want to know?" Is it a comment thread? Or is it building an app? And if it is building an app, you have to think "Is this worth the wait? And is it worth the resources that are required to do it?"

In this case, we thought of Google Forms. If someone fills in the form, you can see the result as a row on a spreadsheet. This meant that even if it was still updating, even if results were still coming in, I could open up the spreadsheet and see all of the results straight away.

I could have tried to do the work in Google, but I downloaded it into Microsoft Excel and then did things like sort it from low to high; I also found the entries where people had written out numbers (instead of putting digits) for how much they spent, and fixed all of those. I decided to exclude as little as I could. So rather than taking only valid responses, I tried to fix what I had. Some people had used foreign currencies, so I converted them to sterling, all of which was a bit painstaking.

But the whole analysis was done in a few hours, and I knocked out the obviously silly entries. A lot of people decided to point out that they spent nothing on tickets. That's a bit facetious, but fine. That was less than a hundred out of over seven thousand entries.

Then there were a few dozen who put in obviously fake high amounts to try to distort the results. Things like ten million pounds. So that left me with a set that I could use with the normal data principles we use every day. I did what's called a "pivot table." I did some averaging. That kind of thing.

We didn't have any idea how much momentum the project would have, so it was just me working with the Sports blog editor. We put our heads together and thought this might be a fun project. We did it, start to finish, in 24 hours. We had the idea, we put something up at lunchtime, we put it on the front of the site, we saw it was proving quite popular, we kept it on the front of the site for the rest of the day, and we presented the results online the next morning.

We decided to use Google Docs because it gives complete control over the results. I didn't have to use anyone else's analytic tools. I can put it easily into a database software or into spreadsheets. When you start using specialist polling software, you are often restricted to using their tools. If the information we'd been asking for was particularly sensitive, we might have hesitated before using Google and thought about doing something "in-house." But generally, it is very easy to drop a Google Form into a Guardian page and it's virtually invisible to the user that we are using one. So it is very convenient.

In terms of advice for data journalists who want to use crowdsourcing, you have to have very specific things you want to know. Ask things that get multiple choice responses as much as possible. Try to get some basic demographics of who you are talking to so you can see if your sample might be biased. If you are asking for amounts and things like this, try in the guidance to specify that it's in digits, that they have to use a specific currency, and things like that. A lot won't, but the more you hold their hand throughout, the better. And always, always, add a comment box because a lot of people will fill out the other fields but what they really want is to give you their opinion on the story. Especially on a consumer story or an outrage.

— *Marianne Bouchart, Data Journalism Blog, interviewing James Ball, the Guardian*

Using and Sharing Data: the Black Letter, the Fine Print, and Reality

In this section we'll have a quick look at the state of the law with respect to data and databases, and what you can do to open up your data using readily available public licenses and legal tools. Don't let any of the following dampen your enthusiasm for data-driven journalism. Legal restrictions on data usually won't get in your way, and you can easily make sure they won't get in the way of others using data you've published.

To state the obvious, obtaining data has never been easier. Before the widespread publishing of data on the Web, even if you had identified a dataset you needed, you'd need to ask whoever had a copy to make it accessible to you, possibly involving paper and the post or a personal visit. Now, you have your computer ask their computer to send a copy to your computer. Conceptually similar, but you have a copy right now, and they (the creator or publisher) haven't done anything, and probably have no idea that you have downloaded a copy.

What about downloading data with a program (sometimes called "scraping") and terms of service (ToS)? Consider the previous paragraph: your browser is just such a program. Might ToS permit access by only certain kinds of programs? If you have inordinate amounts of time and money to spend reading such documents and perhaps asking a lawyer for advice, by all means, do. But usually, just don't be a jerk: if your program hammers a site, your network may well get blocked from accessing the site in question —and perhaps you will have deserved it. There is now a large body of practice around accessing and scraping data from the web. If you plan to do this, reading about examples at a site like ScraperWiki will give you a head start.

Once you have some data of interest, you can query, pore over, sort, visualize, correlate, and perform any other kind of analysis you like using your copy of the data. You can publish your analysis, which can cite any data. There's a lot to the catchphrase "facts are free" (as in free speech), but maybe this is only a catchphrase among those who think too much about the legalities of databases, or even more broadly (and more wonkily), data governance.

What if, being a good or aspiring-to-be-good data-driven journalist, you intend to publish not just your analysis, including some facts or data points, but also the datasets/ databases you used—and perhaps added to—in conducting your analysis? Or maybe you're just curating data and haven't done any analysis (good: the world needs data curators). If you're using data collected by some other entity, there could be a hitch. (If your database is wholly assembled by you, read the next paragraph anyway as motivation for the sharing practices in the next next paragraph.)

If you're familiar with how copyright restricts creative works—if the copyright holder hasn't given permission to use a work (or the work is in the public domain or your use might be covered by exceptions and limitations such as fair use) and you use—distribute, perform, etc.—the work anyway, the copyright holder could force you to stop. Although facts are free, collections of facts can be restricted very similarly, though there's more variation in the relevant laws than there is for copyright as applied to creative works. Briefly, a database can be subject to copyright, as a creative work. In many jurisdictions, by the "sweat of the brow," merely assembling a database, even in an uncreative fashion, makes the database subject to copyright. In the United States in particular, there tends to be a higher minimum of creativity for copyright to apply (Feist v. Rural, a case about a phone book, is the U.S. classic if you want to look it up). But in some jurisdictions there are also "database rights" that restrict databases, separate from copyright (though there is lots of overlap in terms of what is covered, in particular where creativity thresholds for copyright are nearly nonexistent). The best known of such are the European Union's *sui generis* database rights. Again, especially if you're in Europe, you may want to make sure you have permission before publishing a database from some other entity.

Obviously such restrictions aren't the best way to grow an ecosystem of data-driven journalism (nor are they good for society at large—social scientists and others told the EU they wouldn't be before *sui generis* came about, and studies since have shown them to be right). Fortunately, as a publisher of a database, you can remove such restrictions from the database (assuming it doesn't have elements that you don't have permission to grant further permissions around), essentially by granting permission in advance. You can do this by releasing your database under a public license or public domain dedication—just as many programmers release their code under a free and open source license, so that others can build on their code (as data-driven journalism often involves code, not just data, of course you should release your code too, so that your data collection and analysis are reproducible). There are lots of reasons for opening up your data. For example, your audience might create new visualizations or applications with it that you can link to—as the Guardian does with their data visualization Flickr pool. Your datasets can be combined with other datasets to give you and your readers greater insight into a topic. Things that others do with your data might give you leads for new stories, or ideas for stories, or ideas for other data-driven projects. And they will certainly bring you kudos.

Figure 4-14. Open Data badges (Open Knowledge Foundation)

When one realizes that releasing works under public licenses is a necessity, the question becomes, which license? That tricky question will frequently be answered by the project or community whose work you're building on, or that you hope to contribute your work to—use the license they use. If you need to dig deeper, start from the set of licenses that are free and open—meaning that anyone has permission, for any use (attribution and sharing alike might be required). What the Free Software Definition and Open Source Definition do for software, the Open Knowledge Definition (*http://opendefini tion.org/*) does for all other knowledge, including databases: define what makes a work open, and what open licenses allow users to do.

You can visit the Open Knowledge Definition website to see the current set of licenses which qualify (*http://opendefinition.org/licenses/*). In summary, there are basically three classes of open licenses:

Public domain dedications
  These also serve as maximally permissive licenses; there are no conditions put upon using the work.

Permissive or attribution-only licenses
  Giving credit is the only substantial condition of these licenses.

Copyleft, reciprocal, or share-alike licenses
  These also require that modified works, if published, be shared under the same license.

Note if you're using a dataset published by someone else under an open license, consider the above paragraph a very brief guide as to how to fulfill the conditions of that open license. The licenses you're most likely to encounter, from Creative Commons, Open Data Commons, and various governments, usually feature a summary that will easily allow you to see what the substantial conditions are. Typically the license will be noted on a web page from which a dataset may be downloaded (or "scraped", as of course, web pages can contain datasets) or in a conspicuous place within the dataset itself, depending on format. This marking is what you should do as well, when you open up your datasets.

Going back to the beginning, what if the dataset you need to obtain is still not available online, or behind a some kind of access control? Consider, in addition to asking for access yourself, requesting that the data to be opened up for the world to reuse. You could give some pointers to some of the great things that can happen with their data if they do this.

Sharing with the world might bring to mind that privacy and other considerations and regulations might come into play for some datasets. Indeed, just because open data lowers many technical and copyright and copyright-like barriers, doesn't mean you don't have to follow other applicable laws. But that's as it always was, and there are tremendous resources and sometimes protections for journalists should your common sense indicate a need to investigate those.

Good luck! But in all probability you'll need more of it for other areas of your project than you'll need for managing the (low) legal risks.

— *Mike Linksvayer, Creative Commons*

Understanding Data

Once you've got your data, what do you do with it? What should you look for? What tools should you use? This section opens with some ideas on improving your data literacy, tips for working with numbers and statistics, and things to bear in mind while working with messy, imperfect and often undocumented datasets. We go on to learn about how to get stories from data, data journalists' tools of choice, and how to use data visualization to give you insights into the topic you're looking at.

Become Data Literate in Three Simple Steps

Just as literacy refers to "the ability to read for knowledge, write coherently, and think critically about printed material," data-literacy is the ability to consume for knowledge, produce coherently, and think critically about data. Data literacy includes statistical literacy, but also understanding how to work with large datasets, how they were produced, how to connect various datasets, and how to interpret them.

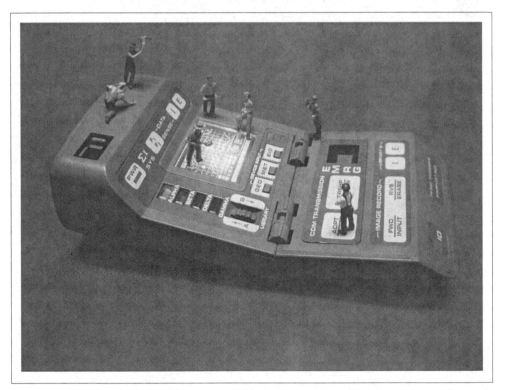

Figure 5-1. Digging into data (photo by JDHancock, http://www.flickr.com/photos/jdhancock/3386035827/)

Poynter's News University offers math classes for journalists (*http://www.newsu.org/courses/math-journalists*), in which reporters get help with concepts such as percentage changes and averages. Interestingly enough, these concepts are being taught simultaneously near Poynter's offices, in Floridian schools to fifth grade pupils (age 10-11), as the curriculum attests (*http://bit.ly/k12-courses*).

That journalists need help in math topics normally covered before high school shows how far newsrooms are from being data-literate. This is a problem. How can a data journalist make use of a bunch of numbers on climate change if she doesn't know what a confidence interval means? How can a data reporter write a story on income distribution if he cannot tell the mean from the median (*http://bit.ly/karenberger-mean-median*)?

A reporter certainly does not need a degree in statistics to become more efficient when dealing with data. When faced with numbers, a few simple tricks can help her get a much better story. As Max Planck Institute professor Gerd Gigerenzer says (*http://bit.ly/ddjnet-numeracy*), better tools will not lead to better journalism if they are not used with insight.

Even if you lack any knowledge of math or stats, you can easily become a seasoned data-journalist by asking 3 very simple questions.

1. How was the data collected?

Amazing GDP growth

The easiest way to show off with spectacular data is to fabricate it. It sounds obvious, but data as commonly commented upon as GDP figures can very well be phony. Former British ambassador Craig Murray reports in his book, *Murder in Samarkand* (*http://amzn.to/murder-samarkand*), that growth rates in Uzbekistan are subject to intense negotiations between the local government and international bodies. In other words, it has nothing to do with the local economy.

GDP is used as the number one indicator because governments need it to watch over their main source of income—VAT. When a government is not funded by VAT, or when it does not make its budget public, it has no reason to collect GDP data and will be better off fabricating them.

Crime is always on the rise

"Crime in Spain grew by 3%," writes El Pais (*http://bit.ly/elpais-numeracy*). Brussels is prey to increased crime from illegal aliens and drug addicts, says RTL (*http://bit.ly/rtl-numeracy*). This type of reporting based on police-collected statistics is common, but it doesn't tell us much about violence.

We can trust that within the European Union, the data isn't tampered with. But police personnel respond to incentives. When performance is linked to clearance rate, for instance, policemen have an incentive to report as much as possible on incidents that don't require an investigation. One such crime is smoking pot. This explains why drug-related crimes in France increased fourfold in the last 15 years while consumption remained constant.

What you can do

When in doubt about a number's credibility, always double-check, just as you'd have if it had been a quote from a politician. In the Uzbek case, a phone call to someone who's lived there for a while suffices ("Does it feel like the country is 3 times as rich as it was in 1995, as official figures show?").

For police data, sociologists often carry out victimization studies, in which they ask people if they are subject to crime. These studies are much less volatile than police data. Maybe that's the reason why they don't make headlines.

Other tests let you assess precisely the credibility of the data, such as Benford's law, but none will replace your own critical thinking.

2. What's in there to learn?

Risk of Multiple Sclerosis doubles when working at night

Surely any German in her right mind would stop working night shifts after reading this headline (*http://bit.ly/dmsg-numeracy*). But the article doesn't tell us what the risk really is in the end.

Take 1,000 Germans. A single one will develop MS over his lifetime. Now, if every one of these 1,000 Germans worked night shifts, the number of MS sufferers would jump to 2. The additional risk of developing MS when working in shifts is 1 in 1,000, not 100%. Surely this information is more useful when pondering whether to take the job.

On average, 1 in every 15 Europeans totally illiterate

The above headline looks frightening. It is also absolutely true. Among the 500 million Europeans, 36 million probably don't know how to read. As an aside, 36 million are also under 7 (data from Eurostat; *http://bit.ly/eurostat-numeracy*).

When writing about an average, always think "an average of what?" Is the reference population homogeneous? Uneven distribution patterns explain why most people drive better than average, for instance. Many people have zero or just one accident over their lifetime. A few reckless drivers have a great many, pushing the average number of accidents way higher than what most people experience. The same is true of the income distribution: most people earn less than average.

What you can do

Always take the distribution and base rate into account. Checking for the mean and median, as well as mode (the most frequent value in the distribution) helps you gain insights in the data. Knowing the order of magnitude makes contextualization easier, as in the MS example. Finally, reporting in natural frequencies (1 in 100) is way easier for readers to understand than using percentage (1%).

3. How reliable is the information?

The sample size problem

"80% dissatisfied with the judicial system", says a survey reported in Zaragoza-based Diaro de Navarra (*http://bit.ly/diariodenavarra*). How can one extrapolate from 800 respondents to 46 million Spaniards? Surely this is full of hot air.

When researching a large population (over a few thousand), you rarely need more than a thousand respondents to achieve a margin of error under 3%. It means that if you were to retake the survey with a totally different sample, 19 times out of 20, the answers you'll get will be within a 3 percentage points interval of the value you would have found, had you asked every single person.

Drinking tea lowers the risk of stroke

Articles about the benefits of tea-drinking are commonplace. This short item in Die Welt (*http://bit.ly/welt-tea*) saying that tea lowers the risk of myocardial infarction is no exception. Although the effects of tea are seriously studied by some, many pieces of research fail to take into account lifestyle factors, such as diet, occupation, or sports.

In most countries, tea is a beverage for the health-conscious upper classes. If researchers don't control for lifestyle factors in tea studies, they tell us nothing more than "rich people are healthier—and they probably drink tea."

What you can do

The math behind correlations and error margins in the tea studies are certainly correct, at least most of the time. But if researchers don't look for co-correlations (e.g., drinking tea correlates with playing sports), their results are of little value.

As a journalist, it makes little sense to challenge the numerical results of a study, such as the sample size, unless there are serious doubts about it. However, it is easy to see if researchers failed to take relevant pieces of information into account.

— *Nicolas Kayser-Bril, Journalism++*

Tips for Working with Numbers in the News

- The best tip for handling data is to enjoy yourself. Data can appear forbidding. But allow it to intimidate you and you'll get nowhere. Treat it as something to play with and explore and it will often yield secrets and stories with surprising ease. So handle it simply as you'd handle other evidence, without fear or favor. In particular, think of this as an exercise in imagination. Be creative by thinking of the alternative stories that might be consistent with the data and explain it better, then test them against more evidence. "What other story could explain this?" is a handy prompt to think about how this number, this obviously big or bad number, this clear proof of this or that, might be nothing of the sort.

- Don't confuse skepticism about data with cynicism. Skepticism is good; cynicism has simply thrown up its hands and quit. If you believe in data journalism (and you probably do, or you wouldn't be reading this book), then you must believe that data has something far better to offer than the lies and damned lies of caricature or the killer facts of swivel-eyed headlines. Data often gives us profound knowledge, if used carefully. We need to be neither cynical nor naive, but alert.

- If I tell you that drinking has gone up during the recession, you might tell me it's because everyone is depressed. If I tell you that drinking is down, you might tell me it's because everyone is broke. In other words, what the data says makes no difference to the interpretation that you are determined to put on it, namely that things are terrible one way or the other. If it goes up, it's bad; if it goes down, it's bad. The point here is that if you believe in data, try to let it speak before you slap on your own mood, beliefs, or expectations. There's so much data about that you will often be able to find confirmation of your prior beliefs if you simply look around a bit. In other words, data journalism, to me at least, adds little value if you are not open-minded. It is only as objective as you strive to make it, and not by virtue of being based on numbers.

- Uncertainty is OK. We associate numbers with authority and certainty. Often as not, the answer is that there is no answer, or the answer may be the best we have but still wouldn't hit a barn door for accuracy. I think we should say these things. If that sounds like a good way of killing stories, I'd argue that it's a great way of raising new questions. Equally, there can often be more than one legitimate way of cutting the data. Numbers don't have to be either true or false.

- The investigation is a story. The story of how you tried to find out can make great journalism, as you go from one piece of evidence to another—and this applies in spades to the evidence from data, where one number will seldom do. Different sources provide new angles, new ideas, and richer understanding. I wonder if we're too hung up on wanting to be authoritative and tell people the answer—and so we miss a trick by not showing the sleuthing.

- The best questions are the old ones: is that really a big number? Where did it come from? Are you sure it counts what you think it counts? These are generally just prompts to think around the data, the stuff at the edges that got squeezed by looking at a single number, the real-life complications, the wide range of other potential comparisons over time, group or geography; in short, context.

— *Michael Blastland, freelance journalist*

Basic Steps in Working with Data

There are at least three key concepts you need to understand when starting a data project:

- Data requests should begin with a list of questions you want to answer.
- Data often is messy and needs to be cleaned.
- Data may have undocumented features.

Figure 5-2. Messy data

Know the Questions You Want to Answer

In many ways, working with data is like interviewing a live source. You ask questions of the data and get it to reveal the answers. But just as a source can only give answers about which he has information, a dataset can only answer questions for which it has the right records and the proper variables. This means that you should consider carefully what questions you need to answer even before you acquire your data. Basically, you work backward. First, list the data-evidenced statements you want to make in your story. Then decide which variables and records you would have to acquire and analyze in order to make those statements.

Consider an example involving local crime reports. Let's say you want to do a story looking at crime patterns in your city, and the statements you want to make involve the times of day and the days of a week in which different kinds of crimes are most likely to happen, as well as what parts of town are hot spots for various crime categories.

You would realize that your data request has to include the date and the time each crime was reported, the kind of crime (murder, theft, burglary, etc.) as well as the address of where the crime occurred. So Date, Time, Crime Category, and Address are the minimum variables you need to answer those questions.

But be aware that there are a number of potentially interesting questions that this four-variable dataset *can't* answer, like the race and gender of victims, or the total value of stolen property, or which officers are most productive in making arrests. Also, you may only be able to get records for a certain time period, like the past three years, which would mean you couldn't say anything about whether crime patterns have changed over a longer period of time. Those questions may be outside of the planned purview of your story, and that's fine. But you don't want to get into your data analysis and suddenly decide you need to know what percentage of crimes in different parts of town are solved by arrest.

One lesson here is that it's often a good idea to request *all* the variables and records in the database, rather than the subset that could answer the questions for the immediate story. (In fact, getting all the data can be cheaper than getting a subset, if you have to pay the agency for the programming necessary to write out the subset.) You can always subset the data on your own, and having access to the full dataset will let you answer new questions that may come up in your reporting and even produce new ideas for follow-up stories. It may be that confidentiality laws or other policies mean that some variables, such as the identities of victims or the names of confidential informants, can't be released. But even a partial database is much better than none, as long as you understand which questions the redacted database can and can't answer.

Cleaning Messy Data

One of the biggest problems in database work is that often you will be using data for analysis reasons that has been gathered for bureaucratic reasons. The problem is that the standard of accuracy for those two is quite different.

For example, a key function of a criminal justice system database is to make sure that defendant Jones is brought from the jail to be in front of Judge Smith at the time of his hearing. For that purpose, it really doesn't matter a lot if Jones' birth date is incorrect, or that his street address is misspelled, or even if his middle initial is wrong. Generally, the system still can use this imperfect record to get Jones to Smith's courtroom at the appointed time.

But such errors can skew a data journalist's attempts to discover the patterns in the database. For that reason, the first big piece of work to undertake when you acquire a new dataset is to examine how messy it is and then clean it up. A good quick way to look for messiness is to create frequency tables of the categorical variables, the ones that would be expected to have a relatively small number of different values. (When using Excel, for instance, you can do this by using Filter or Pivot Tables on each categorical variable.)

Take "Gender," an easy example. You may discover that your Gender field includes any of a mix of values like these: Male, Female, M, F, 1, 0, MALE, FEMALE, etc., including misspellings like "Femal". To do a proper gender analysis, you must standardize—decide on M and F, perhaps—and then change all the variations to match the standards. Another common database with these kinds of problems are American campaign finance records, where the Occupation field might list "Lawyer," "Attorney," "Atty," "Counsel," "Trial Lawyer," and any of a wealth of variations and misspellings; again, the trick is to standardize the occupation titles into a shorter list of possibilities.

Data cleanup gets even more problematic when working with names. Are "Joseph T. Smith", "Joseph Smith," "J.T. Smith," "Jos. Smith," and "Joe Smith" all the same person? It may take looking at other variables like address or date of birth, or even deeper research in other records, to decide. But tools like Google Refine can make the cleanup and standardization task faster and less tedious.

Dirty Data

Thanks to the generally strong public records laws in the United States, getting data here isn't as big a problem as it can be in many other countries. But once we get it, we still face the problems of working with data that has been gathered for bureaucratic reasons, not for analytic reasons. The data often is "dirty," with values that aren't standardized. Several times I have received data that doesn't match up to the supposed file layout and data dictionary that accompanies it. Some agencies will insist on giving you the data in awkward formats like .pdf, which have to be converted. Problems like these make you appreciate it when you do get an occasional no-hassle dataset.

— *Steve Doig, Walter Cronkite School of Journalism, Arizona State University*

Data May Have Undocumented Features

The Rosetta Stone of any database is the so-called data dictionary. Typically, this file (it may be text or PDF or even a spreadsheet) will tell you how the data file is formatted (delimited text, fixed width text, Excel, dBase, etc.), the order of the variables, the names of each variable, and the datatype of each variable (text string, integer, decimal, etc.) You will use this information to help you properly import the data file into the analysis software you intend to use (Excel, Access, SPSS, Fusion Tables, any of various flavors of SQL, etc.)

The other key element of a data dictionary is an explanation of any codes being used by particular variables. For instance, Gender may be coded so that "1=Male" and

"0=Female." Crimes may be coded by your jurisdiction's statute numbers for each kind of crime. Hospital treatment records may use any of hundreds of 5-digit codes for the diagnoses of the conditions for which a patient is being treated. Without the data dictionary, these datasets could be difficult or even impossible to analyze properly.

But even with a data dictionary in hand, there can be problems. An example happened to reporters at the Miami Herald in Florida some years ago when they were doing an analysis of the varying rates of punishment that different judges were giving to people arrested for driving while intoxicated. The reporters acquired the conviction records from the court system and analyzed the numbers in the three different punishment variables in the data dictionary: amount of prison time given, amount of jail time given, and amount of fine given. These numbers varied quite a bit amongst the judges, giving the reporters' evidence for a story about how some judges were harsh and some were lenient.

But for every judge, about 1-2 percent of the cases showed no prison time, no jail time, and no fine. So the chart showing the sentencing patterns for each judge included a tiny amount of cases as "No punishment," almost as an afterthought. When the story and chart was printed, the judges howled in complaint, saying the Herald was accusing them of breaking a state law that required that anyone convicted of drunk driving be punished.

So the reporters went back to Clerk of the Court's office that had produced the data file and asked what had caused this error. They were told that the cases in question involved indigent defendants with first-time arrests. Normally they would be given a fine, but they had no money. So the judges were sentencing them to community service, such as cleaning litter along the roads. As it turned out, the law requiring punishment had been passed after the database structure had been created. So all the court clerks knew that in the data, zeros in each of the prison-jail-fine variables meant community service. However, this *wasn't* noted in the data dictionary, and therefore caused a Herald correction to be written.

The lesson in this case is to always ask the agency giving you data if there are any undocumented elements in the data, whether it is newly created codes that haven't been included in the data dictionary, changes in the file layout, or anything else. Also, always examine the results of your analysis and ask "Does this make sense?" The Herald reporters were building the chart on deadline and were so focused on the average punishment levels of each judge that they failed to pay attention to the scant few cases that seemed to show no punishment. They should have asked themselves if it made sense that all the judges seemed to be violating state law, even if only to a tiny degree.

— *Steve Doig, Walter Cronkite School of Journalism, Arizona State University*

The £32 Loaf of Bread

A story for Wales On Sunday about how much the Welsh government is spending on prescriptions for gluten-free products, contained the headline figure (*http://bit.ly/wale sonline-gluten-free*) that it was paying £32 for a loaf of bread. However, this was actually 11 loaves that cost £2.82 each.

The figures, from a Welsh Assembly written answer and a Welsh NHS statistics release, listed the figure as cost per prescription item. However, they gave no additional definition in the data dictionary of what a prescription item might refer or how a separate quantity column might define it.

The assumption was that it referred to an individual item—e.g., a loaf of bread—rather than what it actually was, a pack of several loaves.

No one, neither the people who answered the written answer nor the press office, when it was put to them, raised the issue about quantity until the Monday after the story was published.

So do not assume that the background notes for government data will help explain what information is being presented or that the people responsible for the data will realize the data is not clear even when you tell them your mistaken assumption.

Generally newspapers want things that make good headlines, so unless something obviously contradicts an interpretation, it is usually easier to go with what makes a good headline and not check too closely and risk the story collapsing, especially on deadline.

Figure 5-3. Prescriptions for gluten-free bread costing Welsh taxpayers £32 (WalesOnline)

But journalists have a responsibility to check ridiculous claims, even if it means that this drops the story down the news list.

— *Claire Miller, WalesOnline*

Start With the Data, Finish With a Story

To draw your readers in, you have to be able to hit them with a headline figure that makes them sit up and take notice. You should almost be able to read the story without having to know that it comes from a dataset. Make it exciting and remember who your audience is as you go.

One example of this can be found in a project carried out by the Bureau of Investigative Journalism using the EU Commission's Financial Transparency System (*http://bit.ly/ec-fts*). The story was constructed by approaching the dataset with specific queries in mind.

We looked through the data for key terms like "cocktail," "golf," and "away days." This allowed us to determine what the Commission had spent on these items and raised plenty of questions and storylines to follow up.

But key terms don't always give you what you want—sometimes you have to sit back and think about what you're really asking for. During this project we also wanted to find out how much commissioners spent on private jet travel but as the dataset didn't contain the phrase "private jet" we had to get the name of their travel providers by other means. Once we knew the name of the service provider to the Commission, "Abelag," we were able to query the data to find out how much was being spent on services provided by Abelag.

With this approach, we had a clearly defined objective in querying the data—to find a figure that would provide a headline; the color followed.

Another approach is to start with a blacklist and look for exclusions. An easy way to pull storylines from data is to know what you shouldn't find in there! A good example of how this can work is illustrated by the collaborative EU Structural Funds project between the Financial Times and the Bureau of Investigative Journalism.

We queried the data, based on the Commission's own rules about what kinds of companies and associations should be prohibited from receiving structural funds. One example was expenditure on tobacco and tobacco producers.

By querying the data with the names of tobacco companies, producers, and growers, we found data that revealed that British American Tobacco was receiving €1.5m for a factory in Germany.

As the funding was outside the rules of Commission expenditure, it was a quick way to find a story in the data.

You never know what you might find in a dataset, so just have a look. You have to be quite bold and this approach generally works best when trying to identify obvious characteristics that will show up through filtering (the biggest, extremes, most common, etc.).

— *Caelainn Barr, Citywire*

Data Stories

Data journalism can sometimes give the impression that it is mainly about presentation of data—such as visualizations that quickly and powerfully convey an understanding of an aspect of the figures, or interactive searchable databases that allow individuals to look up places like their own local street or hospital. All this can be very valuable, but like other forms of journalism, data journalism should also be about stories. So what are the kinds of stories you can find in data? Based on my experience at the BBC, I have drawn up a list, or "typology," of different kinds of data stories.

I think it helps to bear this list below in mind, not only when you are analyzing data, but also at the stage before that, when you are collecting it (whether looking for publicly available datasets or compiling freedom of information requests).

Measurement
> The simplest story; counting or totaling something: "Local councils across the country spent a total of £x billion on paper clips last year." But it's often difficult to know if that's a lot or a little. For that, you need context, which can be provided by:

Proportion
> "Last year local councils spent two-thirds of their stationery budget on paper clips."

Internal comparison
> "Local councils spend more on paper clips than on providing meals-on-wheels for the elderly."

External comparison
> "Council spending on paper clips last year was twice the nation's overseas aid budget."

There are also other ways of exploring the data in a contextual or comparative way:

Change over time
> "Council spending on paper clips has trebled in the past four years."

"League tables"
> These are often geographical or by institution, and you must make sure the basis for comparison is fair (e.g., taking into account the size of the local population). "Borsetshire Council spends more on paper clips for each member of staff than any other local authority, at a rate four times the national average."

Or you can divide the data subjects into groups:

Analysis by categories
> "Councils run by the Purple Party spend 50% more on paper clips than those controlled by the Yellow Party."

Or you can relate factors numerically:

Association
> "Councils run by politicians who have received donations from stationery companies spend more on paper clips, with spending increasing on average by £100 for each pound donated."

But, of course, always remember that correlation and causation are not the same thing.

So if you're investigating paper clip spending, are you also getting the following figures?

- Total spending to provide context?
- Geographical/historical/other breakdowns to provide comparative data?
- The additional data you need to ensure comparisons are fair, such as population size?
- Other data that might provide interesting analysis to compare or relate the spending to?

— *Martin Rosenbaum, BBC*

Data Journalists Discuss Their Tools of Choice

Psssss. That is the sound of your data decompressing from its airtight wrapper. Now what? What do you look for? And what tools do you use to get stuck in? We asked data journalists to tell us a bit about how they work with data. Here is what they said:

> At the Guardian Datablog, we really like to interact with our readers and allowing them to replicate our data journalism quickly means they can build on the work we do and sometimes spot things we haven't. So the more intuitive the data tools, the better. We try to pick tools that anyone could get the hang of without learning a programming language or having special training and without a hefty fee attached.

> We're currently using Google products quite heavily for this reason. All the datasets we tidy and release are available as a Google Spreadsheet, which means people with a Google account can download the data, import it into their own account and make their own charts, sort the data and create pivot tables, or they can import the data into a tool of their choice.

> To map data, we use Google Fusion tables. When we create heat maps in Fusion, we share our KML shape files so that readers can download and build their own heat maps —maybe adding extra layers of data onto the Datablog's original map. The other nice feature of these Google tools is that they work on the many platforms our readers use to access the blog, such as their desktop, their mobile, and tablets.

> In addition to Google Spreadsheets and Fusion, we use two other tools in our daily work. The first is Tableau, to visualize multi-dimensional datasets; and the second is ManyEyes, for quick analysis of data. None of these tools are perfect, so we continue to look for better visualization tools that our readers will enjoy.

> — Lisa Evans, *the Guardian*

> Am I ever going to be a coder? Very unlikely! I certainly don't think that all reporters need to know how to code. But I do think it is very valuable for them to have a more general awareness of what is possible and know how to talk to coders.

> If you're starting out, walk, don't run. You need to persuade your colleagues and editors that working with data can get you stories that you wouldn't otherwise get and that it's well worth doing. Once they see the value of this approach, you can expand into doing more complex stories and projects.

My advice is to learn Excel and do some simple stories first. Start out small and work your way up to database analysis and mapping. You can do so much in Excel—it's an extremely powerful tool and most people don't even use a fraction of its functionality. If you can, go on a course on Excel for journalists, such as the one offered by the Centre for Investigative Journalism.

With respect to interpreting data: don't take this lightly. You have to be conscientious. Pay attention to detail and question your results. Keep notes on how you're processing the data and keep a copy of the original data. It is easy to make a mistake. I always do my analysis two or three times practically from scratch. Even better would be to get your editor or someone else to analyze the data separately and compare the results.

— Cynthia O'Murchu, *Financial Times*

The ability to write and deploy complex software as quickly as a reporter can write a story is a pretty new thing. It used to take a lot longer. Things changed thanks to the development of two free/open source rapid development frameworks: Django and Ruby on Rails, both of which were first released in the mid-2000s.

Django, which is built on top of the Python programming language, was developed by Adrian Holovaty and a team working in a newsroom—the Lawrence Journal-World in Lawrence, Kansas. Ruby on Rails was developed in Chicago by by David Heinemeier Hansson and 37Signals, a web application company.

Though the two frameworks take different approaches to the "MVC pattern," they're both excellent and make it possible to build even very complex web applications very quickly. They take away some of the rudimentary work of building an app. Things like creating and fetching items from the database, and matching URLs to specific code in an app are built into the frameworks, so developers don't need to write code to do basic things like that.

While there hasn't been a formal survey of news app teams in the U.S., it is generally understood that most teams use one of these two frameworks for database-backed news apps. At ProPublica, we use Ruby on Rails.

The development of rapid web server "slice" provisioning services like Amazon Web Services also took away some of what used to make deploying a web app a slow process.

Apart from that, we use pretty standard tools to work with data: Google Refine and Microsoft Excel to clean data; SPSS and R to do statistics; ArcGIS and QGIS to do GIS; Git for source code management; TextMate, Vim and Sublime Text for writing code; and a mix of MySQL, PostgreSQL and SQL Server for databases. We built our own JavaScript framework called "Glass" that helps us build front-end heavy apps in JavaScript very quickly.

— Scott Klein, *ProPublica*

Sometimes the best tool can be the simplest tool—the power of a spreadsheet is easy to underestimate. But using a spreadsheet back when everything was in DOS enabled me to understand a complex formula for the partnership agreement for the owners of The Texas Rangers—back when George W. Bush was one of the key owners. A spreadsheet can help me flag outliers or mistakes in calculations. I can write clean-up scripts and more. It is a basic in the toolbox for a data journalist.

That said, my favorite tools have even more power—SPSS for statistical analysis and mapping programs that enable me to see patterns geographically.

— Cheryl Phillips, *The Seattle Times*

I'm a big fan of Python. Python is a wonderful open source programming language that is easy to read and write (e.g., you don't have to type a semi-colon after each line). More importantly, Python has a tremendous user base and therefore has plugins (called packages) for literally everything you need.

I would consider Django as something rarely needed by data journalists. It is a Python web application framework—that is, a tool to create big, database-driven web applications. It is definitely too heavyweight for small interactive infographics.

I also use QGis, which is an open source toolkit providing a wide range of GIS functionality needed by data journalists who deal with geodata every now and then. If you need to convert geospatial data from one format into another, then QGis is what you need. It can handle nearly every geodata format out there (Shapefiles, KML, GeoJSON, etc.). If you need to cut out a few regions, QGis can do this as well. Plus there is a huge community around QGis, so you find tons of resources like tutorials (*http://bit.ly/goettingen-tuto rial*) out in the web.

R was created mainly as a scientific visualization tool. It is hard to find any visualization method or data wrangling technique that is not already built into R. R is a universe in its own, the mecca of visual data analysis. One drawback is that you need to learn (yet another) programming language, as R has its own language. But once you have taken the initial climb on the learning curve, there's no tool more powerful than R. Trained data journalists can use R to analyze huge datasets that extend the limits of Excel (for instance, if you have a table with a million rows).

What's really nice about R is that you're able to keep an exact "protocol" of what you're doing with the data throughout the entire process—from reading a CSV file to generating charts. If the data changes, you can regenerate the chart using one click. If someone is curious about the integrity of your chart, you can show the exact source, which allows everyone to recreate the exact chart on their own (or maybe find the mistakes you made).

NumPy + MatPlotLib is kind of a way of doing the same thing in Python. It's an option if you're already well trained in Python. In fact, NumPy and MatPlotLib are two examples of Python packages. They can be used for data analysis and data visualization, and are both limited to static visualizations. They cannot be used to create interactive charts with tooltips and more advanced stuff.

I'm not using MapBox, but I've heard it is a great tool if you want to provide more sophisticated maps based on OpenStreetMap. It allows you, for instance, to customize the map styles (colors, labels, etc). There's also a companion of MapBox, called Leaflet. Leaflet is basically a higher level JavaScript library for mapping that allows you to easily switch between map providers (OSM, MapBox, Google Maps, Bing, etc.).

RaphaelJS is a rather low-level visualization library that allows you to work with basic primitives (like circles, lines, text), and to animate them, add interactions, etc. There's nothing like a ready-to-use bar chart in it, so you have to draw a set of rectangles yourself.

However, the good thing about Raphael is that everything you create will also work in Internet Explorer. That's not the case with many other (amazing) visualization libraries like d3. Sadly, so many users are still using IE and no newsroom can afford to ignore 30% of their users.

Besides RaphaelJS, there's also the option of creating a Flash fallback for IE. That is basically what The New York Times is doing. This means that you have to develop each application twice.

I'm still not convinced about the "best" process of shipping visualization for IE and modern browsers. Often I find that RaphaelJS applications can run horribly slow on IE, around ten times slower than they run in Flash using modern browsers. So Flash fallbacks might be a better option if you want to provide high-quality animated visualizations for all users.

— Gregor Aisch, *Open Knowledge Foundation*

My go-to tool is Excel, which can handle the majority of CAR problems and has the advantages of being easy to learn and available to most reporters. When I need to merge tables, I typically use Access, but then export the merged table back into Excel for further work. I use ESRI's ArcMap for geographic analyses; it's powerful and is used by the agencies that gather geocoded data. TextWrangler is great for examining text data with quirky layouts and delimiters, and can do sophisticated search-and-replace with regular expressions. When statistical techniques like linear regression are needed, I use SPSS; it has a friendly point-and-click menu. For really heavy lifting, like working with datasets that have millions of records that may need serious filtering and programmed variable transformations, I use SAS software.

— Steve Doig, *Walter Cronkite School of Journalism*

Our tools of choice include Python and Django for hacking, scraping, and playing with data; and PostGIS, QGIS, and the MapBox toolkit for building crazy web maps. R and NumPy + MatPlotLib are currently battling for supremacy as our kit of choice for exploratory data analysis, though our favorite data tool of late is homegrown: CSVKit. More or less everything we do is deployed in the cloud.

— Brian Boyer, *Chicago Tribune*

At La Nacion we use:

- Excel for cleaning, organizing and analyzing data;
- Google Spreadsheets for publishing and connecting with services such as Google Fusion Tables and the Junar Open Data Platform;
- Junar for sharing our data and embedding it in our articles and blog posts;
- Tableau Public for our interactive data visualizations;
- Qlikview, a very fast business intelligence tool to analyze and filter large datasets;
- NitroPDF for converting PDFs to text and Excel files; and
- Google Fusion Tables for map visualizations.

— Angélica Peralta Ramos, *La Nacion (Argentina)*

As a grassroots community without any technical bias, we at Transparency Hackers use a lot of different tools and programming languages. Every member has it's own set of preferences and this great variety is both our strength and our weakness. Some of us are actually building a "Transparency Hacker Linux Distribution," which we could live-boot anywhere and start hacking data. This toolkit has some interesting tools and libraries for handling data like Refine, RStudio and OpenOffice Calc (usually an overlooked tool by savvy people, but really useful for quick/small stuff). Also, we've been using Scraperwiki quite a lot to quickly prototype and save data results online.

For data visualization and graphs, there are a lot of tools we like. Python and NumPy are pretty powerful. A few people in the community have been playing with R, but at the end of the day I still think Javascript plotting graph libs like d3, Flot, and RaphaelJS end up being used in the majority of our projects. Finally, we've been experimenting a lot with mapping, and Tilemill has been a really interesting tool to work with.

— Pedro Markun, *Transparência Hacker*

Using Data Visualization to Find Insights in Data

Visualization is critical to data analysis. It provides a front line of attack, revealing intricate structure in data that cannot be absorbed in any other way. We discover unimagined effects, and we challenge imagined ones.

— William S. Cleveland (from Visualizing Data, *Hobart Press*)

Data by itself, consisting of bits and bytes stored in a file on a computer hard drive, is invisible. In order to be able to see and make any sense of data, we need to visualize it. In this section I'm going to use a broader understanding of the term *visualizing*, that includes even pure textual representations of data. For instance, just loading a dataset into a spreadsheet software can be considered as data visualization. The invisible data suddenly turns into a visible "picture" on our screen. Thus, the question should not be whether journalists need to visualize data or not, but which kind of visualization may be the most useful in which situation.

In other words: when does it makes sense to go beyond the table visualization? The short answer is: *almost always*. Tables alone are definitely not sufficient to give us an overview of a dataset. And tables alone don't allow us to immediately identify patterns within the data. The most common example here are geographical patterns that can only be observed after visualizing data on a map. But there are also other kinds of patterns, which we will see later in this section.

Using Visualization to Discover Insights

It is unrealistic to expect that data visualization tools and techniques will unleash a barrage of ready-made stories from datasets. There are no rules, no "protocol" that will guarantee us a story. Instead, I think it makes more sense to look for "insights," which can be artfully woven into stories in the hands of a good journalist.

Every new visualization is likely to give us some insights into our data. Some of those insights might be already known (but perhaps not yet proven), while other insights might be completely new or even surprising to us. Some new insights might mean the beginning of a story, while others could just be the result of errors in the data, which are most likely to be found by visualizing the data.

In order to make finding insights in data more effective, I find the process discussed in Figure 5-4 (and the rest of this section) to be very helpful.

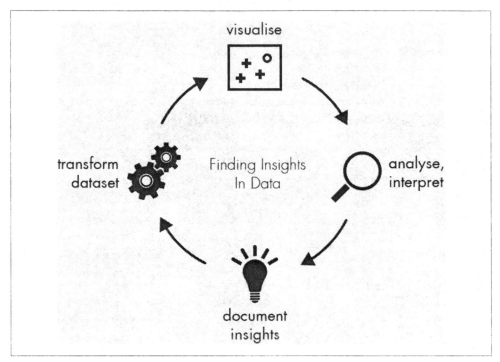

Figure 5-4. Data insights: a visualization (Gregor Aisch)

Learn how to visualize data

Visualization provides a unique perspective on the dataset. You can visualize data in lots of different ways.

Tables are very powerful when you are dealing with a relatively small number of data points. They show labels and amounts in the most structured and organized fashion and reveal their full potential when combined with the ability to sort and filter the data. Additionally, Edward Tufte suggested including small chart pieces within table columns—for instance, one bar per row or a small line chart (since then also known as a sparkline). But still, as mentioned earlier, tables clearly have their limitations. They are great to show you one-dimensional outliers like the top 10, but they are poor when it comes to comparing multiple dimensions at the same time (for instance, population per country over time).

Major Groups	Apr-07		Apr-08	% YoY		% MoM		%Wt	
Food	2,532		2,588	2.2		-0.3		40.9	
Hospitality & Service Industries	1,159		1,195	3.1		0.1		18.7	
Household Goods	858		933	8.7		0.5		13.9	
Other, Pharma, Watches	552		625	13.3		-0.8		8.9	
Department Stores	482		500	3.8		0.1		7.8	
Clothing & Soft Goods	421		453	7.6		0.3		6.8	
Recreational Goods	198		222	16.5		0.4		3.1	
Total Retail Sales	6,194.2		6,515.1	5.2		-0.1			

Group	Apr-07		Apr-08	% YoY		% MoM		%Wt	
Food									
Supermarkets & Grocery Stores	1,675		1,793	7.0		-0.3		27.0	
Takeaway Food	374		271	-27.5		-2.2		6.0	
Liquor	282		309	9.8		0.9		4.5	
Other Food	202		215	6.4		0.8		3.3	
Hospitality & Service Industries									
Hotels & Licensed Clubs	647		747	15.5		0.9		10.4	
Cafes & Restaurants	456		389	-14.8		-0.7		7.4	
Selected Services	56		59	5.4		-4.8		0.9	
Other, Pharma, Watches									
Other Retailing	243		256	5.3		-1.9		3.9	
Pharmaceutical, Cosmetic & Toiletry	216		266	23.3		0.2		3.5	
Watch & Jewellery	93		103	10.6		-0.4		1.5	
Department Stores									
Department Stores	482		500	3.8		0.1		7.8	
Household Goods									
Furniture & Floor Covering	407		464	14.0		1.6		6.6	
Domestic Hardware & Houseware	282		254	-10.0		-0.2		4.6	
Domestic Appliances & Recorded Music	169		214	27.0		-1.0		2.7	
Clothing & Soft Goods									
Clothing	308		331	7.6		0.4		5.0	
Other Clothing Related	113		122	7.9		0.0		1.8	
Recreational Goods									
Newspaper, Book & Stationery	113		139	22.7		1.2		1.8	
Other Recreational Goods	77		83	7.4		-1.0		1.2	

Figure 5-5. Tips from Tufte: sparklines (Gregor Aisch)

Charts, in general, allow you to map dimensions in your data to visual properties of geometric shapes. There's much written about the effectiveness of individual visual properties, and the short version is this: color is difficult, position is everything. In a scatterplot, for instance, two dimensions are mapped to the to the x- and y-position. You can even display a third dimension to the color or size of the displayed symbols. Line charts are especially suited for showing temporal evolutions, while bar charts are perfect for comparing categorical data. You can stack chart elements on top of each other. If you want to compare a small number of groups in your data, displaying multiple instances of the same chart is a very powerful way (also referred to as small multiples). In all charts you can use different kinds of scales to explore different aspects in your data (e.g., linear or log scale).

In fact, most of the data we're dealing with is somehow related to actual people. The power of maps is to reconnect the data to our very physical world. Imagine a dataset of geolocated crime incidents. Crucially, you want to see *where* the crimes happen. Also maps can reveal geographic relations within the data (e.g., a trend from North to South, or from urban to rural areas).

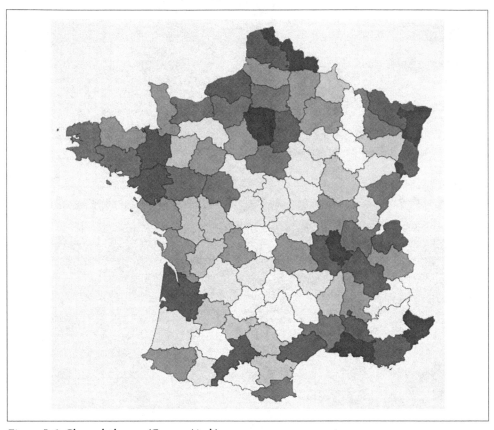

Figure 5-6. Choropleth map (Gregor Aisch)

Speaking of relations, the fourth most important type of visualization is a graph. Graphs are all about showing the interconnections (edges) in your data points (nodes). The position of the nodes is then calculated by more or less complex graph layout algorithms which allow us to immediately see the structure within the network. The trick of graph visualization in general is to find a proper way to model the network itself. Not all datasets already include relations, and even if they do, it might not be the most interesting aspect to look at. Sometimes it's up to the journalist to define edges between nodes. A perfect example of this is the U.S. Senate Social Graph (*http://slate.me/senate -social*), whose edges connect senators that voted the same in more than 65% of the votes.

Analyze and interpret what you see

Once you have visualized your data, the next step is to learn something from the picture you created. You could ask yourself:

- What can I see in this image? Is it what I expected?

- Are there any interesting patterns?
- What does this mean in the context of the data?

Sometimes you might end up with a visualization that, in spite of its beauty, might seem to tell you nothing of interest about your data. But there is almost always *something* that you can learn from any visualization, however trivial.

Document your insights and steps

If you think of this process as a journey through the dataset, the documentation is your travel diary. It will tell you where you have traveled to, what you have seen there, and how you made your decisions for your next steps. You can even start your documentation before taking your first look at the data.

In most cases when we start to work with a previously unseen dataset, we are already full of expectations and assumptions about the data. Usually there is a reason why we are interested in that dataset that we are looking at. It's a good idea to start the documentation by writing down these initial thoughts. This helps us to identify our bias and reduces the risk of misinterpretation of the data by just finding what we originally wanted to find.

I really think that the documentation is the most important step of the process—and it is also the one we're most likely to tend to skip. As you will see in the example below, the described process involves a lot of plotting and data wrangling. Looking at a set of 15 charts you created might be very confusing, especially after some time has passed. In fact, those charts are only valuable (to you or any other person you want to communicate your findings) if presented in the context in which they have been created. Hence you should take the time to make some notes on things like:

- Why have I created this chart?
- What have I done to the data to create it?
- What does this chart tell me?

Transform data

Naturally, with the insights that you have gathered from the last visualization, you might have an idea of what you want to see next. You might have found some interesting pattern in the dataset which you now want to inspect in more detail.

Possible transformations are:

Zooming
  To have look at a certain detail in the visualization

Aggregation
  To combine many data points into a single group

Filtering
> To (temporarily) remove data points that are not in our major focus

Outlier removal
> To get rid of single points that are not representative for 99% of the dataset.

Let's consider that you have visualized a graph, and what came out of this was nothing but a mess of nodes connected through hundreds of edges (a very common result when visualizing so-called *densely connected networks*). One common transformation step would be to filter some of the edges. If, for instance, the edges represent money flows from donor countries to recipient countries, we could remove all flows below a certain amount.

Which Tools to Use

The question of tools is not an easy one. Every data visualization tool available is good at something. Visualization and data wrangling should be easy and cheap. If changing parameters of the visualizations takes you hours, you won't experiment that much. That doesn't necessarily mean that you don't need to learn how to use the tool. But once you learned it, it should be really efficient.

It often makes a lot of sense to choose a tool that covers both the data wrangling and the data visualization issues. Separating the tasks in different tools means that you have to import and export your data very often. Here's a short list of some data visualization and wrangling tools:

- Spreadsheets like LibreOffice, Excel or Google Docs
- Statistical programming frameworks like R (r-project.org) or Pandas (pandas.py-data.org)
- Geographic Information Systems (GIS) like Quantum GIS, ArcGIS, or GRASS
- Visualization Libraries like d3.js (mbostock.github.com/d3), Prefuse (prefuse.org), or Flare (flare.prefuse.org)
- Data wrangling tools like Google Refine or Datawrangler
- Non-programming visualization software like ManyEyes or Tableau Public (tableausoftware.com/products/public)

The sample visualizations in the next section were created using R, which is kind of a Swiss Army knife of (scientific) data visualization.

An Example: Making Sense of US Election Contribution Data

Let us have look at the US Presidential Campaign Finance database, which contains about 450,000 contributions to US presidential candidates. The CSV file is 60 megabytes and way too big to handle easily in a program like Excel.

In the first step I will explicitly write down my initial assumptions on the FEC contributions dataset:

- Obama gets the most contributions (since he is the president and has the greatest popularity).
- The number of donations increases as the time moves closer to election date.
- Obama gets more small donations than Republican candidates.

To answer the first question, we need to *transform* the data. Instead of each single contribution, we need to sum the total amounts contributed to each candidate. After *visualizing* the results in a sorted table, we can confirm our assumption that Obama would raise the most money:

Candidate	Amount ($)
Obama, Barack	72,453,620.39
Romney, Mitt	50,372,334.87
Perry, Rick	18,529,490.47
Paul, Ron	11,844,361.96
Cain, Herman	7,010,445.99
Gingrich, Newt	6,311,193.03
Pawlenty, Timothy	4,202,769.03
Huntsman, Jon	2,955,726.98
Bachmann, Michelle	2,607,916.06
Santorum, Rick	1,413,552.45
Johnson, Gary Earl	413,276.89
Roemer, Charles E. *Buddy* III	291,218.80
McCotter, Thaddeus G	37,030.00

Even though this table shows the minimum and maximum amounts and the order, it does not tell very much about the underlying patterns in candidate ranking. Figure 5-7 is another view on the data, a chart type that is called a "dot chart," in which we can see everything that is shown in the table *plus* the patterns within the field. For instance, the dot chart allows us to immediately compare the distance between Obama and Romney, and Romney and Perry, without needing to subtract values. (Note: the dot chart was created using R. You can find links to the source code at the end of this chapter).

Now, let us proceed with a bigger picture of the dataset. As a first step, I *visualized* all contributed amounts over time in a simple plot. We can see that almost all donations are very, very small compared to three really big outliers. Further investigation reveals that these huge contributions are coming from the "Obama Victory Fund 2012" (also

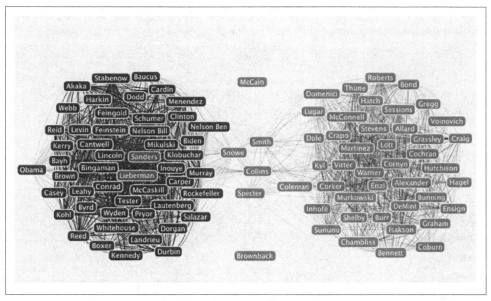

Figure 5-7. Visualizations to spot underlying patterns (Gregor Aisch)

known as Super PAC) and were made on June 29th ($450k), September 29th ($1.5mio), and December 30th ($1.9mio).

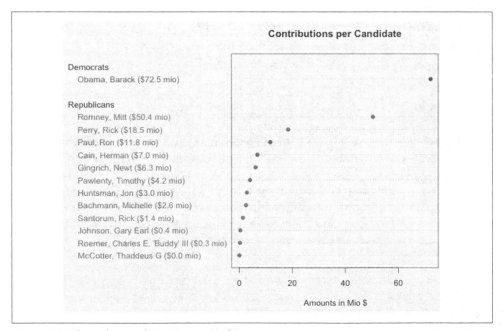

Figure 5-8. Three clear outliers (Gregor Aisch)

While the contributions by Super PACs alone is undoubtedly the biggest story in the data, it might be also interesting to look beyond it. The point now is that these big contributions disturb our view on the smaller contributions coming from individuals, so we're going to remove them from the data. This transform is commonly known as outlier removal. After visualizing again, we can see that most of the donations are within the range of $10k and -$5k.

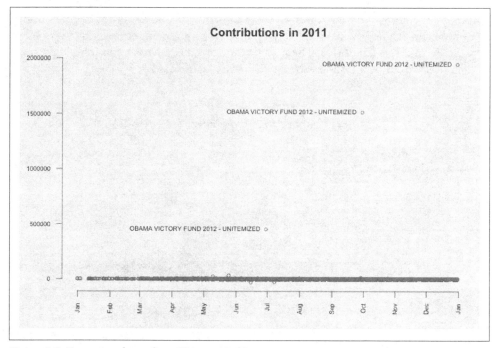

Figure 5-9. Removing the outliers (Gregor Aisch)

According to the contribution limits placed by the FECA, individuals are not allowed to donate more than $2500 to each candidate. As we see in the plot, there are numerous donations made above that limit. In particular, two big contributions in May attract our attention. It seems that they are *mirrored* in negative amounts (refunds) in June and July. Further investigation in the data reveals the following transactions:

- On May 10, *Stephen James Davis*, San Francisco, employed at Banneker Partners (attorney), has donated **$25,800** to Obama.

- On May 25, *Cynthia Murphy*, Little Rock, employed at the Murphy Group (public relations), has donated **$33,300** to Obama.

- On June 15, the amount of **$30,800** was refunded to *Cynthia Murphy*, which reduced the donated amount to **$2500**.

- On July 8, the amount **$25,800** was refunded to *Stephen James Davis*, which reduced the donated amount to $0.

What's interesting about these numbers? The $30,800 refunded to Cynthia Murphy equals the maximum amount individuals may give to national party committees per year. Maybe she just wanted to combine both donations in one transaction, which was rejected. The $25,800 refunded to Stephen James Davis possibly equals the $30,800 minus $5000 (the contribution limit to any other political committee).

Another interesting finding in the last plot is a horizontal line pattern for contributions to Republican candidates at $5000 and -$2500. To see them in more detail, I visualized just the Republican donations. The resulting graphic is one great example of patterns in data that would be invisible without data visualization.

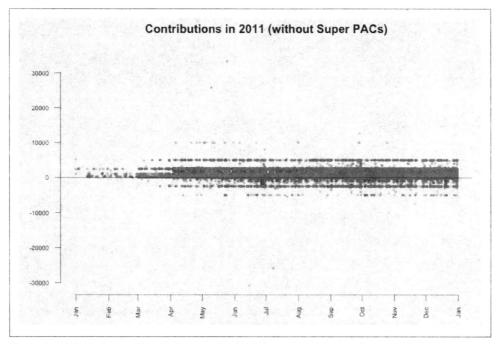

Figure 5-10. Removing outliers 2 (Gregor Aisch)

What we can see is that there are many $5000 donations to Republican candidates. In fact, a look up in the data returns that these are 1243 donations, which is only 0.3% of the total number of donations, but since those donations are evenly spread across time, the line appears. The interesting thing about the line is that donations by individuals were limited to $2500. Consequently, every dollar above that limit was refunded to the donors, which results in the second line pattern at -$2500. In contrast, the contributions to Barack Obama don't show a similar pattern.

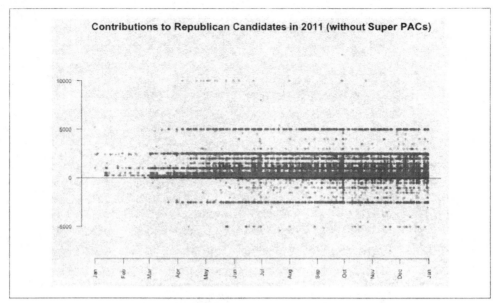

Figure 5-11. Removing outliers 3 (Gregor Aisch)

So, it might be interesting to find out why thousands of Republican donors did not notice the donation limit for individuals. To further analyze this topic, we can have a look at the total number of $5k donations per candidate.

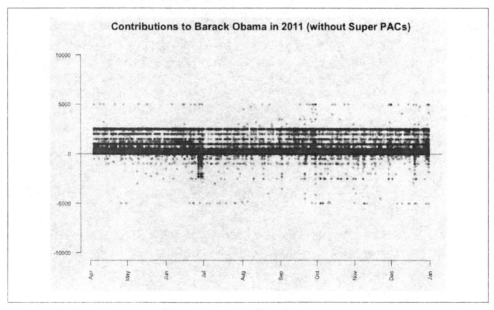

Figure 5-12. Donations per candidate (Gregor Aisch)

Of course, this is a rather distorted view since it does not consider the total amounts of donations received by each candidate. The next plot shows the percentage of $5k donations per candidate.

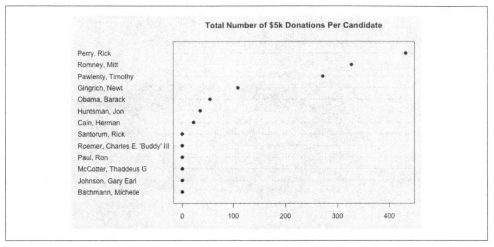

Figure 5-13. Where does the senator's money come from?: donations per candidate (Gregor Aisch)

What To Learn From This

Often, such a visual analysis of a new dataset feels like an exciting journey to an unknown country. You start as a foreigner with just the data and your assumptions, but with every step you make, with every chart you render, you get new insights about the topic. Based on those insights, you make decisions for your next steps and what issues are worth further investigation. As you might have seen in this chapter, this process of visualizing, analyzing and transformation of data could be repeated nearly infinitely.

Get the Source Code

All of the charts shown in this chapter were created using the wonderful and powerful software R. Created mainly as a scientific visualization tool, it is hard to find any visualization or data wrangling technique that is not already built into R. For those who are interested in how to visualize and wrangle data using R, here's the source code of the charts generated in this chapter:

- dotchart: contributions per candidate (*https://gist.github.com/1769733*)
- plot: all contributions over time (*https://gist.github.com/1816161*)
- plot: contributions by authorized committees (*https://gist.github.com/1816169*)

There is also a wide range of books and tutorials available.

— *Gregor Aisch, Open Knowledge Foundation*

Delivering Data

Once you've had a good look at your data and decided that there's something interesting to write about, how can you deliver it to the public? This section opens with short anecdotes about how leading data journalists have served their data up to their readers—from infographics to open data platforms to download links. Then we take a more extended look at how to build news apps, and the ins and outs of data visualization. Finally, we take a look at what you can do to engage your audience around your project.

Presenting Data to the Public

There are lots of different ways to present your data to the public—from publishing raw datasets with stories, to creating beautiful visualizations and interactive web applications. We asked leading data journalists for tips on how to present data to the public.

To Visualize or Not to Visualize?

There are times when data can tell a story better than words or photos, and this is why terms like "news application" and "data visualization" have attained buzzword status in so many newsrooms of late. Also fueling interest is the bumper crop of (often free) new tools and technologies designed to help even the most technically challenged journalist turn data into a piece of visual storytelling.

Tools like Google Fusion Tables, Many Eyes, Tableau, Dipity, and others make it easier than ever to create maps, charts, graphs, or even full-blown data applications that heretofore were the domain of specialists. But with the barrier to entry now barely a speed bump, the question facing journalists is now less about whether you can turn your dataset into a visualization, but whether you should. Bad data visualization (*http://bit.ly/niemanlab-wordcloud*) is worse in many respects than none at all.

— *Aron Pilhofer, New York Times*

Using Motion Graphics

With a tight script, well-timed animations, and clear explanations, motion graphics can serve to bring complex numbers or ideas to life, guiding your audience through the story. Hans Rosling's video lectures are a good example of how data can come to life to tell a story on the screen. Whether or not you agree with their methodology, I also think the Economist's Shoe-throwers' index (*http://econ.st/shoethrowers*) is a good example of using video to tell a numbers-based story. You wouldn't, or shouldn't, present this graphic as a static image. There's far too much going on. But having built up to it step by step, you're left with an understanding of how and why they got to this index. With motion graphics and animated shorts, you can reinforce what your audience is hearing. A voice-over with explanatory visuals provides a very powerful and memorable way of telling a story.

— *Lulu Pinney, freelance infographic designer*

Telling the World

Our workflow usually starts in Excel. It is such an easy way to quickly work out if there's something interesting in the data. If we have a sense that there is something in it, then we go to the news desk. We're really lucky as we sit right next to the main news desk at the Guardian. Then we look at how we should visualize it or show it on the page.

Then we write the post that goes with it. When I'm writing I usually have a cut-down version of the spreadsheet next to the text editor. Often I'll do bits of analysis while I'm writing to pick out interesting things. Then I'll publish the post and spend a bit of time Tweeting about it, writing to different people, and making sure that it is linked to from all the right places.

Half of the traffic from some of our posts will come from Twitter and Facebook. We're pretty proud that the average amount of time spent on a Datablog article is 6 minutes, compared to an average of 1 minute for the rest of the Guardian website. 6 minutes is a pretty good number, and time spent on the page is one of the key metrics when analyzing our traffic.

This also helps to convince our colleagues about the value of what we're doing. That and the big data-driven stories that we've worked on that everyone else in the newsroom knows: COINS, WikiLeaks, and the UK riots. For the COINS spending data, we had 5-6 specialist reporters at the Guardian working to give their views about the data when it was released by the UK government. We also had another team of 5-6 when the UK government spending over £25k data was released—including well-known reporters like Polly Curtis. WikiLeaks was also obviously very big, with lots of stories about Iraq and Afghanistan. The riots were also pretty big, with over 550k hits in two days.

But it is not just about the short term hits: it is also about being a reliable source of useful information. We try to be the place where you can get good, meaningful information on topics that we cover.

— *Simon Rogers, the Guardian*

Publishing the Data

We often will embed our data onto our site in a visualization and in a form that allows for easy download of the dataset. Our readers can explore the data behind the stories through interacting in the visualization or using the data themselves in other ways. Why is this important? It increases the transparency of The Seattle Times. We are showing the readers the same data that we used to draw powerful conclusions. And who uses it? Our critics for sure, as well as those just interested in the story and all of its ramifications. By making the data available we also can enlist tips from these same critics and general readers on what we may have missed and what more we could explore—all valuable in the pursuit of journalism that matters.

— *Cheryl Phillips, The Seattle Times*

Opening Up Your Data

Giving news consumers easy access to the data we use for our work is the right thing to do for several reasons. Readers can assure themselves that we aren't torturing the data to reach unfair conclusions. Opening up our data is in the social science tradition of allowing researchers to replicate our work. Encouraging readers to study the data can generate tips that may lead to follow-up stories. Finally, engaged readers interested in your data are likely to return again and again.

— *Steve Doig, Walter Cronkite School of Journalism, Arizona State University*

Starting an Open Data Platform

At La Nación, publishing open data is an integral part of our data journalistic activities. In Argentina there is no Freedom of Information Act and no national data portal, so we feel strongly about providing our readers with access to the data that we use in our stories.

Hence we publish raw structured data through our integrated Junar (*http://data.lana cion.com.ar*) platform as well as in Google Spreadsheets. We explicitly enable and encourage others to reuse our data, and we explain a bit about how to do this with documentation and video tutorials (*http://bit.ly/lanacion-tutorials*).

Furthermore, we're presenting some of these datasets and visualizations in our Nación Data blog (*http://blogs.lanacion.com.ar/data/*). We're doing this in order to evangelize about data and data publishing tools in Argentina, and show others how we gathered our data, how we use it, and how they can reuse it.

Since we opened the platform in February 2012 , we've received suggestions and ideas for datasets, mostly from academic and research people, as well as students from universities that are very thankful every time we reply with a solution or specific dataset. People are also engaging with and commenting on our data on Tableau, and several times we have been the most commented and top viewed item on the service. In 2011, we had 7 out of the top 100 (*http://bit.ly/tableau-7-100*) most viewed visualizations.

— *Angélica Peralta Ramos, La Nación (Argentina)*

Making Data Human

As the discussion around big data bounds into the broader consciousness, one important part has been conspicuously missing—the human element. While many of us think about data as disassociated, free-floating numbers, they are in fact measurements of tangible (and very often human) things. Data are tethered to the real lives of real people, and when we engage with the numbers, we must consider the real-world systems from which they came.

Take, for example, location data, which is being collected right now on hundreds of millions of phones and mobile devices. It's easy to think of these data (numbers that represent latitude, longitude, and time) as "digital exhaust," but they are in fact distilled moments from our personal narratives. While they may seem dry and clinical when read in a spreadsheet, when we allow people to put their own data on a map and replay them, they experience a kind of memory replay that is powerful and human.

At the moment, location data is used by a lot of third parties—application developers, big brands, and advertisers. While the second parties (telecoms and device managers) own and hold the data, the first party in this equation—you—has neither access or control over this information. At the NYTimes R&D group, we have launched a prototype project called OpenPaths (*https://openpaths.cc*) to both allow the public to explore their own location data, and to experience the concept of data ownership. After all, people should have control of these numbers that are so closely connected to their own lives and experiences.

Journalists have a very important role in bringing this inherent humanity of data to light. By doing so, they have the power to change public understanding—both of data and of the systems from which the numbers emerged.

— *Jer Thorp, Data Artist in Residence: New York Times R&D Group*

Open Data, Open Source, Open News

2012 may well be the year of open news. It's at the heart of our editorial ideology and a key message in our current branding. Amidst all this, it's clear that we need an open process for data-driven journalism. This process must not only be fuelled by open data, but also be enabled by open tools. By the end of the year, we hope to be able to accompany every visualization we publish with access to both the data behind it and the code that powers it.

Many of the tools used in visualization today are closed source. Others come with restrictive licenses that prohibit the use of derivative data. The open source libraries that do exist often solve a single problem well but fail to offer a wider methodology. All together, this makes it difficult for people to build on each other's work. It closes conversations rather than them opening up. To this end, we are developing a stack of open tools for interactive storytelling—the Miso Project (@themisoproject).

We are discussing this work with a number of other media organizations. It takes community engagement to realize the full potential of open source software. If we're successful, it will introduce a fundamentally different dynamic with our readers. Contributions can move beyond commenting to forking our work, fixing bugs, or reusing data in unexpected ways.

— *Alastair Dant, the Guardian*

Add A Download Link

In the past few years, I've worked with a few gigabytes of data for projects or articles, from scans of typewritten tables from the 1960s to the 1.5 gigabytes of cables released by WikiLeaks. It's always been hard to convince editors to systematically publish source data in an open and accessible format. Bypassing the problem, I added "Download the Data" links within articles, pointing to the archives containing the files or the relevant

Google docs. The interest from potential reusers was in line with what we see in government-sponsored programs (i.e., very, very low). However, the few instances of reuse provided new insights or spurred conversations that are well worth the few extra minutes per project!

— *Nicolas Kayser-Bril, Journalism++*

Know Your Scope

Know your scope. There's a big difference between hacking for fun and engineering for scale and performance. Make sure you've partnered with people who have the appropriate skill set for your project. Don't forget design. Usability, user experience, and presentation design can greatly affect the success of your project.

— *Chrys Wu, Hacks/Hackers*

How to Build a News App

News applications are windows into the data behind a story. They might be searchable databases, sleek visualizations, or something else altogether. But no matter what form they take, news apps encourage readers to interact with data in a context that is meaningful to them: looking up crime trends in their area, checking the safety records of their local doctor, or searching political contributions to their candidate of choice.

More than just high-tech infographics, the best news apps are durable products. They live outside the news cycle, often by helping readers solve real-world problems, or answering questions in such a useful or novel way that they become enduring resources. When journalists at ProPublica wanted to explore the safety of American kidney dialysis clinics, they built an application (*http://projects.propublica.org/dialysis/*) that helped users check whether their hometown facility was safe. Providing such an important and relevant service creates a relationship with users that reaches far beyond what a narrative story can do alone.

Therein lies both the challenge and the promise of building cutting-edge news apps: creating something of lasting value. Whether you are a developer or a manager, any discussion about how to build a great news app should start with a product development mentality: keep a laser focus on the user, and work to get the most bang for your buck. So before you start building, it helps to ask yourself three questions, discussed in the following sections.

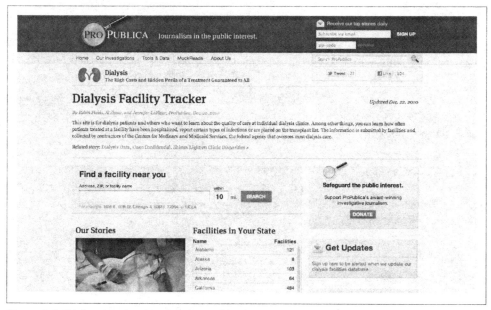

Figure 6-1. Dialysis Facility Tracker (ProPublica)

Who Is My Audience and What Are Their Needs?

News apps don't serve the story for its own sake—they serve the user. Depending on the project, that user might be a dialysis patient who wants to know about the safety record of her clinic, or even a homeowner unaware of earthquake hazards near his home. No matter who it is, any discussion about building a news app, like any good product, should start with the people who are going to use it.

A single app might serve many users. For instance, a project called Curbwise (*http://curbwise.com/*), built by the Omaha (Nebraska) World-Herald serves homeowners who believe they are being overtaxed; curious residents who are interested in nearby property values; and real estate workers trying to keep track of recent sales. In each of those cases, the app meets a specific need that keeps users coming back.

Homeowners, for instance, might need help gathering information on nearby properties so they can argue that their taxes are unfairly high. Pulling together that information is time-consuming and complicated, a problem Curbwise solves for its users by compiling a user-friendly report (*http://curbwise.com/how-to-protest*) of all the information they need to challenge their property taxes to local authorities. Curbwise sells that report for $20, and people pay for it because it solves a real problem in their lives.

Whether your app solves a real-world problem like Curbwise or supplements the narrative of a story with an interesting visualization, always be aware of the people who will be using it. Concentrate on designing and building features based on their needs.

How Much Time Should I Spend on This?

Developers in the newsroom are like water in the desert: highly sought-after and in short supply. Building news apps means balancing the daily needs of a newsroom against the long-term commitments it takes to build truly great products.

Say your editor comes to you with an idea: the City Council is set to have a vote next week about whether to demolish several historic properties in your town. He suggests building a simple application that allows users to see the buildings on a map.

As a developer, you have a few options. You can flex your engineering muscle by building a gorgeous map using custom software. Or you can use existing tools like Google Fusion Tables or open source mapping libraries and finish the job in a couple hours. The first option will give you a better app; but the second might give you more time to build something else with a better chance of having a lasting impact.

Just because a story lends itself to a complex, beautiful news app doesn't mean you need to build one. Balancing priorities is critical. The trick is to remember that every app you build comes at a cost: namely, another potentially more impactful app you could have been working on instead.

How Can I Take Things to the Next Level?

Building high-end news apps can be time-consuming and expensive. That's why it always pays to ask about the payoff. How do you elevate a one-hit wonder into something special?

Creating an enduring project that transcends the news cycle is one way. But so is building a tool that saves you time down the road (and open sourcing it!), or applying advanced analytics to your app to learn more about your audience.

Lots of organizations build Census maps to show demographic shifts in their cities. But when the Chicago Tribune news apps team built theirs (*http://bit.ly/chicago-census*), they took things to the next level by developing tools and techniques to build those maps quickly, which they then made available (*http://bit.ly/chicagotribune-maps*) for other organizations to use.

At my employer, the Center for Investigative Reporting, we coupled a simple searchable database with a fine-grained event tracking framework that allowed us to learn, among other things, how much users value serendipity and exploration in our news apps.

At the risk of sounding like a bean-counter, always think about return on investment (*http://bit.ly/cironline-return*). Solve a generic problem; create a new way to engage users; open source parts of your work; use analytics to learn more about your users; or even find cases like Curbwise where part of your app might generate revenue.

Wrapping Up

News application development has come a long way in a very short time. News Apps 1.0 were a lot like Infographics 2.0—interactive data visualizations, mixed with searchable databases, designed primarily to advance the narrative of the story. Now, many of those apps can be designed by reporters on deadline using open source tools, freeing up developers to think bigger thoughts.

News Apps 2.0, where the industry is headed, is about combining the storytelling and public service strengths of journalism with the product development discipline and expertise of the technology world. The result, no doubt, will be an explosion of innovation around ways to make data relevant, interesting and especially useful to our audience—and at the same time, hopefully helping journalism do the same.

— *Chase Davis, Center for Investigative Reporting*

News Apps at ProPublica

A news application is a big interactive database that tells a news story. Think of it like you would any other piece of journalism. It just uses software instead of words and pictures.

By showing each reader data that is specific to them, a news app can help each reader understand a story in a way that's personally meaningful to them. It can help a reader understand their personal connection to a broad national phenomenon, and help them attach what they know to what they don't know, and thereby encourage a deep understanding of abstract concepts.

We tend to build news apps when we have a dataset (or think we can acquire a dataset) that is national in scope yet granular enough to expose meaningful details.

A news app should tell a story, and just like any good news story, it needs a headline, a byline, a lead, and a nut graph. Some of these concepts can be hard to distinguish in a piece of interactive software, but they're there if you look closely.

Also, a news app should be generative, meaning it should generate more stories and more reporting. ProPublica's best apps have been used as the basis for local stories.

For instance, take our Dollars for Docs news app (*http://projects.propublica.org/docdol lars*). It tracked, for the first time, millions of dollars of payments by drug companies to doctors, for consulting, speaking, and so on. The news app we built lets readers look up their own doctor and see the payments they've received. Reporters at other news organizations also used the data. More than 125 local news organizations, including the Boston Globe, Chicago Tribune, and the St. Louis Post-Dispatch did investigative stories on local doctors based on Dollars for Docs data.

A few of these local stories were the result of formal partnerships, but the majority were done quite independently—in some cases, we didn't have much, if any, knowledge that the story was being worked on until it came out. As a small but national news organization, this kind of thing is crucial for us. We can't have local knowledge in 125 cities, but if our data can help reporters who have local knowledge tell stories with impact, we're fulfilling our mission.

One of my favorite news apps is the Los Angeles Times's Mapping L.A. (*http://projects .latimes.com/mapping-la/neighborhoods/*), which started out as a crowdsourced map of Los Angeles's many neighborhoods, which up until Mapping L.A. launched, had no independent, widely-accepted set of boundaries. After the initial crowdsourcing project, the Times has been able to use neighborhoods as a framing device for great data reporting—things like crime rate by neighborhood, school quality by neighborhood, etc., which they wouldn't have been able to do before. So not only is Mapping L.A. both broad and specific, it's generative, and it tells people's own stories.

The resources necessary to build a news app range pretty widely. The New York Times has dozens of people working on news apps and on interactive graphics. But Talking Points Memo (*http://polltracker.talkingpointsmemo.com/*) made a cutting edge political poll tracker app with two staffers, neither of whom had computer science degrees.

Like most newsroom-based coders, we follow a modified Agile methodology to build our apps. We iterate quickly and show drafts to the other folks in the newsroom we're working with. Most importantly, we work really closely with reporters and read their drafts—even early ones. We work much more like reporters than like traditional programmers. In addition to writing code, we call sources, gather information, and build expertise. It would be pretty difficult to make a good news app using material we don't understand.

Why should newsrooms be interested in producing data-driven news apps? Three reasons: It's great journalism, it's hugely popular—ProPublica's most popular features are news apps—and if we don't do it, somebody else will. Think of all the scoops we'd miss! Most importantly, newsrooms should know that they can all do this too. It's easier than it looks.

— *Scott Klein, ProPublica*

Visualization as the Workhorse of Data Journalism

Before you launch into trying to chart or map your data, take a minute to think about the many roles that static and interactive graphic elements play in your journalism.

In the reporting phase, visualizations can:

- Help you identify themes and questions for the rest of your reporting
- Identify outliers: good stories, or perhaps errors, in your data
- Help you find typical examples
- Show you holes in your reporting

Visualizations also play multiple roles in publishing. They can:

- Illustrate a point made in a story in a more compelling way
- Remove unnecessarily technical information from prose
- Particularly when they are interactive and allow exploration, provide transparency about your reporting process to your readers

These roles suggest you should start early and often with visualizations in your reporting, whether or not you start electronic data or records. Don't consider it a separate step, something to be considered after the story is largely written. Let this work help guide your reporting.

Getting started sometimes means just putting the notes you've already taken in a visual form. Consider the graphic in Figure 6-2, which ran in the Washington Post in 2006.

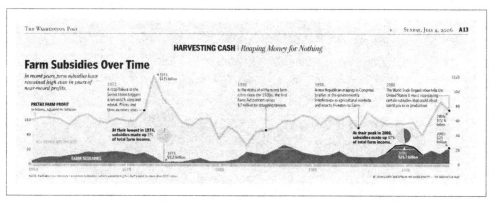

Figure 6-2. Farm Subsidies Over Time (Washington Post)

It shows the portion of farm income associated with subsidies and key events over the past 45 years, and was built over a series of months. Finding data that could be used over time with similar definitions and similar meanings was a challenge. Investigating all of the peaks and troughs helped us keep context in mind as we did the rest of our reporting. It also meant that one chore was pretty much finished before the stories were written.

Here are some tips for using visualization to start exploring your datasets.

Tip 1: Use small multiples to quickly orient yourself in a large dataset

I used this technique at the Washington Post when we were looking into a tip that the George W. Bush administration was awarding grants on political, not substantive, grounds. Most of these aid programs are done by formula, and others have been funded for years, so we were curious whether we might see the pattern by looking at nearly 1,500 different discretionary streams.

I created a graph for each program, with the red dots indicating a presidential election year and the green dots indicating a congressional year. The problem: yes, there was a spike in the six months before the presidential election in several of these programs—the red dots with the peak numbers next to them—but it's the wrong election year. The pattern consistently showed up during the 2000 presidential election between Al Gore and George W. Bush, not the 2004 election.

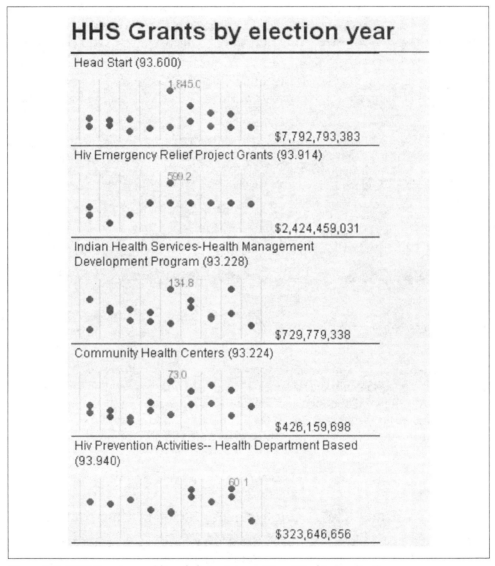

Figure 6-3. HHS Grants: sparklines help in story-spotting (Washington Post)

This was really easy to see in a series of graphs rather than a table of numbers, and an interactive form let us check various types of grants, regions and agencies. Maps in small multiples can be a way to show time and place on a static image that's easy to compare—sometimes even easier than an interactive.

This example was created with a short program written in PHP, but it's now much easier to do with Excel 2007 and 2010's sparklines. Edward Tufte, the visualization expert, invented these "intense, simple, word-like graphics" to convey information in a glance across a large dataset. You now see them everywhere, from the little graphs under stock market quotations to win-loss records in sports.

Tip 2: Look at your data upside down and sideways

When you're trying to understand a story or a dataset, there's no wrong way to look at it; try it every way you can think of, and you'll get a different perspective. If you're reporting on crime, you might look at one set of charts with change in violent crimes in a year; another might be the percent change; the other might be a comparison to other cities; and another might be a change over time. Use raw numbers, percentages, and indexes.

Look at them on different scales. Try following the rule that the x-axis must be zero. Then break that rule and see if you learn more. Try out logarithms and square roots for data with odd distributions.

Keep in mind the research done on visual perception. William Cleveland's experiments showed that the eye sees change in an image when the average slope is about 45 degrees. This suggests you ignore the admonitions to always start at zero and instead work toward the most insightful graphic. Other research in epidemiology has suggested you find a target level as a boundary for your chart. Each of these ways helps you see the data in different ways. When they've stopped telling you anything new, you know you're done.

Tip 3: Don't assume

Now that you've looked at your data a variety of ways, you've probably found records that don't seem right—you may not understand what they meant in the first place, or there are some outliers that seem like they are typos, or there are trends that seem backwards.

If you want to publish anything based on your early exploration or in a published visualization, you have to resolve these questions and you can't make assumptions. They're either interesting stories or mistakes; interesting challenges to common wisdom or misunderstanding.

It's not unusual for local governments to provide spreadsheets filled with errors, and it's also easy to misunderstand government jargon in a dataset.

First, walk back your own work. Have you read the documentation, its caveats and does the problem exist in the original version of the data? If everything on your end seems right, then it's time to pick up the phone. You're going to have to get it resolved if you plan to use it, so you might as well get started now.

That said, not every mistake is important. In campaign finance records, it's common to have several hundred postal codes that don't exist in a database of 100,000 records. As long as they're not all in the same city or within a candidate, the occasional bad data record just doesn't matter.

The question to ask yourself is: if I were to use this, would readers have a fundamentally accurate view of what the data says?

Tip 4: Avoid obsessing over precision

The flip side of not asking enough questions is obsessing over precision before it matters. Your exploratory graphics should be generally correct, but don't worry if you have various levels of rounding, if they don't add up to exactly 100 percent or if you are missing one or two years' data out of 20. This is part of the exploration process. You'll still see the big trends and know what you have to collect before it's time for publication.

In fact, you might consider taking away labeling and scale markers, much like the charts above, to even better get an overall sense of the data.

Tip 5: Create chronologies of cases and events

At the start of any complex story, begin building chronologies of key events and cases. You can use Excel, a Word document, or a special tool like TimeFlow for the task, but at some point you will find a dataset you can layer behind. Reading through it periodically will show you what holes are in your reporting that have to be filled out.

Tip 6: Meet with your graphics department early and often

Brainstorm about possible graphics with the artists and designers in your newsroom. They will have good ways to look at your data, suggestions of how it might work interactively, and know how to connect data and stories. It will make your reporting much easier if you know what you have to collect early on, or if you can alert your team that a graphic isn't possible when you can't collect it.

Tips For Publication

You might have spent only a few days or few hours on your exploration, or your story might have taken months to report. But as it becomes time to move to publication, two aspects become more important.

Remember that missing year you had in your early exploration? All of a sudden, you can't go any further without it. All of that bad data you ignored in your reporting? It's going to come back to haunt you. The reason is that you can't write around bad data. For a graphic, you either have everything you need or you don't, and there's no middle ground.

Match the effort of the data collection with the interactive graphic

There's no hiding in an interactive graphic. If you are really going to have your readers explore the data any way they want, then every data element has to be what it claims to be. Users can find any error at any time, and it could haunt you for months or years. If you're building your own database, it means you should expect to proofread, fact check, and copyedit the entire database. If you're using government records, you should decide how much spot-checking you'll do, and what you plan to do when you find the inevitable error.

Design for two types of readers

The graphic—whether it's a standalone interactive feature or a static visualization that goes with your story—should satisfy two different kinds of readers. It should be easy to understand at a glance, but complex enough to offer something interesting to people who want to go further. If you make it interactive, make sure your readers get something more than a single number or name.

Convey one idea, then simplify

Make sure there is one single thing you want people to see? Decide on the overwhelming impression you want a reader to get, and make everything else disappear. In many cases, this means removing information even when the Internet allows you to provide everything. Unless your main purpose is in transparency of reporting, most of the details you collected in your timeline and chronology just aren't very important. In a static graphic, it will be intimidating. In an interactive graphic, it will be boring.

— *Sarah Cohen, Duke University*

Using Visualizations to Tell Stories

Data visualization merits consideration for several reasons. Not only can it be strikingly beautiful and attention getting—valuable social currency for sharing and attracting readers—it also leverages a powerful cognitive advantage: fully half of the human brain is devoted to processing visual information. When you present a user with an information graphic, you are reaching them through the mind's highest-bandwidth pathway. A well-designed data visualization can give viewers an immediate and profound impression, and cut through the clutter of a complex story to get right to the point.

But unlike other visual media—such as still photography and video—data visualization is also deeply rooted in measurable facts. While aesthetically engaging, it is less emotionally charged, more concerned with shedding light than heat. In an era of narrowly-focused media that is often tailored towards audiences with a particular point of view, data visualization (and data journalism in general) offers the tantalizing opportunity for storytelling that is above all driven by facts, not fanaticism.

Moreover, like other forms of narrative journalism, data visualization can be effective for both breaking news—quickly imparting new information like the location of an accident and the number of casualties—and for feature stories, where it can go deeper into a topic and offer a new perspective, to help you see something familiar in a completely new way.

Seeing the Familiar in a New Way

In fact, data visualization's ability to test conventional wisdom is exemplified by an interactive graphic published by The New York Times in late 2009, a year after the global economic crisis began (*http://nyti.ms/employment-lines*). With the United States' national unemployment rate hovering near 9 percent, users could filter the US population by various demographic and educational filters to see how dramatically rates varied. As it turned out, the rate ranged from less than 4% for middle-aged women with advanced degrees to nearly half of all young black men who had not finished high school, and moreover this disparity was nothing new—a fact underscored by fever lines showing the historic values for each of these groups.

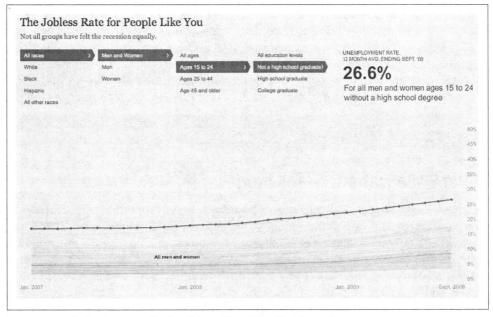

Figure 6-4. The Jobless Rate for People Like You (New York Times)

Even after you've stopped looking it, a good data visualization gets into your head and leaves a lasting mental model of a fact, trend, or process. How many people saw the animation distributed by tsunami researchers (*http://1.usa.gov/tsunami-animation*) in December 2004, which showed cascading waves radiating outward from an Indonesian earthquake across the Indian Ocean, threatening millions of coastal residents in South Asia and East Africa?

Data visualizations—and the aesthetic associations they engender—can even become cultural touchstones, such as the representation of deep political divisions in the United States after the 2000 and 2004 elections, when "red" Republican-held states filled the heartland and "blue" Democratic states clustered in the Northeast and far West. Never mind that in the US media before 2000, the main broadcast networks had freely switched between red and blue to represent each party, some even choosing to alternate every four years. Thus some Americans' memories of Ronald Reagan's epic 49-state "blue" landslide victory (*http://bit.ly/infobarrel-map*) for the Republicans in 1984.

But for every graphic that engenders a visual cliché, another comes along to provide powerful factual testimony, such as The New York Times' 2006 map (*http://nyti.ms/ diaspora-graphic*) that used differently sized circles to show where hundreds of thousands of evacuees from New Orleans were now living, strewn across the continent by a mixture of personal connections and relocation programs. Would these "stranded" evacuees ever make it back home?

So now that we've discussed the power of data visualization, it's fair to ask: when should we use it, and when should we *not* use it? First, we'll look at some examples of where data visualization might be useful to help tell a story to your readers.

Showing Change Over Time

Perhaps the most common use of data visualization—as personified by the humble fever chart—is to show how values have changed over time. The growth of China's population since 1960 (*http://bit.ly/google-china-population*) or the spike in unemployment since the economic crash of 2008 are good examples. But data visualization also can very powerfully show change over time through other graphic forms. The Portuguese researcher Pedro M. Cruz used animated circle charts to dramatically show the decline of western European empires (*http://pmcruz.com/visual-experiments/visualizing -empires*) since the early 19th century. Sized by total population, Britain, France, Spain, and Portugal pop like bubbles as overseas territories achieve independence. There go Mexico, Brazil, Australia, India, and wait for it...there go many African colonies in the early sixties, nearly obliterating France.

A graph by the Wall Street Journal (*http://on.wsj.com/tech-empire*) shows the number of months it took a hundred entrepreneurs to reach the magic number of $50 million in revenues. Created using the free charting and data analysis tool Tableau Public, the comparison resembles the trails of multiple airplanes taking off, some fast, some slow, some heavy, plotted over each other.

Speaking of airplanes, another interesting graph showing change over time plots the market share of major US airlines (*http://nyti.ms/airline-merger*) during several decades of industry consolidation. After the Carter administration deregulated passenger aviation, a slew of debt-financed acquisitions created national carriers out of smaller regional airlines, as this graphic by The New York Times illustrates.

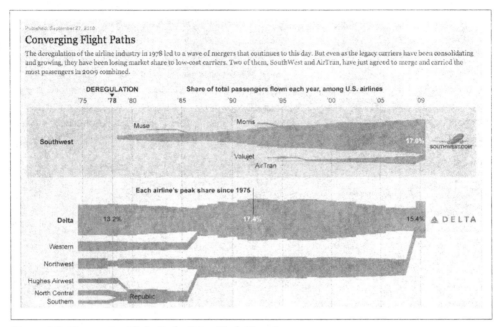

Figure 6-5. Converging Flight Paths (New York Times)

Given that almost all casual readers view the horizontal "x" axis of a chart as representing time, sometimes it's easy to think that *all* visualizations should show change over time.

Comparing Values

However, data visualization also shines in the area of helping readers compare two or more discrete values, whether to put in context the tragic loss of servicemen and women in the Iraq and Afghan conflicts (by comparing them to the scores of thousands killed in Vietnam and the millions who died in World War II, as the BBC did in an animated slideshow (*http://bbc.in/animated-slideshow*) accompanying their casualties database); or when National Geographic, using a very minimalist chart (*http://bit.ly/ngm-hearts*), showed how much more likely you were to die of heart disease (1 in 5 chance) or stroke (1 in 24) than, say airplane crashes (1 in 5,051) or a bee sting (1 in 56,789) by showing the relative odds of dying (all overshadowed by a huge arc representing the odds of dying overall: 1 in 1!).

Figure 6-6. Counting the human cost of war (BBC)

BBC, in collaboration with the agency Berg Design, also developed the website "Dimensions" (*http://bit.ly/ngm-hearts*), which let you overlay the outlines of major world events—the Deepwater Horizon oil spill or the Pakistan floods, for example—over a Google map of your own community (*http://howbigreally.com/*).

Showing Connections and Flows

France's introduction of high-speed rail in 1981 didn't literally make the country smaller, but a clever visual representation shows how much less time it now takes to reach different destinations than by conventional rail. A grid laid over the country appears square in the "before" image, but is squashed centrally towards Paris in the "after" one, showing not just that outbound destinations are "closer," but that the greatest time gains occur in the first part of the journey, before the trains reach unimproved tracks and have to slow down.

For comparisons between two separate variables, look at Ben Fry's chart evaluating the performance of Major League Baseball teams relative to their payrolls (*http://benfry .com/salaryper/*). In the left column, the teams are ranked by their record to date, while on the right is the total of their player salaries. A line drawn in red (underperforming) or blue (overperforming) connects the two values, providing a handy sense of which team owners are regretting their expensive players gone bust. Moreover, scrubbing across a timeline provides a lively animation of that season's "pennant race" to the finish.

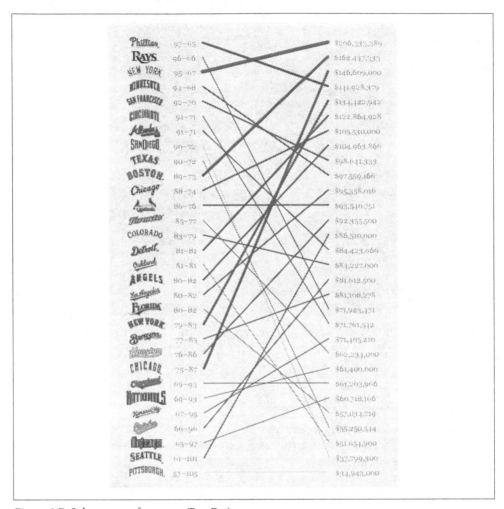

Figure 6-7. Salary vs. performance (Ben Fry)

Designing With Data

Similar in a way to graphing connections, flow diagrams also encode information into the connecting lines, usually by thickness and/or color. For example, with the Eurozone in crisis and several members incapable of meeting their debts, The New York Times sought to untangle the web of borrowing (*http://nyti.ms/eurozone-crisis*) that tied EU members to their trading partners across the Atlantic and in Asia. In one "state" of the visualization, the width of the line reflects the amount of credit passing from one country to another, where a yellow to orange color ramp indicates how "worrisome" it is— i.e., unlikely to be paid back!

On a happier topic, National Geographic magazine produced a deceptively simple chart showing the connections of three US cities (*http://bit.ly/sankey-wine*)—New York, Chicago and Los Angeles—to major wine-producing regions, and how the transportation methods bringing product from each of the sources could result in drastically different carbon footprints, making Bordeaux a greener buy for New Yorkers than California wine, for example.

"SourceMap," a project started at MIT's business school, uses flow diagrams to take a rigorous look at global procurement for manufactured products, their components and raw materials. Thanks to a lot of heavy research, a user can now search for products ranging from Ecco brand shoes (*http://sourcemap.com/view/1760*) to orange juice (*http://sourcemap.com/view/1011*) and find out from what corners of the globe it was sourced from, and its corresponding carbon footprint.

Showing Hierarchy

In 1991, the researcher Ben Shneiderman invented a new visualization form called the "treemap" (*http://www.cs.umd.edu/hcil/treemap-history/*) consisting of multiple boxes concentrically nested inside of each other. The area of a given box represents the quantity it represents, both in itself and as an aggregate of its contents. Whether visualizing a national budget by agency and subagency (*http://openspending.org/*), visualizing the stock market by sector and company, or a programming language by classes and subclasses, the treemap is a compact and intuitive interface for mapping an entity and its constituent parts. Another effective format is the dendrogram, which looks like a more typical organization chart, where subcategories continue to branch off a single originating trunk.

Figure 6-8. OpenSpending.org (Open Knowledge Foundation)

Browsing Large Databases

While sometimes data visualization is very effective at taking familiar information and showing it in a whole new light, what happens when you have brand-new information that people want to navigate? The age of data brings with it startling new discoveries almost every day, from Eric Fischer's brilliant geographic analyses of Flickr snapshots (*http://bit.ly/flickr-analysis*) to New York City's release of thousands of previously confidential teacher evaluations (*http://projects.wsj.com/nyc-teachers/*).

These datasets are at their most powerful when users can dig in and drill down to the information that is most relevant to them.

In early 2010, The New York Times was given access to Netflix's normally private records of what areas rent which movies the most often. While Netflix declined to disclose raw numbers, The Times created an engaging interactive database (*http://nyti .ms/interactive-database*) that let users browse the top 100-ranked rentals in 12 US metro areas, broken down to the postal code level. A color-graded "heatmap" overlaid on each community enabled users to quickly scan and see where a particular title was most popular.

Toward the end of that same year, the Times published the results of the United States decennial census (*http://nyti.ms/census-explorer*)—just hours after it was released. The interface, built in Adobe Flash, offered a number of visualization options and allowed users to browse down to every single census block in the nation (out of 8.2 million) to see the distribution of residents by race, income, and education. Such was the resolution of the data that when looking through the dataset in the first hours after publication, you wondered if you might be the first person in the world to explore that corner of the database.

Similar laudable uses of visualization as a database front-end include the BBC's investigation of traffic deaths (*http://bbc.in/road-deaths*), and many of the attempts to quickly index large data dumps like WikiLeaks' release of the Iraq and Afghanistan war logs.

The 65k Rule

Upon receiving the first dump of Afghan war log data from WikiLeaks, the team processing it started talking about how excited they were to have access to 65,000 military records.

This immediately set alarms ringing amongst those who had experience with Microsoft Excel. Thanks to an historic limitation in the way that rows are addressed, the Excel import tool won't process more than 65,536 records. In this case, it emerged that a mere 25,000 rows were missing!

The moral of this story (aside from avoiding using Excel for such tasks), is to always be suspicious of anyone boasting about 65,000 rows of data.

— *Alastair Dant, the Guardian*

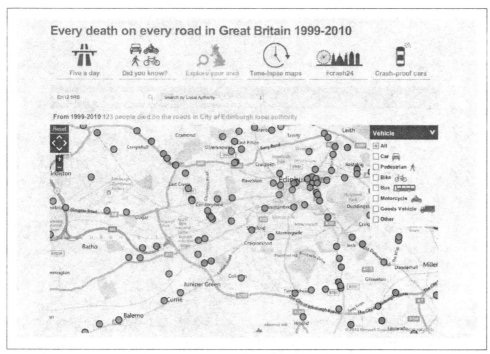

Figure 6-9. Every death on the road in Great Britain 1999-2010 (BBC)

Envisioning Alternate Outcomes

In The New York Times, Amanda Cox's "porcupine chart" of tragically optimistic US deficit projections (*http://nyti.ms/porcupine-graph*) over the years shows how sometimes what happened is less interesting than what didn't happen. Cox's fever line showing the surging budget deficit after a decade of war and tax breaks shows how unrealistic expectations of the future can turn out to be.

Bret Victor, a longtime Apple interface designer (and originator of the "kill math" theory of visualization to communicate quantitative information), has prototyped a kind of *reactive document (http://worrydream.com/#!/TenBrighterIdeas)*. In his example, energy conservation ideas include editable premises, whereby a simple step like shutting off lights in empty rooms could save Americans the output of from 2 to 40 coal plants. Changing the percentage referenced in the middle of a paragraph of text causes the text in the rest of the page to update accordingly!

For more examples and suggestions, here is a list of different uses for visualizations, maps and interactive graphics compiled by Matthew Ericson of The New York Times (*http://bit.ly/ericson-links*).

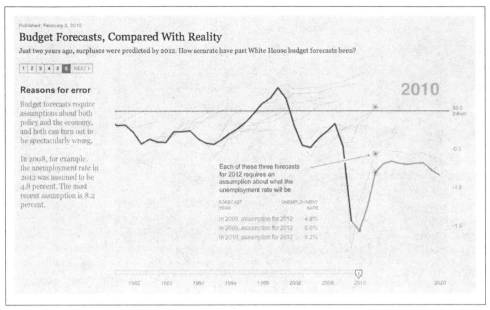

Figure 6-10. Budget Forecasts, Compared With Reality (New York Times)

When Not To Use Data Visualization

In the end, effective data visualization depends on good, clean, accurate, and meaningful information. Just as many good quotes, facts, and descriptions power good narrative journalism, data visualization is only as good as the data that fuels it.

When your story can be better told through text or multimedia
> Sometimes the data alone does not tell the story in the most compelling way. While a simple chart illustrating a trend line or summary statistic can be useful, a narrative relating the real-world consequences of an issue can be more immediate and impactful to a reader.

When you have very few data points
> It has been said, "a number in isolation doesn't mean anything." A common refrain from news editors in response to a cited statistic is, "compared to what?" Is the trend going up or down? What is normal?

When you have very little variability in your data, no clear trend, or conclusion
> Sometimes you plot your data in Excel or a similar charting app and discover that the information is noisy, has a lot of fluctuation, or has a relatively flat trend. Do you raise the baseline from zero to just below the lowest value, in order to give the line some more shape? No! Sounds like you have ambiguous data and need to do more digging and analysis.

When a map is not a map
> Sometimes the spatial element is not meaningful or compelling, or distracts attention from more pertinent numeric trends, like change over time or showing similarities between non-adjacent areas.

When a table would do
> If you have relatively few data points but have information that might be of use to some of your readers, consider just laying out the data in tabular form. It's clean, easy to read and doesn't create unrealistic expectations of "story." In fact, tables can be a very efficient and elegant layout for basic information.

— *Geoff McGhee, Stanford University*

Different Charts Tell Different Tales

In this digital world, with the promise of immersive 3D experiences, we tend to forget that for such a long time we only had ink on paper. We now think of this static, flat medium as a second class citizen, but in fact over the hundreds of years we've been writing and printing, we've managed to achieve an incredible wealth of knowledge and practices to represent data on the page. While interactive charts, data visualizations, and infographics are all the rage, they forego many of the best practices we've learned. Only when you look back through the history of accomplished charts and graphs can we understand that bank of knowledge and bring it forward into new mediums.

Some of the most famous charts and graphs came out of the need to better explain dense tables of data. William Playfair was a Scottish polyglot who lived in the late 1700s to early 1800s. He singlehandedly introduced the world to many of the same charts and graphs we still use today. In his 1786 book, *Commercial and Political Atlas*, Playfair introduced the bar chart to clearly show the import and export quantities of Scotland in a new and visual way.

He then went on to popularize the dreaded pie chart in his 1801 book *Statistical Breviary*. The need for these new forms of charts and graphs came out of commerce, but as time passed, others appeared and were used to save lives. In 1854 John Snow created his now famous "Cholera Map of London" by adding a small black bar over each address where an incident was reported. Over time, an obvious density of the outbreak could be seen and action taken to curb the problem.

As time passed, practitioners of these new chart and graphs got bolder and experimented further, pushing the medium toward what we know today. André-Michel Guerry was the first to publish the idea of a map where individual regions were different colors based on some variable. In 1829 he created the first choropleth by taking regions in France and shading them to represent crime levels. Today we see such maps used to show political polling regions, who voted for whom, wealth distribution, and many other geographically linked variables. It seems like such a simple idea, but even today, it is difficult to master and understand if not used wisely.

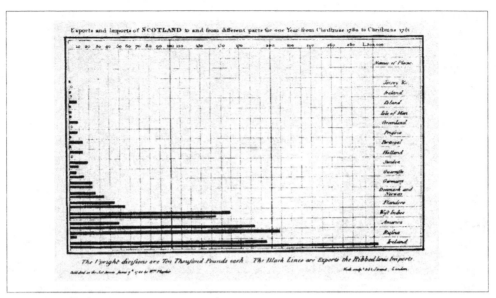

Figure 6-11. An early bar chart (William Playfair)

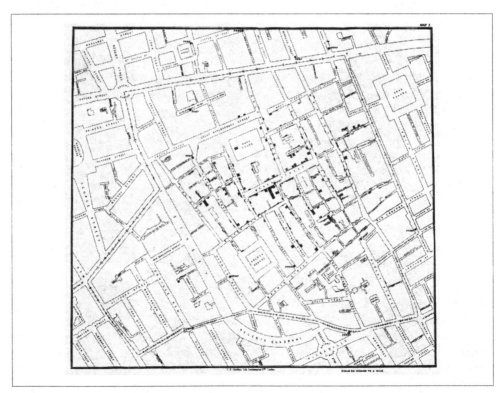

Figure 6-12. Cholera map of London (John Snow)

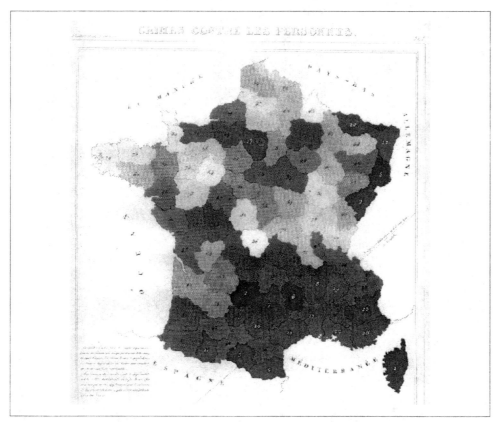

Figure 6-13. Choropleth map of France showing crime levels (André-Michel Guerry)

There are many tools a good journalist needs to understand and have in their toolbox for constructing visualizations. Rather than jump right in at the deep end, an excellent grounding in charts and graphs is important. Everything you create needs to originate from a series of atomic charts and graphs. If you can master the basics, then you can move onto constructing more complex visualizations which are made up from these basic units.

Two of the most basic chart types are bar charts and line charts. While they are very similar in their use cases, they can also differ greatly in their meaning. Let's take for instance, company sales for each month of the year. We'd get 12 bars representing the amount of money brought in each month (Figure 6-14).

Let's look into why this should be bars rather than a line graph. Line graphs are ideal for continuous data. With our sales figures, it is the sum of the month, not continuous. As a bar, we know that in January, the company made $100 and in February it made $120. If we made this a line graph, it would still represent $100 and $120 on the first of each month, but with the line graph we estimate that on the 15th it looks as it the

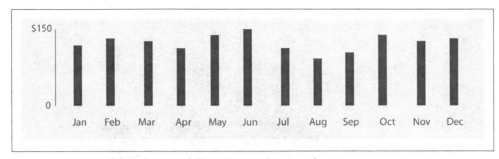

Figure 6-14. A simple bar chart: useful to represent discrete information

company made $110. Which isn't true. Bars are used for discrete units of measurement, whereas lines are used when it is a continuous value, such as temperature.

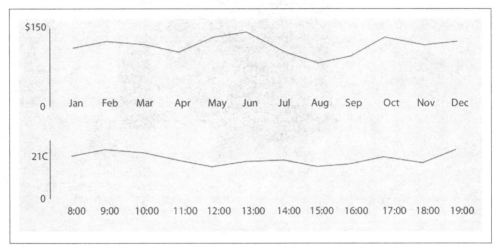

Figure 6-15. Simple line graphs: useful to represent continuous information

We can see that at 8:00 the temperature was 20C and at 9:00 it was 22C. If we look at the line to guess the temperature at 8:30 we'd say 21C, which is a correct estimate since temperature is continuous and every point isn't a sum of other values; it represents the exact value at that moment or an estimate between two exact measurements.

Both the bar and line have a stacked variation (Figure 6-17). This is an excellent story-telling tool that can work in different ways. Let's take, for example, a company that has 3 locations.

For each month we have 3 bars, one for each of the shops—36 total for the year. When we place them next to each other (Figure 6-16), we can quickly see in which month which store was earning the most. This is one interesting and valid story, but there is another hidden within the same data. If we stack the bars, so we only have one for each month, we now lose the ability to easily see which store is the biggest earner, but now we can see which months the company does the best business as a whole.

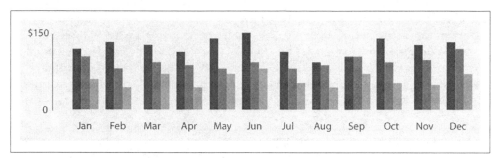

Figure 6-16. A grouped bar graph

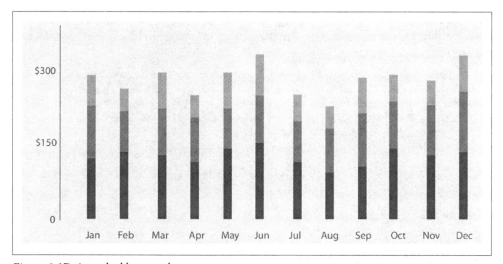

Figure 6-17. A stacked bar graph

Both of these are valid displays of the same information, but they are two different stories using the same starting data. As a journalist, the most important aspect of working with the data is that you first choose the story you are interested in telling. Is it which month is the best for business, or is it which store is the flagship? This is just a simple example, but it is really the whole focus of data journalism—asking the right question before getting too far. The story will guide the choice of visualization.

The bar chart and line graph are really the bread and butter of any data journalist. From there you can expand into histograms, horizon graphs, sparklines, stream graphs, and others, which all share similar properties and are suited for slightly different situations —including the amount of data or data sources, and location of the graphic in terms of the text.

In journalism, one of the very commonly used charting features is a map. Time, amount, and geography are common to maps. We always want to know how much is on one area versus another or how the data flows from one area to another. Flow diagrams and choropleths are very useful tools to have in your skill set when dealing with visualizations for journalism. Knowing how to color-code a map properly without misrepresenting or misleading readers is key. Political maps are usually color-coded as all or nothing for certain regions, even if a candidate only won one part of the country by 1%. Coloring does not have to be a binary choice; gradients of color based on groups can be used with care. Understanding maps is a large part of journalism. Maps easily answer the WHERE part of the 5 W's.

Once you have mastered the basic type of charts and graphs, you can then begin to build-up more fancy data visualizations. If you don't understand the basics, then you are building on a shaky foundation. In much the way you learn how to be a good writer —keeping sentences short, keeping the audience in mind, and not overcomplicating things to make yourself sound smart, but rather conveying meaning to the reader— you shouldn't go overboard with the data either. Starting small is the most effective way to tell the story, slowly building only when needed.

> Vigorous writing is concise. A sentence should contain no unnecessary words, a paragraph no unnecessary sentences, for the same reason that a drawing should have no unnecessary lines and a machine no unnecessary parts. This requires not that the writer make all his sentences short, or that he avoid all detail and treat his subjects only in outline, but that every word tell.
>
> — William Strunk Jr., *Elements of Style (1918)*

It is OK to not use every piece of data in your story. You shouldn't have to ask permission to be concise, it should be the rule.

— *Brian Suda, (optional.is)*

Data Visualization DIY: Our Top Tools

What data visualization tools are out there on the Web that are easy to use—and free? Here on the Datablog and Datastore (*http://www.guardian.co.uk/data*), we try to do as much as possible using the Internet's powerful free options.

That may sound a little disingenuous, in that we obviously have access to the Guardian's amazing graphics and interactive teams for those pieces where we have a little more time—such as this map of public spending (*http://bit.ly/guardian-spending*; created using Adobe Illustrator) or this Twitter riots interactive (*http://bit.ly/guardian-riots*).

But for our day-to-day work, we often use tools that anyone can—and create graphics that anyone else can too.

So, what do we use?

Google Fusion Tables

This online database and mapping tool (*http://www.google.com/fusiontables/Home/*) has become our default for producing quick and detailed maps, especially those where you need to zoom in. You get all the high resolution of Google Maps but it can open a lot of data—100 MB of CSV, for instance. The first time you try it, Fusion tables may seem a little tricky—but stick with it. We used it to produce maps like the Iraq one in Figure 6-18 and also border maps like Figure 6-19, about homelessness.

Figure 6-18. The WikiLeaks war logs (the Guardian)

The main advantage is the flexibility—you can can upload a KML file of regional borders, say—and then merge that with a data table. It's also getting a new user interface, which should make it easier to use.

You don't have to be a coder to make one—and this Fusion layers tool (*http://bit.ly/fusion-layers*) allows you to bring different maps together or to create search and filter options, which you can then embed on a blog or a site.

This excellent tutorial by Google's Kathryn Hurley (*http://bit.ly/fusiontables-tutorial*) is a great place to start.

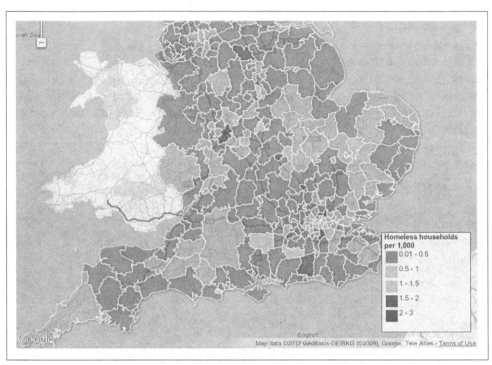

Figure 6-19. Homelessness interactive map (the Guardian)

 Use shpescape (*http://www.shpescape.com/*) to convert official .shp files into Fusion tables for you to use. Also, watch out for overcomplicated maps—Fusion can't cope with more than a million points in one cell.

Tableau Public

If you don't need the unlimited space of the professional edition, Tableau Public (*http://www.tableausoftware.com/public*) is free. With it you can make pretty complex visualizations with up to 100,000 rows simply and easily. We use it when we need to bring different types of charts together, as in this map of top tax rates around the world (*http://bit.ly/guardian-top-tax*; which also has a bar chart).

Or you can even use it as a data explorer, which is what we did in Figure 6-20 with the US federal elections spending data (*http://bit.ly/guardianelections-us*; although we ran out of space in the free public version...something to watch out for). Tableau also needs the data formatted in quite specific ways for you to get the most out of it. But get through that and you have something intuitive that works well. La Nación in Argentina has built its entire data journalism operation around Tableau (*http://blogs.lanacion.com.ar/data/*), for instance.

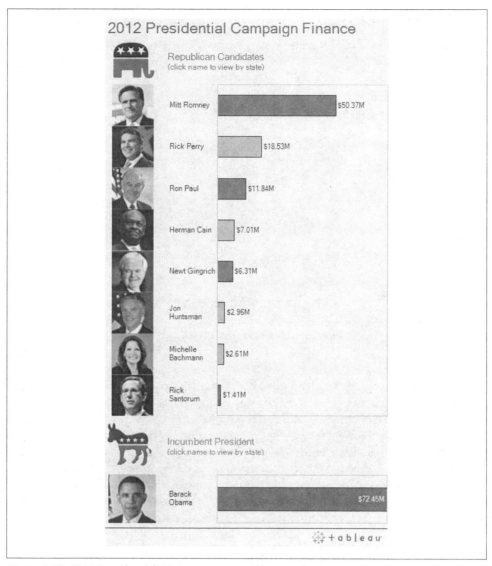

Figure 6-20. *2012 Presidential Campaign Finance (the Guardian)*

Tableau has some good online tutorials for you to start with, at *http://www.tableausoft ware.com/learn/training*.

 Tableau is designed for PCs, although a Mac version is in the works. Use a mirror such as parallels to make it work.

Google Spreadsheet Charts

You can access this tool at *http://www.google.com/google-d-s/spreadsheets/*.

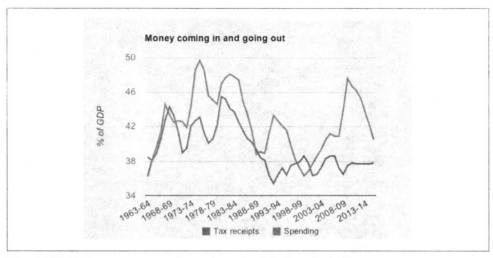

Figure 6-21. UK government spending and taxation (the Guardian)

After something simple (like a bar or line chart, or a pie chart), you'll find that Google spreadsheets (which you create from the documents bit of your Google account) can create some pretty nice charts—including the animated bubbles used by Hans Rosling's Gapminder (*http://www.gapminder.org/*). Unlike the charts API (*http://code.google.com/apis/chart/*), you don't need to worry about code; it's pretty similar to making a chart in Excel, in that you highlight the data and click the chart widget. The customization options are worth exploring too; you can change colors, headings, and scales. They are pretty design-neutral, which is useful in small charts. The line charts have some nice options too, including annotation options.

 Spend some time with the chart customization options; you can create your own color palette.

Datamarket

Better known as a data supplier, Datamarket is actually a pretty nifty tool for visualizing numbers too (*http://bit.ly/datamarket-explore*). You can upload your own or use some of the many datasets they have to offer, but the options do get better if you get the Pro account.

Datamarket works best with time series data, but check out their extensive data range.

Many Eyes

If ever a site needed a bit of TLC, it's IBM's Many Eyes (*http://ibm.co/ibm-manyeyes*). When it launched, created by Fernanda B. Viégas (*http://fernandaviegas.com/*) and Martin Wattenberg (*http://www.bewitched.com/*), it was a unique exercise in allowing people to simply upload datasets and visualize them. Now, with its creators working for Google, the site feels a little unloved with its muted color palettes; it hasn't seen much new in the way of visualizations for some time.

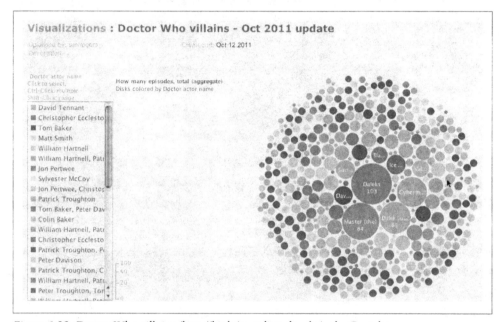

Figure 6-22. Doctor Who villains (http://bit.ly/guardian-dr-who); the Guardian

You can't edit the data once you've uploaded it, so make sure you get it right before you create it.

Color Brewer

Not strictly a visualization tool, Color Brewer (*http://colorbrewer2.org/*) is really for choosing map colors. You can choose your base color and get the codes for the entire palette.

And Some More

If none of these are for you, it's also worth checking out this DailyTekk piece (*http://bit.ly/dailytekk-infographic*), which has even more options. The ones above aren't the only tools, just those we use most frequently. There are lots of others out there too, including:

- Chartsbin (*http://chartsbin.com/*), a tool for creating clickable world maps
- iCharts (*http://www.icharts.net/*), which specializes in small chart widgets
- Geocommons (*http://geocommons.com/*), which shares data and boundary data to create global and local maps
- Oh, and there's also piktochart.com (*http://piktochart.com/*), which provides templates for those text/numbers visualizations that are popular at the moment.

— *Simon Rogers, the Guardian*

How We Serve Data at Verdens Gang

News journalism is about bringing new information to the reader as quickly as possible. The fastest way may be a video, a photo, a text, a graph, a table, or a combination of these. Concerning visualizations, the purpose should be the same: quick information. New data tools enable journalists to find stories they couldn't otherwise find, and present stories in new ways. Here are a few examples showing how we serve data at the most read newspaper in Norway, Verdens Gang (VG).

Numbers

This story (*http://bit.ly/vg-lotto*) is based on data from the Norwegian Bureau of Statistics, taxpayer data, and data from the national Lotto monopolist. In this interactive graph, the reader could find different kinds of information from each Norwegian county and municipality. The actual table is showing the percent of the income used on games. It was built using Access, Excel, MySql, and Flash.

Networks

We used social network analysis to analyze the relations between 157 sons and daughters of the richest people in Norway. Our analysis showed that heirs of the richest persons in Norway also inherited their parents' network. Altogether, there were more than 26,000 connections, and the graphics were all finished manually using Photoshop. We used Access, Excel, Notepad, and the social network analysis tool Ucinet.

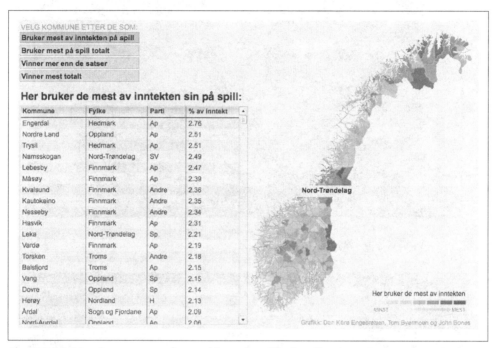

Figure 6-23. Mapping taxpayers data and Lotto data (Verdens Gang)

Maps

In this animated heatmap combined with a simple bar chart (*http://bit.ly/vg-heatmap*), you can see crime incidents occur on a map of downtown Oslo, hour by hour, over the weekend for several months. In the same animated heatmap, you can see the number of police officers working at the same time. When crime really is happening, the number of police officers is at the bottom. It was built using ArcView with Spatial Analyst.

Figure 6-24. Rich birds of a feather flock together (Verdens Gang)

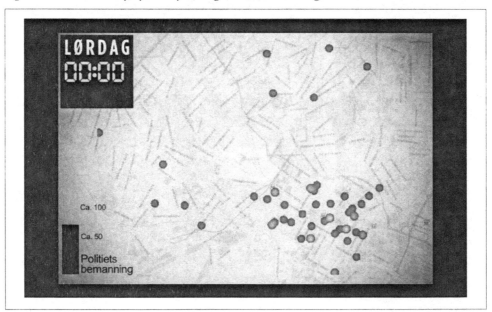

Figure 6-25. Animated heat map (Verdens Gang)

Text Mining

For this visualization (*http://bit.ly/vg-vis*), we text mined speeches held by the seven Norwegian party leaders during their conventions. All speeches were analyzed, and the analyses supplied angles for some stories. Every story was linked to the graph, and the readers could explore and study the language of politicians. This was built using Excel, Access, Flash, and Illustrator. If this had been built in 2012, we would have made the interactive graph in JavaScript.

Figure 6-26. Text mining speeches from party leaders (Verdens Gang)

Concluding Notes

When do we need to visualize a story? Most of the times we do not need to, but sometimes we want to do so to help our readers. Stories containing a huge amount of data quite often need visualization. However, we have to be quite critical when choosing what kind of data we are going to present. We know all kinds of stuff when we report about something, but what does the reader really need to know for the story? Perhaps a table is enough, or a simple graph showing a development from year A to year C. When working with data journalism, the point is not necessarily to present huge amounts of data. It's about journalism!

There has been a clear trend in the last 2-3 years to create interactive graphs and tables that enable the reader to drill down into different themes. A good visualization is like a good picture. You understand what it is about just by looking at it for a moment or two. The more you look at the visual, the more you see. The visualization is bad when the reader does not know where to start or where to stop, and when the visualization is overloaded by details. In this scenario, perhaps a piece of text would be better?

— *John Bones, Verdens Gang*

Public Data Goes Social

Data is invaluable. Access to data has the potential to illuminate issues in a way that triggers results. Nevertheless, poor handling of data can put facts in an opaque structure that communicates nothing. If it doesn't promote discussion or provide contextual understanding, data may be of limited value to the public.

Nigeria returned to democracy in 1999 after lengthy years of military rule. Probing the facts behind data was taken as an affront to authority and was seen to be trying question the stained reputation of the junta. The Official Secrets Act compelled civil servants not to share government information. Even thirteen years after the return to democracy, accessing public data can be a difficult task. Data about public expenditure communicates little to the majority of the public, who are not well-versed in financial accounting and complex arithmetic.

With the rise of mobile devices and an increasing number of Nigerians online, with BudgIT we saw a huge opportunity to use data visualization technologies to explain and engage people around public expenditure. To do this, we have had to engage users across all platforms and to reach out to citizens via NGOs. This project is about making public data a social object and building an extensive network that demands change.

To successfully engage with users, we have to understand what they want. What does the Nigerian citizen care about? Where do they feel an information gap? How can we make the data relevant to their lives? BudgIT's immediate target is the average literate Nigerian connected to online forums and social media. In order to compete for the limited attention of users immersed in a wide variety of interests (gaming, reading, socializing) we need to present the data in a brief and concise manner. After broadcasting a snapshot of the data as a Tweet or an infographic, there's an opportunity for a more sustained engagement with a more interactive experience to give users a bigger picture.

When visualizing data, it is important to understand the level of data literacy of our users. As beautiful and sophisticated as they may be, complex diagrams and interactive

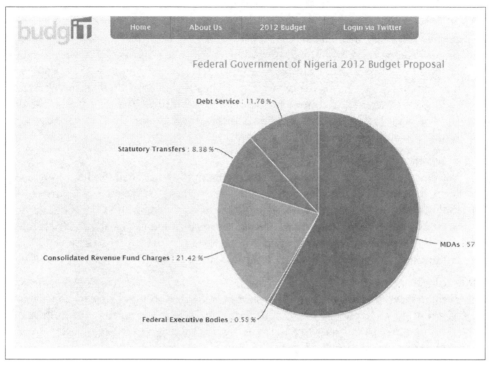

Figure 6-27. The BudgIT cut app (BudgIT Nigeria)

applications might not meaningfully communicate to our users based on their previous experiences with interpreting data. A good visualization will speak to the user in a language they can understand, and bring forth a story that they can easily connect with.

We have engaged over 10,000 Nigerians over the budget, and we profile them into three categories to ensure that optimum value is delivered. The categories are briefly explained below:

Occasional users
>These are users who want information simply and quickly. They are interested in getting a picture of the data, not detailed analytics. We can engage them via tweets or interactive graphics.

Active users
>Users who stimulate discussion, and use the data to increase their knowledge of a given area or challenge the assumptions of the data. For these users, we want to provide feedback mechanisms and the possibility to share insights with their peers via social networks.

Data hogs
>These users want raw data for visualization or analysis. We simply give them the data for their purposes.

With BudgIT, our user engagement is based on the following:

Stimulating discussion around current trends

> BudgIT keeps track of online and offline discussions and seeks to provide data around these topics. For example, with the fuel strikes in January 2012, there was constant agitation among the protesters on the need to reinstate fuel subsidies and reduce extravagant and unnecessary public expenditure. BudgIT tracked the discussion via social media and in 36 busy hours, built an app that allows citizens to reorganize the Nigerian budget.

Good feedback mechanisms

> We engage with users through discussion channels and social media. Many users want to know about stories behind the data and many ask for our opinion. We make sure that our responses only explain the facts behind the data and are not biased by our personal or political views. We need to keep feedback channels open, actively respond to comments, and engage the users creatively to ensure that the community built around the data is sustained.

Make it local

> For a dataset targeted at a particular group, BudgIT aims to localize its content and to promote a channel of discussion that connects to the needs and interests of particular groups of users. In particular, we're interested in engaging users around issues they care about via SMS.

After making expenditure data available on yourbudgit.com, we reach out to citizens through various NGOs. We also plan to develop a participatory framework where citizens and government institutions can meet in town halls to define key items in the budget that need to be prioritized.

The project has received coverage in local and foreign media, from CP-Africa (*http://bit.ly/cp-africa-budget*) to the BBC (*http://bbc.in/africa-budget*). We have undertaken a review of the 2002-2011 budgets for the security sector for an AP journalist, Yinka Ibukun. Most media organizations are "data hogs" and have requested data from us to use for their reportage. We are planning further collaborations with journalists and news organizations in the coming months.

— *Oluseun Onigbinde, BudgIT Nigeria*

Engaging People Around Your Data

Almost as important as publishing the data in the first place is getting a reaction from your audience. You're human; you're going to make mistakes, miss things, and get the wrong idea from time to time. Your audience is one of the most useful assets that you've got. They can fact-check and point out things that you may not have considered.

Engaging that audience is tricky, though. You're dealing with a group of people who've been conditioned over years of Internet use to hop from site to site, leaving nothing but a sarcastic comment in their wake. Building a level of trust between you and your users is crucial; they need to know what they're going to get, know how they can react to it and offer feedback, and know that that feedback is going to be listened to.

But first you need to think about what audience you've got, or want to get. That will both inform and be informed by the kind of data that you're working with. If it's specific to a particular sector, then you're going to want to explore particular communications with that sector. Are there trade bodies that you can get in touch with that might be willing to publicize the resources that you've got and the work that you've done to a wider audience? Is there a community website or a forum that you can get in touch with? Are there specialist trade publications that may want to report on some of the stories that you're finding in the data?

Social media is an important tool, too, though it again depends on the type of data that you're working with. If you're looking at global shipping statistics, for example, you're unlikely to find a group on Facebook or Twitter that'll be especially interested in your work. On the other hand, if you're sifting through corruption indices across the world, or local crime statistics, that's likely to be something that's going to be of interest to a rather wider audience.

When it comes to Twitter, the best approach tends to be to contact high-profile figures, briefly explaining why your work is important, and including a link. With any luck, they'll retweet you to their readers, too. That's a great way to maximize exposure to your work with minimum effort—though don't badger people!

Once you've got people on the page, you need to think about how your audience going to interact with your work. Sure, they might read the story that you've written and look at the infographics or maps, but giving your users an outlet to respond is immensely valuable. More than anything, it's likely to give you greater insight into the subject you're writing about, informing future work on the topic.

Firstly, it goes without saying that you need to publish the raw data alongside your articles. Either host the data in comma-separated plain text, or host it in a third-party service like Google Docs. That way, there's only one version of the data around, and you can update it as necessary if you find errors in the data that need correcting later. Better still, do both. Make it as easy as possible for people to get hold of your raw materials.

Then start to think about if there's other ways that you can get the audience to interact. Keep an eye on metrics on which parts of your datasets are getting attention—it's likely that the most trafficked areas could have something to say that you might have missed. For example, you might not think to look at the poverty statistics in Iceland, but if those cells are getting plenty of attention, then there might be something there worth looking at.

Think beyond the comment box, too. Can you attach comments to particular cells in a spreadsheet? Or a particular region of an infographic? While most embeddable publishing systems don't necessarily allow for this, it's worth taking a look at if you're creating something a little more bespoke. The benefits that it can bring to your data can't be underestimated.

Make sure that other users can see those comments too—they have almost as much value as the original data, in a lot of cases, and if you keep that information to yourself, then you're depriving your audience of that value.

Finally, other people might want to publish their own infographics and stories based on the same sources of data—think about how best to link these together and profile their work. You could use a hashtag specific to the dataset, for example, or if it's highly pictorial, then you could share it in a Flickr group.

Having a route to share information more confidentially could be useful too—in some cases it might not be safe for people to publicly share their contributions to a dataset, or they might simply not be comfortable doing so. Those people may prefer to submit information through an email address, or even an anonymous comments box.

The most important thing you can do with your data is share it as widely and openly as possible. Enabling your readers to check your work, find your mistakes, and pick out things that you might have missed will make both your journalism—and the experience for your reader—infinitely better.

— *Duncan Geere, Wired.co.uk*

About the Editors

Jonathan Gray is Head of Community and Culture at the Open Knowledge Foundation (*http://okfn.org*), an award-winning non-profit organization dedicated to promoting open data, open content, and the public domain in a wide variety of different fields. He founded several data journalism projects at the OKFN, including OpenSpending.org, which maps public spending around the world, and Europe's Energy, which puts EU energy targets into context. He is doing research in philosophy and the history of ideas at Royal Holloway, University of London. More about him can be found at *jonathangray.org*.

Liliana Bounegru is editor of DataDrivenJournalism.net and project manager on data journalism at the European Journalism Centre (*http://www.ejc.net/*). Her work includes coordinating the Data Journalism Awards and co-editing the Data Journalism Handbook. Liliana also works as a researcher on the collaborative research project EMAPS (Electronic Maps to Assist Public Science) and is a Research MA candidate in Media Studies at the University of Amsterdam. Her research focuses on the impact of technology on media, culture, and society. She blogs at *lilianabounegru.org*.

Lucy Chambers is a Community Coordinator at the Open Knowledge Foundation. She works on the OKFN's OpenSpending.org project and Spending Stories, a Knight News Challenge Winner 2011—helping journalists build context around and fact check spending data. She also coordinates the data-driven journalism activities of the Foundation, running training sessions for journalists on how to find, work with, and present data.

About the Project Coordinators

The European Journalism Centre (*http://www.ejc.net/*) provides training to enhance the quality of journalistic coverage of European current affairs and to provide strategic support for the European media.

The Open Knowledge Foundation (*http://okfn.org/*) seeks a world in which open knowledge is ubiquitous and routine—both online and offline—and promotes open knowledge because of its potential to deliver far-reaching societal benefits.

Have it your way.

CPSIA information can be obtained at www.ICGtesting.com
Printed in the USA
LVOW122212120712

289892LV00003B/1/P